# MIGRANT BRĀHMAṆAS IN NORTHERN INDIA

# MIGRANT BRĀHMAṆAS IN NORTHERN INDIA

## Their Settlement and General Impact

*c.* A.D. 475–1030

SWATI DATTA (née SEN GUPTA)

MOTILAL BANARSIDASS
Delhi Varanasi Patna Bangalore Madras

*First Edition : 1989*

MOTILAL BANARSIDASS
Bungalow Road, Jawahar Nagar, Delhi-110007

*Branches:*
Chowk, Varanasi 221001
Ashok Rajpath, Patna 800004
24 Race Course Road, Bangalore 560001
120 Royapettah High Road, Mylapore, Madras 600004



ISBN: 81-208-0067-2

The publication of this book has been financially supported by the Indian Council of Historical Research. The responsibility for the facts stated, opinions expressed or conclusions reached, is entirely that of the author. The Indian Council of Historical Research accepts no responsibility for them.

PRINTED IN INDIA
BY JAINENDRA PRAKASH JAIN AT SHRI JAINENDRA PRESS, A-45 NARAINA INDUSTRIAL AREA, PHASE I, NEW DELHI 110028 AND PUBLISHED BY NARENDRA PRAKASH JAIN FOR MOTILAL BANARSIDASS, DELHI 110007.

To my parents
DR SARADINDU BHUSAN GUPTA
*and*
URMILA GUPTA

# Contents

# Preface

The internal mobility of the Brāhamaṇas in Northern India has been recorded in inscriptions and land charters as early as the 5th and 6th centuries A.D. This feature of their life has been studied, albeit casually by a few: P. Niyogi, in her *Brahmanic Settlements in Different Subdivisions of Ancient Bengal*, writes about the movement of Brāhmaṇas to and from Bengal; B.N. Sharma in *The Social and Cultural History of Northern India*, catalogues a handful of instances of migration within the whole of Northern India; two short articles by B. Upadhyaya (*JBRS* XXXXXV p. 308-312) and N. Dasgupta (*IC* XIII p. 157-162) also deal with the subject. Encouraged by the findings and the views of these scholars, I have made a more detailed study, which this book attempts to present. It gives a full picture of the migrant Brāhmaṇas in Northern India between c. 475 and 1030 A.D.

This work is based on my thesis which was approved for the degree of Doctor of Philosophy by Patna University in 1979.

In the preparation of this book, I have received advice and help from various authorities. Professor B.P. Majumdar, formerly Head of the Department of History, Patna University, has given me invaluable guidance: to him I owe a debt of immeasurable gratitude. I am also grateful to late Dr. B.C. Sen (Sanskrit College, Calcutta), Professor J.N. Sarkar (former Head of the Department of History, Jadavpur University), Sri S.K. Bose (formerly Principal, B.N. College, Patna), Professor R.S. Sharma (University of Delhi), Professor Y. Mishra (retired Professor, Patna University), Professor R.K. Chaudhary (Post-graduate department of History, Bhagalpur University), Professor B.N. Mukherjee (University of Calcutta), Dr. B.K. Sinha and Dr. H.P. Dvivedi (both of Patna University), Professor J.G. de Casparis of the

Indologisch Institut, Holland, and Professor A.D.H. Bivar (London School of Oriental and African Studies). I acknowledge my appreciation for the courtesy and consideration shown to me by the staff of the various libraries in Patna and of the library of the London School of Oriental and African Studies. My special thanks are due to Messrs Motilal Banarsidass, who have kindly taken much interest in the publication of the book.

'Garvyk' Swati Datta
Newton Avenue,
Wick,
Scotland

# Abbreviations

| | | |
|---|---|---|
| BSDSAB | — | *Brahmanic Settlements in Different Subdivisions of Ancient Bengal*, by P. Niyogi |
| CA | — | *The Classical Age* |
| CII | — | *Corpus Inscriptionum Indicarum* |
| DHNI | — | *Dynastic History of Northern India*, by H.C. Ray |
| EB | — | *Encyclopaedia Britannica* |
| EBSGP | — | *The Early Brahmanical System of Gotra And Pravara*, by J. Brough |
| EI | — | *Epigraphia Indica* |
| ESS | — | *Encyclopaedia of the Social Sciences* |
| HB | — | *History of Bengal I*, edited by R.C. Majumdar |
| HCSL | — | *History of Classical Sanskrit Literature*, by M. Krishnamachariar |
| HDS | — | *History of Dharmaśāstra* |
| HIL | — | *History of Indian Literature I*, by M. Winternitz |
| HRS | — | *Contributions to the History of the Hindu Revenue System*, by U.N. Ghoshal |
| HSL | — | *History of Sanskrit Literature I*, by S.N. Dasgupta and S.K. De |
| IA | — | *Indian Antiquary* |
| IC | — | *Indian Culture* |
| IEG | — | *Indian Epigraphical Glossary*, by D.C. Sircar |
| IHC | — | *Proceedings of the Indian History Congress* |
| IHQ | — | *Indian Historical Quarterly* |
| IK | — | *The Age of Imperial Kanauj* |

| | | |
|---|---|---|
| IO | — | *Inscriptions of Orissa* |
| JAHRS | — | *Journal of the Andhra Historical Research Society* |
| JAS | — | *Journal of the Asiatic Society* |
| JASB | — | *Journal of the Asiatic Society of Bengal* |
| JBBRAS | — | *Journal of the Bombay Branch of the Royal Asiatic Society* |
| JBORS | — | *Journal of the Bihar and Orissa Research Society* |
| JBRS | — | *Journal of the Bihar Research Society* |
| JOIB | — | *Journal of the Oriental Institute of Baroda* |
| KS | — | *Kāmarūpa-Śāsanāvalī* |
| OHRJ | — | *Orissa Historical Research Journal* |
| RAT | — | *Rāṣṭrakūṭas and their Times*, by A.S. Altekar |
| RT | — | *Rājataraṅgiṇī of Kalhaṇa* (English Translation by M.A. Stein) |
| SCHNI | — | *Social And Cultural History of Northern India*, by B.N. Sharma |
| SE | — | *The Struggle For Empire* |
| SGAMI | — | *Studies in the Geography of Ancient and Mediaeval India*, by D.C. Sircar |
| SHCGEG | — | *Studies in the Historical and Cultural Geography and Ethnography of Gujarat*, by H.D. Sankalia |
| SSAAMI | — | *Studies in the Society and Administration of Ancient and Mediaeval India*, by D.C. Sircar |
| TBIGC | — | *Two Brāhmaṇical Institutions: Gotra and Caraṇa*, by G.S. Ghurye |
| TLB | — | *The Topographical List of the Bṛhatsaṁhitā*, by J.F. Fleet, edited by K.K. Dasgupta |
| VA | — | *The Vedic Age* |

# Introduction

Migration involves the movement of human beings who, voluntarily or otherwise leave their ancestral homes to settle elsewhere for security and better prospects. This phenomenon is common to all ages. This book deals with the migration of Brāhmaṇas in Northern India between c. 475-1030 A.D.

This period was characterised by long drawn out political disturbances. In the years following the Hūṇa invasion of North India in the middle of the 5th century, the imperial power of the Guptas gradually declined. Their empire began to break up and new ruling families like the Maitrakas of Valabhī, the Gurjaras of Broach and the Cāḷukyas of Bādāmi appeared on the scene. Their conflicts with their neighbours to maintain their frontiers created an atmosphere of unrest. The death of Harṣavardhana soon after c. 646 A.D., added to the existing turmoil. It marked the beginning of the struggle for supremacy over Kanauj, which had become a symbol of imperial status. The Pālas, the Rāṣṭrakūṭas and the Gurjara Pratihāras and the Paramāras clashed in their attempts to capture and hold Kanauj. Later the Tomaras and Cāhamānas fought with one another over the Madhyadeśa region. Their antagonism was so deep-rooted, that they failed to present a united front against the invasions of Sultan Mahmūd of Ghazni. The latter, from about c. 1000 A.D. made repeated inroads into Northern India, thereby weakening its political structure. Even after his death in c. 1030 A.D., the struggle for supremacy between the Indian rulers continued unchecked. It is to this long period of tensions, insecurity and instability, i.e., c. 475-1030 A.D., that the migration of a large number of Brāhmaṇas can be attributed.

The ancient Indian inscriptions and charters in the volumes of *Epigraphia Indica, Corpus Inscriptionum Indicarum,*

*Indian Historical Quarterly*, Journals of the Bihar and Orissa Research Society, the Orissa Historical Research Journals and the Journals and Proceedings of the Asiatic Societies of Bengal and Bombay, yield valuable information. Literary sources like the *Kāmarūpa-Śāsanāvalī* of. Padmanath Bhattacharya, the *Gauḍalekhamālā* of A.K. Maitreya, the *Rājataraṅgiṇī* of Kalhaṇa, Alberuni's *India*, the *Kathāsaritasāgara* (Ocean of Stories, edited by Penzer), the *Harṣacarita, Karpūramañjarī* and *Daśakumāracarita*, all record instances of migration.

A study of these sources reveals the reasons which have been responsible for migration on a wide scale. The inscriptions do not ascribe any reason for the movements. Yet an examination of the political situation of the time, together with social and economic factors like excessive population and famines, helps us to ascribe some causes, which, however, are essentially hypothetical. The number of people who migrated during a century, or within decades, can never be known. But a broad idea of the number of migrants can be gathered from the inscriptions. In the years preceding c. 750 A.D., instances of migration were few in number, and were mostly confined to Gujarat. Later they became more frequent when Brāhmaṇas began to travel longer distances. During these years, particular regions appear as centres of emigration and the mainstream of movement was towards Orissa.

Prompted by their gregarious instincts, the migrant Brāhmaṇas, took up residence in *bhaṭṭa* or Brāhmaṇa villages. Men with common *gotra* affiliations and similar origins, often had the tendency to live together in the same place. Almost all of them had specific Vedic qualifications. Others, with specialised education and training and endowed with literary genius, served their patrons as teachers, court poets, ministers, priests, astrologers, military officials and writers.

Most of the migrant Brāhmaṇas became beneficiaries of the ruling kings and their feudatories. In the earlier phase of the period under survey, they received plots of land of various sizes. But later on, mostly one or more villages were donated to them. Generally the lands were cultivable and the donees were given the right to levy a varying range of taxes. The financial status of the migrant Brāhmaṇas depended on the geographical situation and nature of the donated lands and the privilege of collecting taxes.

On the basis of the above, an attempt has been made to assess the position of the migrant Brāhmaṇas. The manner in which they were received in their new surroundings, their accomplishments, and their contributions to the life and culture of the times, have been worked out as far as possible.

# Chapter I

## Problems and History of Migration

People, in the process of movement involving the abandonment of their ancestral homes and the search for new permanent domicile, have since the earliest times, travelled far and near. The movement was sometimes confined to the boundaries of their home-land—at others it extended over the whole country; or from one country to another, or even from one continent to another. Physical factors, as well as political and socio-economic causes, have all played their part in human migrations.

### World Phenomena

The life of early man, was considerably influenced by geographical factors and the surroundings in which he lived. Movement of ice-sheets and volcanic eruptions compelled the occupants of northern Eurasia, North America and North-West Europe, to abandon their homes. In some cases, the search for a fresh environment led to a radical change in the choice of a new home of a migrating people. The Āryans, according to some scholars, left the deserts and oases of Central Asia, for the richer and more fertile regions of the Punjab and upper Ganges valley.

Sudden population movements in historical times, like the outburst of the Hyksos from the desert and steppe regions sometime before 1500 B.C., have been attributed to climatic changes or pulsation. The "pulsation theory", which presupposes century-long periods of increasing dryness, alternating with periods of increasing rainfall, has been used by E. Huntingdon[1], to explain great nomad movements. According to him, during very dry periods, the pastoral nomads of Central Asia, were forced by a shortage of pastures, to emigrate and prey on the lands of their sedentary neighbours.

The urge for wealth and loot too, combined with scarcity of food and population pressure, set in motion large numbers of pastoral nomads from Central Asia, Mongolia, Turkestan and the neighbouring territories. As the grazing fields became disproportionate to the increasing population, new grazing grounds had to be sought. The comparatively prosperous condition of their sedentary neighbours tempted the nomads. Being lured by the wealth and facilities available in those agricultural tracts, the nomads fought successfully and settled down in these regions. The sedentary people in ancient times were living on the shores of the North Baltic and Mediterranean Seas and the Atlantic, Pacific and Indian Oceans. A large part of continental Europe and Asia was unsettled and the nomadic people crossed mountains and seas and surged from the borders of China to the Danube and the Rhine.[2] Asian and European history provide ample examples of the movement and settlement of nomadic and other tribes. The Semites may have infiltrated from Arabia and Syria into Mesopotamia, establishing Kish and Mari as their chief centres. Later, the Hittites, the Mitannis, the Hurrians and the Kassites migrating from their original homes somewhere between the Baltic and the Black Sea, probably in the plains of southern Russia,[3] gradually infiltrated into different parts of western Asia. As regards the parent group from which some of these tribes broke away, viz. the Indo-Europeans, the migrations of its various branches affected Asia as well as Europe. The Āryans travelled across the plateau of Asia Minor, finally entering India. In Europe meanwhile, another branch moved northwards along the Volga and westwards across the open plains of Poland and Germany, reaching Denmark and the Rhine, Scotland, Greenland and England.

Invasions too compelled people to leave their ancestral homes. In the course of their movements, the nomads came into conflicts with other people and tribes, which frequently led to a displacement and exodus of the vanquished. In Asia, a branch of the Great Yueh-chi, drove away the Śakas who moving further to the south-west, came to Bactria, where they put an end to the Greek rule. From Baluchistan they travelled to the mouth of the Indus and then towards Gujarat. Meanwhile one of the tribes of the Great Yueh-chi, the Kuṣāṇas became masters of Kabul and Kandahar. In southern China, Chinese expansion forced the Tai or Shan people into Siam and Indo-China. Even in the twentieth century, during World War II, panic-stricken people fled before the onslaught of the Germans. From 1933 to 1939, France gave asylum to Jews from Germany, Austria and Czechoslovakia, as well as to many Italians and Poles. In India, as a result of the demands before and after the partition in 1947, Hindus and Sikhs in large numbers, fled from West Pakistan into India, and Muslims from India into West Pakistan and the then East Pakistan. After 1950 again, Hindus from East Pakistan came to settle in various places in India, while Muslims from India migrated to the then East Pakistan. However, religious and political differences within the population itself, were partially responsible for these movements.

Famines sometimes forced men to leave their homes and move to more congenial places. In mediaeval Europe, people in flight from famine-stricken areas, were a common feature. The potato famine in Ireland between 1846 and 1851 was the most disastrous in western Europe in the nineteenth century. It became a major factor in the emigration of over a million people within a decade. In India such famines had been frequent in the past. Later famines in Bengal in 1776 and in Bombay and Madras during 1876 and 1877, compelled ryots in many villages to abandon their homes.[4] In the U.S.A. in 1934-1935, drought forced ruined farmers to leave the "dust-bowl" of the great plains and flee to California.

Government policy in religious, social, economic, political and foreign spheres, was often responsible for migration. The exodus of the Hebrews from Egypt, recorded in the *Old Testament* can be attributed to religious persecution. In the seventeenth century, similar migrations of fugitives began from England and France. Due to the religious policy of James I many Puritans in 1620 fled from England in the Mayflower to the western part of modern U.S.A. In recent times the religious views and racial consciousness of the Jews have made them victims of harassment.

Sometimes, the socio-economic policy of a government, forced dissidents to emigrate. During and after the civil war in Russia in-between 1919 and 1922 a large number of anti-Communist Russians fled to the democratic countries of Europe. In Germany, when the Nazi party took control of the government in 1933, many migrated to western Europe and the U.S.A.

Agreements between nations and treaty adjustments have resulted in transfer and exchange of population involving migration. This assumed especially immense proportions during World War II. The total number of Europeans expelled, deported, evacuated and transferred upto 1943, has been estimated at 30,000,000.[5] At the close of the War a fresh redistribution of European population took place, so that about 25,000,000 people[6] were settled permanently in the course of various population movements between 1944 and 1947.

Changed modes of production, over-population, poverty, and the desire for individual betterment, have resulted in international migrations, in Great Britain, in the U.S.S.R. and in other countries. The radical changes in agricultural organization and technique and the spread of enclosures in England in the sixteenth, seventeenth and eighteenth centuries created a surplus of rural population, part of which was forced to emigrate. In the early years of the U.S.S.R. the collectivization of agriculture and the industrialization projects of the government led men and women to urban centres.

Migratory movements are at times the result of differential population pressure. They help to equalize the economic density, which is the ratio between the number of inhabitants and the resources at their disposal. Pressure of population combined with other factors, like necessities of extension of trade, the desire for political and cultural expansion, political discontent and unsatisfactory economic conditions. All this in the ancient world led to the founding of the Greek colonies scattered from the Black Sea to the western Mediterranean, and the Roman colonies in Spain, Gaul and north-western Africa.

In modern times over-population involving poverty and lack of employment forced many to enter into a contract-labour or indenture for a number of years. They agreed on the basis of this to leave their home country and to work in the plantations and industries of the developing countries, in return for food and clothes. In 1834, businessmen in Mauritius began to import indentured coolies from India, a step that finally brought many Indians to Mauritius, British Guiana, Trinidad, Jamaica and the other islands of the British West Indies.[7] Indians also migrated to Natal, Tanganyika, Kenya and Uganda and others to the French colonies and Dutch Guiana. Most of the indentured labourers, even after the stipulated number of years, preferred to remain where they had migrated. They set up colonies of permanent settlers financially better off than their fellowmen in their home country. Even within India, as in many other countries, people are driven to migrate to find employment.

Although the system of indentured labour gradually died out, migrations in quest of better economic prospects continued. Not unknown even in early times this desire had led to the individual migration of artisans and craftsmen. Glass workers left the ancient centres of their industry in Syria, and set up glass-houses in Italy after 100 B.C. and also in northern France[8]. An Italian bronze worker is known to have transferred his business from Lucania to Rhodes, while a silk manufacturer, of Antioch, spent his life in Naples. In the present day, international movements of traders and businessmen is known in India. The Marwaris, the most prosperous of business classes in the country left their home-land in Marwar which provides neither sufficient food, nor opportunities nor facilities for trade. To run their business houses, they have settled permanently in Assam, West Bengal, Bihar, Madras and Kerala, which are far-off from Rajasthan. Migrations in search of better economic prospects, have now become a very common occurrence. Qualified men, like doctors, engineers, businessmen, and others, who are nevertheless dissatisfied with their economic situation at home, seek individual betterment in wealthier countries abroad. Migrations from England to Canada, the U.S.A., Australia and New Zealand, and from India to England, Europe, Australia, Canada and the U.S.A., take place frequently, although immigration rules and legislations have restricted such movements to a considerable extent.

## Northern India (c. 475-1030 A.D.)

In Northern India, migrations of Brāhmaṇas from one part of the country to another, are recorded in inscriptions consisting mostly of land-grant charters, dating as far back as the fifth and sixth centuries of the Christian era. Many of the factors responsible for migration mentioned above can be applied to these Brāhmaṇas and will be discussed a few pages hereafter. For the sake of convenience, the history of their migration and the pattern that it took during the period c. 475-1030 A.D. is being studied in various phases.

It must be pointed out that many of the place-names that occur in the charters have either not yet been identified at all or have not yet been located with certainty. Consequently there are records in which sometimes the original habitat of the donee and sometimes his place of residence has been identified, but not the village granted. Again there are cases, where merely the donated lands have been located, but not the Brāhmaṇa's original home, or the place where he first took up residence. Apart from this, there are a number of other land-grants, where it has not been possible to trace the modern place-names of either the Brāhmaṇa's ancestral home, or the region to which he migrated. A list of records consulted for this purpose has been appended at the end.

Mention must also be made of the problem of determining the trend of migration or the nature of movements. However, only in such cases where the Brāhmaṇas are known to have emigrated from one place and taken up residence in another before receiving a grant, can any definite idea be formed about the pattern of migration, i.e. whether the movement was from town to village or *vice versa*, or whether it was merely from village to village and town to town. Lack of identification of place-names becomes a serious problem here, as it makes it difficult to decide, whether a place was a village or a town. Moreover in many cases, the mention of only larger geographical units or localities from where Brāhmaṇas emigrated e.g. the Madhyadeśa, Ṭakāri, Kolāñca and where they settled down, e.g. Oḍra-*viṣaya* and Oḍra-*deśa* further aggravates the problem. However, where there is definite mention of towns and villages or the places have been identified by modern scholars without any doubt, there it is possible to arrive at some conclusion with regard to the pattern of migration.

**History of Migrations in Northern India c. 475-606 A.D.**

With the decline of the imperial Guptas, some new dynasties like the Pāṇḍuvaṁśis, the Maitrakas and the early Kalacuris appeared on the political horizon. It is from the charters of these dynasties that a few instances of migration are known in the early period of our survey.

In the sixth century, the Pāṇḍuvaṁśis were consolidating their power in South Kośala, or the present Raipur-Bilaspur-Sambalpur region of Madhya Pradesh. The fourth ruler in the line was Mahāśiva Tīvara who flourished in the later half of the sixth century A.D.[9] In his fifth regnal year he issued the Bonda Plates. They record the grant of two localities, Bondaka and Avaḍika, adjoining Bondaka, in the Piharāja-*bhukti* made collectively to a number of Brāhmaṇas. The names of three of them were Avanti-Vikramopādhyāya, Lāṭa-Phalihasvāmin and Yoraṅga-Viṣṇubhavasvāmin.[10] As the editor of the charter, D.C. Sircar points out, the fact that these place names are attached to the names of the Brāhmaṇas shows that they probably came from Avanti or western Malwa, Lāṭa or central and southern Gujarat, and possibly Yoraṅga, a place which has not yet been identified. He identifies Bondaka, one of the donated villages, with Bonda, situated about two miles from the bank of the Mahānadī, near Balpur in the Raigarh district of Madhya Pradesh. Avaḍika the other locality has not been identified, although the grant itself states that it was situated close to Bondaka. Hence it may be inferred that these Brāhmaṇas emigrated from Malwa and Gujarat, and came to Madhya Pradesh.

In the last quarter of the fifth century A.D., the family of the Maitrakas of Valabhī was rising to prominence in the Kathiawar Peninsula. Several records of this family are available which are dated in the Valabhī era, usually regarded as the same as the Gupta era of c. 319-320 A.D.

Dharasena II of this line, in the year 270/c. 589-590 A.D., issued a charter wherein it is stated, that Asilāpallikā-grāma in Baṇḍarajidri-*taluka* identified with Asawal[11] and Barejadi, seven miles north of Mehmadabad[12] situated in Kheṭaka-*āhāra* or modern Kaira in Gujarat[13], was given to the Brāhmaṇa Viṣṇumitra. He hailed from Ānarttapura,[14] identified with Ānandapura or modern Vaḍnagara in North Gujarat,[15] and was living in Kheṭaka or Kaira, near which he later received a village.

Just as Mahāśiva Tīvara made over two localities to a number of Brāhmaṇas, so too Maitraka Śīlāditya I, by his Navalakhi Plates, dated in the *Gupta* year 286/c. 545-546 A.D.[16] granted the village Bhoṇḍānaka, included within Vaṭanagara-*sthalī* to forty-four Brāhmaṇas, all of whom had emigrated from Samgapurī.[17] Samgapurī has been identified by H.M. Bhadkamkar, the editor of the grant, as Shahapur near Junagadh. But the donated village has not yet been located. As regards Vaṭanagara-*sthalī* in which it lay, the editor is rather uncertain about its identity. He says that Vaṭanagara may be either Vaḍnagara in Baroda or Vaṭapadra which according to Buhler, was the same as modern Vaḍodra or Baroda. He attributes this uncertainty to two reasons. He argues on the basis of a grant dated G.S. 290/c. 609-610 A.D., where several villages with names ending in *ānaka* are found, that there is greater probability of the correctness of the second alternative. On the other hand, the fame of Vaḍnagara as an early habitat of Brāhmaṇas, still preserved in the name of a local cast of Brāhmaṇas, gives greater support to the first supposition. However, as Vaṭanagara or Vaḍnagara is known to have been the home of several Brāhmaṇas in the early period, it is not unlikely, that the donated village may have been situated in its vicinity. Hence all these Brāhmaṇas who had been living in Shahapur near Junagadh, migrated to the Baroda region and received a village, which they were to share among themselves.

Unlike these charters, wherein the original homes of the donees have been located, a copper-plate of Maitraka Dharasena I, refers to two Brāhmaṇa brothers, whose ancestral home has not been identified with certainty. The donees Ajuna and Mankasvāmin, sons of Guhaḍhya, were inhabitants of Sinhapura but at the time of the grant were residing at Kikkaṭāputra.[18] Later they received two fields and a well in Śarkarāpadraka, a village included in the district of Kikkaṭāputra and the Kālāpaka-*pathaka* of Surāṣṭra. Although the village in which the fields were situated is not identified, according to the charter itself, it lay in Surāṣṭra. As regards Sinhapura from where the Brāhmaṇas came, there are four places having the name Siṁhapura, in the Punjab, in the Kaliṅga country, in Rāḍha[19], and in Gujarat. However, as most of the Maitraka charters record migrations within Gujarat itself, it is possible that Sinhapura here is same as Siṁhapura or Sihor in south-east Kathiawar[20], from where the Brāhmaṇas migrated to the Surāṣṭra region, sometime before they received the grant.

While the donees of all the charters mentioned above, are known to have definitely migrated, the donee Brāhmaṇasvāmin of the Abhona Plates of Śaṁkaragaṇa of the *Kalacuri* year 347/c. 596-597 A.D., has been described as being a resident of Kallivana[21] with no mention whatsoever, as to whether he migrated from elsewhere. He received land measuring a hundred *pādāvartas* in the village of Vallisikā, situated in the *viṣaya* of Bhogavardhana. Mirashi, the editor of the grant, has identified Kallivana with modern Kalvana, the chief town of Kalvana-*taluka* in the Nasik district. According to him, Vallisikā the donated village is modern Valsa, seven miles south of Bhogavardhana. He locates Bhogavardhana in the Hyderabad district in modern Andhra Pradesh, and identifies it with Bhokardhan. D.C.Sircar[22], however, suggests that Bhogavardhana-

*viṣaya* may have been another name of the ancient Govardhana or Nasik district of Maharashtra. This latter identification seems to be more appropriate, as the *Kalacuri* territory is known to have comprised northern Maharashtra. In this case, the donee's home and donated village not being far from one another, he may well have lived in Kalvana in the Nasik district, and enjoyed his lands in a village in the same area. However, if Mirashi's view is accepted, he may have had to emigrate from Kalvana in the Nasik district of Maharashtra, to Bhogavardhana in the Hyderabad state of modern Andhra Pradesh. Although nothing has been said with regard to this, as Nasik and Hyderabad are situated at quite a distance from one another, Brāhmaṇa—svāmin must have found it impossible to supervise a village which was far away from his place of residence. Hence this probably necessitated his migration to the Hyderabad region. So this is a doubtful case of migration, and nothing definite can be said until the identification of Bhogavardhana is established beyond doubt.

**c. 606 — 647 A.D.**

In the early years of the seventh century A.D., a branch of the Gurjara family of Rajputana occupied Broach and the regions around it and gradually a large part of Malwa passed into their hands. The Gurjaras of Broach, however, never assumed imperial titles and ruled as feudatories of either the main Gurjara family of Rajputana or of the Cāḷukyas.

A set of Kaira Plates of Gurjara Dadda II, issued in *KS* 380/c. 629-630 A.D., refers to the grant of the village of Śirīshapadraka situated in the *viṣaya* of Akrureśvara. Mirashi the editor of the plates, identifies the village with Sisodra, about eleven miles west by south of Aṅkleśvara, in the Broach District. The grant was made collectively to forty Brāhmaṇas, two among whom were immigrants. The *adhyāpaka* Bhaṭṭi had emigrated from Jambūsaras or Jambūsara, twenty-seven miles to the north of Broach, and at the time of the grant, was a resident of the donated village.[23] Another Brāhmaṇa Bhadra had come from Bharukachchha or Broach and was a resident of Bherajjikā,[24] identified with Borjai in the Broach district, about twelve miles east of Aṅkleśvara near Broach. Together with the other donees, they were to enjoy the income from the donated village.

Two sets of Sankheda Plates, both dated in *KS* 392/ c. 642 A.D., were issued by Dadda II. Both benefited the Brāhmaṇa Sūrya, who was an emigrant from Daśapura, and a resident of the village of Kṣīrasara.[25] He was endowed with two fields bordering on the village of Kṣīrasara. Daśapura is Mandasor in western Malwa. Mirashi the editor of the charters, has identified Kṣīrasara with Khariakua about a mile to the east of Kukadi, eight miles to the west-south-west of Sankheda in the Baroda district. So the donee in this case, migrated from western Malwa to the Baroda district.

While the Gurjaras held sway over the area around Broach, another part of Gujarat was under the Maitrakas of Valabhī. Dhruvasena II Bālāditya, who was a contemporary of Dadda II, issued several charters. In the *Gupta* year 312/c. 632 A.D., the Brāhmaṇa Mātrakāla, an emigrant from Girinagara and resident of Kheṭaka,[26] received from Dhruvasena II, a field in the western quarter of Hastikapallikā-*grāma* in Koṇaka-*pathaka* in Kheṭāhāra-*viṣaya*. Girinagara and Kheṭaka can be identified with Girnar in Kathiawar and Kaira in Gujarat. The donated village has not yet been located, but the Kheṭāhāra-*viṣaya* in which it lay, can be identified with the district of Kaira, where the Brāhmaṇa was living, having already emigrated from Girnar.

By his Nogawa Plates of the *Gupta* year 320/c. 639-640 A.D., Dhruvasena II handed over a hundred *bhuktis* of land on the eastern boundary of the village of Navagrāmaka, which is unidentified but which lay in Mālavaka. D.C. Sircar identifies Mālavaka with Mālava or Malwa and points out that Dhruvasena II, the donor, is known to have granted land in the district of Mālava, apparently in the Mahi valley.[27] So by this time the Maitrakas had acquired a portion of western Malwa. The land was granted jointly to two Brāhmaṇas. One of them, Saṅgaravi, son of Maheśvara, was an emigrant from Jambūsara near Broach, and a resident of Ayānakāgrahāra.[28] However, another set of Nogawa Plates of Dhruvasena II of the year

321/c. 640-641 A.D., also records a grant to two Brāhmaṇas, one of whom has been described as being a resident of Ayānakāgrahāra and a Trivedin of Daśapura. It is possible that Ayānakāgrahāra may have been near Daśapura or Mandasor in Malwa. Hence sometime before the date of the grant, the donee had left his home in Gujarat and had come to western Malwa.

In the year 323/c. 642-643 A.D. Dhruvasena II issued his Amreli Museum Plates, which refer to the Brāhmaṇa Somaśarman, son of Śāmbhakumāraśarman. His family had emigrated from Ānarttapura or Vaḍnagara, and at the time of the grant he was residing at Valabhī[29] or modern Vala near Bhavnagar in Kathiawar. He became the recipient of a field at the northern border of the village Machchoṭikā in the Uttiṇṇaijja division. Both of these localities are unidentified. This much is known according to the charter, that they lay in Surāṣṭra.

Śīlāditya I issued a charter in which the village where the donated plots of land lay, has not yet been located. In the *Gupta* year 287/c. 608 A.D., the Brāhmaṇa Bhaṭṭi, son of Bhaṭṭaguha who had emigrated from Ānarttapura or Ānandapura, and was a resident of Valabhī[30], received from the Maitraka ruler, a hundred and twenty *pādāvartas* of land in the north-east quarter of the Kālāsamaka village, which unfortunately still remains unidentified.

A number of charters, one of the Cāḷukyas and the rest issued by the Maitrakas, give instances of migration, in which the original habitat of the donees have not yet been traced with certainty. Already in the latter part of the sixth century, a powerful Kanarese family called the Cāḷukyas, was consolidating itself in the Deccan, with the capital at Bādāmi in the Bijapur district. They brought a large part of the Deccan and a portion of Gujarat under their control. Pulakeśin II was the most powerful of the early Cāḷukyas. By his Lohaner Plates of *Śaka* 552/c. 630 A.D., he rewarded a Brāhmaṇa Dāmadīkṣita, who had emigrated from Girinagara and at the time of the grant, was living in Lohānagara[31], by granting him a village named Goviyāṇaka which was near the village of Asikheṭaka and was included in Moṣiṇī-*pathaka*. Although Girinagara is usually identified with Girnar in Kathiawar, G.H. Khare who edited the plates, prefers to identify it with one of the four villages, each being called Girnar, in the Igatpuri, Malegaon, Nasik and Baglan *talukas* of the Nasik district. He identifies Lohānagara with modern Lohaner in the Baglan-*taluka*. As regards the donated village Goviyāṇaka it is the same as the modern village of Govana, lying two miles to the south-west of Askheda or Asikheṭaka, in the Baglan-*taluka* of the Nasik district of Maharashtra. If Khare's view is accepted, Dāmadīkṣita migrated over a short distance within Maharashtra itself. Alternately, if Girinagara is the same as Girnar in Kathiawar, he had to travel a greater distance, coming from Kathiawar in Gujarat to the Nasik district of Maharashtra.

Dhruvasena II in the *Gupta* year 313/c. 634 A.D. issued the Goras Copper Plates. In them are mentioned two Brāhmaṇa cousins, Devakula, son of Śarmma and Bhāda, son of Dattila and nephew of Śarmma. They had come from Valāpadra and had settled in Gorakeśa.[32] Valāpadra has not been identified. But according to D.B. Diskalkar who edits the plates, it may be identical with the village of Velāpadra included in Jharisthalī, mentioned in a grant of Dharasena II of Valabhī.[33] Jhari can be identified with modern Jhar in the Amreli district of Kathiawar. If Velāpadra and Valāpadra are the same, they may be traced to modern Valavad, two miles from Sihor in Kathiawar.[34] Gorakeśa where the donees were residing, is the same as the village Goras, in the Mahuva district in former Bhavnagar state. The cousins were given two fields, each of a hundred *pādāvartas*, in Bahumūla-*grāma* in Vaṭapallikā *sthalī*, which are not identified, but which as the plates say, lay within Surāṣṭra.

As regards the Nogawa Plates of Dhruvasena II of the *Gupta* year 320/c. 639-640 A.D., one of its two donees has been discussed earlier. The other donee Agnisvāmin, son of Kumārasvāmin, had emigrated from Udumbaragahvara and was residing at Agastikāgrahāra,[35] neither of which is identified. Together they were given land in the village of Navagrāmaka in Mālavaka or Malwa. A year later in c. 640-641 A.D., Dhruvasena II again issued a set of Nogawa Plates, also to two donees one of whom was an emigrant Brāhmaṇa, Dattasvāmin, son of Budhasvāmin. He had come from Udumbaragahvara and was a resident of Ayānakāgrahāra,[36] both of which are unidentified. However, Ayānakāgrahāra was probably in the vicinity of Daśapura in Malwa. He and his co-donee received a hundred *bhuktis* of land at the southern boundary of the village of Candraputraka in Mālavaka or Mālava.

Pāṇini in his *Gaṇapāṭha* (IV.2.53) describes the Udumbaras as *'Rajanyās'* and he refers to their habitat near the people of Jullundur. The *Bṛhatsaṁhitā* (XIV.4) places them in the northwest with the Kapiṣṭhalas, who according to K.K. Dasgupta (*A Tribal History of Ancient India*, p.39), presumably lived somewhere on the bank of the Ravi. But the Brāhmaṇa donees of the inscription mentioned above, hailed from a place called Udumbaragahvara which possibly can have no connection with the Punjab. Sankalia points out, that the Udumbara tree is very common in the northern and central parts of Gujarat. However, on this basis, it would not be right to conclude without any reservations, that Udumbaragahvara was a village in either of these regions in Gujarat. Udumbara trees grow in other parts of India as well. So the name Udumbaragahvara could well indicate any place which lay in an area where Udumbara trees can be found. So this place remains unidentified.

**c. 647-750 A.D.**

During the period c. 647-750 A.D. several new dynasties began to emerge on the political scene of Northern India. One of these was the early Guhila family of Kiṣkindhapura, a locality in the Udaipur-Dungarpur region of Rajasthan. The first two members of the house, Paḍḍa and Devagaṇa who flourished in the early years of the seventh century, were erstwhile feudatories of Harṣa of Kanauj. The rulers who came after them do not mention the name of the overlord under whom they held a semi-independent position. D.C. Sircar[37], however, thinks that the later Guhilas of Kiṣkindhapura owed allegiance to the Mauryas or Moris, who had possibly extended their hold over a large part of Rajasthan after the death of Harṣavardhana.

Bhāvihita, successor of Devagaṇa, issued a grant in the *Harṣa* year 48. It refers to the Brāhmaṇa Āsaṅgaśarman, son of Indraśarman, whose family hailed from Ujjayinī or Ujjain, but who himself at the time of the grant was a resident of Kuragirikā.[38] He received a village in the Purapaṭṭa-*Viṣaya*, the location of which according to D.C. Sircar was the area around the capital city[39] of Kiṣkindhapura[40] in the Udaipur-Dungarpur region. So the ancestors of Āsaṅgaśarman had left their home in Madhya Pradesh and had come to Rajasthan some time before the date of the grant.

The Maitrakas of Valabhī were still flourishing in the Surāṣṭra region during this period. Dharasena IV in the *Gupta saṁvat* 330/c. 649-650 A.D., handed over the village Desurakṣitijja in Siṁhapallikā-*pathaka* in Kheṭaka-*āhāra*. Desurakṣitijja has been identified with Desor, eight miles south of Thasara. It lay in Kheṭaka or the Kaira district. The beneficiary was the Brāhmaṇa Nārāyaṇamitra, son of Keśavamitra, who had emigrated from Ānarttapura or Vaḍnagara and was residing in the village of Kāsara[41], which, however, is unidentified.

After Dharasena IV a change occurred in the ruling family, as power passed from the line of Dharasena IV to a collateral branch of the Maitrakas, i.e. to the house of Śīlāditya I. Kharagrāha II Dharmāditya of this branch, in the *Gupta* year 337/c. 656-657 A.D., is known to have granted the village of Paṅgulapallikā in Ghṛtālayabhūmi of Śivabhāgapura-*viṣaya*. These places are not identified, but according to Sankalia, Śivabhāgapura-*viṣaya* was in the Gujarat region.[42] The recipient was Nārāyaṇa, son of Keśava,[43] an emigrant from Ānandapura and a resident of Kheṭaka[44] or Kaira.

Śīlāditya III, in *GS* 346/c. 666 A.D., issued two charters. One of these was in favour of the Brāhmaṇa Yajñadatta alias Prakāśa. He was the son of Śrīdharadatta. He had emigrated from Ānandapura and was a resident of Valabhī.[45] He was given two fields, each of a hundred *pādāvartas*. One was in Padmavaṭika-*grāma* in Kalākṣyeṭaka which is unidentified, but which must have been within Surāṣṭra. The other was in an unnamed village in Hastavaprāhāra or modern Hathab in the former Bhavnagar state in Surāṣṭra. The other charter records a grant to three Brāhmaṇas. Two of them, Piṭṭaleśvara, son of Brāhmaṇa Bhaṭṭihari and Piṭṭaleśvara's son Nāga, had come from Girinagara or Girnar and were living in Siṁhapura[46] or Sihor in Kathiawar. With their co-donee, they were given two fields, each measuring fifty *pādāvartas* situated in Vātanumaka-*grāma* and Daccānaka-*grāma* which are unidentified, but were included in Hastavaprāhāra, which lay within Surāṣṭra.

Two Maitraka charters, one dated in the *Gupta* era 350/c.669-670 A.D., and another of *saṁvat* 352/c.671-672 A.D., are said to have belonged to Śīlāditya II. But there seems to be some mistake, as regards either the dates of the grants or the name of the donor. According to R.C. Majumdar, the dates of Śīlāditya III range between c. 662 and 684 A.D.[47] On the basis of this, the donor of the two grants mentioned above, should be Śīlāditya III and not Śīlāditya II. The earlier charter, the Lunsadi Plates refer to the grant of some lands and a pond in the village of Desenaka, which stood at the mouth of the Madhumatī river in the land of Surāṣṭra. The donees were two Brāhmaṇa brothers, emigrants from Dvīpa[48] or modern Diu. By his later grant of *saṁvat* 352/c. 671-672 A.D., Śīlāditya III handed over a field in Dhūṣā village, which has not been located, but which on the evidence of the charter itself lay within Surāṣṭra. The recipient was Magopadatta, son of Kikkaka who like many others had left Ānandapura and had come to settle in Valabhī[49] or Vala.

The Gurjaras still held sway over the Broach region. From Navasari, Jayabhaṭa III of this family, issued a set of plates in *KS* 456/c. 705-706 A.D. In them is mentioned Devasvāmin, also called Kallumbara, son of Datta. He had left his home in Girinagara in Kathiawar and at the time of the grant was living in Śrāddhikāgrahāra,[50] which, however, is unidentified. He was granted the Śamīpadraka village in Korillā-*pathaka*. Mirashi the editor of the plates, identifies Śamīpadraka with Sondarn, seven miles south-west of Karwan and twelve miles north of the Narmadā, and Kōrillā-*pathaka* with Koral, on the northern bank of the Narmadā, about ten miles north-east of Broach. Hence in this case, the migration was confined within Gujarat.

While the main line of the Cāḷukyas was ruling with its headquarters at Bādāmi, another branch closely related to them by family ties, was ruling as the viceroys of the Gujarat region, with Navasari as the provincial capital. Avanijanāśraya Pulakeśirāja, was fourth in the line of these viceroys. From Navasari, he issued a set of plates in *KS* 490/c. 739-740 A.D. By this charter the village Padraka, situated in the *āhāra* and *viṣaya* of Karmaṇeya, was bestowed on the Brāhmaṇa Kāñcala, son of Govindali, who had emigrated from Vanavāsī.[51] According to Mirashi who has edited the charter, the village Padraka is represented by modern Pardi, four miles east of Navasari, in the Surat district. Karmaṇeya *viṣaya* in which it was included, is identical with Kamrej, ten miles to the north-east of Surat. Vanavāsī from where the donee had come, is in North Kanara. So the donee emigrated from North Kanara.

Shortly before the collapse of the Cāḷukyas, a family of the Rāṣṭrakūṭas was gradually coming into prominence in the Deccan. They carved out for themselves in the middle of the seventh century, a small principality in Berar, and gained in importance under Dantidurga who later became the founder of the Rāṣṭrakūṭa empire. His Ellora Plates dated *Śaka* 663/c. 741 A.D., refer to three Brāhmaṇas, Ādityabhaṭṭa, Māula and Govisara, who were emigrants from Navasārikā.[52] They were given the village of Pippalāla in the district of Candrapurī-84. Navasārikā has been identified by D.C. Sircar, with Nausari in the Surat district of South Gujarat.[53] The donated village Pippalāla is the same as modern Pippalala, about thirty-three miles from Ellora near Aurangabad in northern Maharashtra. Hence the three donees went from Gujarat to Maharashtra.

Mention must be made here of two charters, wherein there is no hint of the original homes of two donees, who are described merely as being residents of particular areas. The Prince of Wales Museum Plates of Gurjara Dadda III, dated in *KS* 427/c. 676-677 A.D., record the grant of Uvarivadra village in Korillā-84. The village has not been located, but Korillā has been identified with Koral on the northern bank of the Narmadā, about ten miles north-east of Broach. The village perhaps lay within the sub-division named Korillā, probably comprising eighty-four villages. The donee was an unnamed Brāhmaṇa, a resident of Sāvatthi.[54] The editor S.N. Chakravarti, does not give the identification of Sāvatthi. However, it is perhaps the same as Śrāvasti, referred to in the records of the later period, as being Bengal or U.P. or sometimes in the wide region known as Madhyadeśa, representing the upper and middle Gangetic basin and the Yamunā-Chambal catchment area.[55] As these regions were far away from Gujarat, the donee must have emigrated from his ancestral home, although the word *vāstavya*[56] and not *vinirgata* has been used in the charter.

The second grant belongs to Anantavarman, son of Devendravarman of the early Eastern Gaṅga family, which had its capital at Kaliṅganagara or Mukhalingam, near Srikakulam in modern Andhra Pradesh. In the *Gaṅga* year 204/c. 700 A.D., he issued the Parlakimedi Plates, which record, that the Brāhmaṇa Viṣṇusomācārya, a resident of Śṛṅgaṭikāgrahāra in Kāmarūpa-*viṣaya*[57] got as a donation the village Talatthere in Kroṣṭukavarttani. The donated village is as yet unidentified. However, Kroṣṭukavarttani in which it lay, was the region to the north of the Vaṁśadhārā in the Ganjam district. Śṛṅgaṭikāgrahāra, where the donee lived, is not identified. R.K. Ghoshal the editor of the charter suggests, that the Kāmarūpa-*viṣaya* to which the village belonged, is not in Assam, but possibly is an unknown district of ancient Kaliṅga. He, however, does not put forward any reason to explain his view. Moreover, so far we know of only one Kāmarūpa in Assam. Hence in the absence of any explanation to locate Kāmarūpa elsewhere, it can be surmised that Viṣṇusomācārya had lived in Assam. Although the word *vāstavya* occurs in the record, as Assam is at a great distance from the Ganjam district of Orissa, he must have migrated to the region where he later received a grant.

One record, the Mudgapadra grant of Śryāśraya Śīlāditya, the elder brother of Avanijanāśraya Pulakeśirāja, dated in *KS* 420/c. 668-669 A.D., refers to the grant of Mudgapadra-*grāma* in Vichihāra district. No clue to the identification of this village is available. One of the donees of the grant was Revāditya, son of Bambhasvāmin, whose family hailed from Girinagara[58] in Kathiawar.

A number of Maitraka charters, as well as a Gurjara grant, give the names of Brāhmaṇas who had left their homes whose location has not yet been traced. Dharasena IV issued a charter, recording the grant of two fields, one in Kolamba in the *viṣaya* of Kheṭaka and the other in the village of Duhuduhu of Nagaraka-*pathaka*. None of these places except Kheṭaka can be found on a modern map. However, according to Bühler who edits the grant, Nagaraka-*pathaka* means the area immediately surrounding the town, and he interprets this as surrounding Kheṭaka itself. So the donated fields lay in the vicinity of Kheṭaka. The donee Aditiśarman, son of Bhavīnāgaśarman, was himself a resident of Kheṭaka at the time of the grant. But he had emigrated from Udumbaragahvara,[59] the modern equivalent of which still remains to be found.

Dharasena IV was succeeded by Dhruvasena III of the family of Śīlāditya I. His grant of the year 334/c. 653-654 A.D., refers to the Brāhmaṇa Bhaṭṭibhaṭṭa, son of Bappa, who was a native and inhabitant of Mahichhaka.[60] He received the village of Paṭṭapadraka in the dakṣiṇapaṭṭa of Śivabhāgapura-*viṣaya*. None of these places is identified, although according to Sankalia, Śivabhāgapura-*viṣaya* was in the Gujarat region.

Śīlāditya III by a grant dated *Gupta saṁvat* 342/c. 661-662 A.D. rewarded the Brāhmaṇa Bhūtakumāra, son of Droṇa. He was an emigrant from Gomūtrikā and a resident of Valabhī.[61] He received Loṇāpadraka-*grāma*. Except for Valabhī, the identity of the other places is unknown, although the donated village, as the charter says, lay in Surāṣṭra.

In the *Gupta* year 346/c. 666 A.D., Śīlāditya III made a grant of two fields in Surāṣṭra to three Brāhmaṇas. Two of them have been discussed earlier. The third Soma, son of Dattulika, had originally been living in Kuśaḥrada,[62] which is as yet unidentified. It may be the same as Kāśaḥrada, identical with Kasardra, twelve miles to the north west of Ahmedabad in Gujarat. However, the identification being uncertain, nothing definite can be said about the location of Kuśaḥrada.

Śīlāditya III again features as the donor of two sets of Jesar Plates. The earlier set, dated in the *Gupta* year 347/c. 666-667 A.D. records, that the Brāhmaṇa Dīkṣita Saggala, alias

Prakāśa, was the son of Sāmbadatta, and having emigrated from Puşyaśāmbapura was residing at Valabhī.[63] He was given a hundred *pādāvartas* of land in the village of Kukkapadra in the Kālāpaka-*pathaka* of Surāştra. Neither the donee's original home, nor the village granted to him has been identified. But Kālāpaka the *pathaka* in which village lay, is modern Kalavada, sixty miles north-west of Porbandar. It was included in the Surāştra region.

Another emigrant from the same place Puşyaśāmbapura, figures as the donee of the second set of Jesar Plates of the *Valabhī* year 357/c. 676-677 A.D. His name is not mentioned and he is only referred to as a Dīkşita,[64] and son of Sāmbadatta. He received a hundred and four *pādāvartas* of land on the northern boundary of the village of Madasara, which like Puşyaśāmbapura, cannot be traced. However, the grant specifically mentions that the village was in Surāştra.

A later Maitraka ruler, also named Śīlāditya in the year 403/c. 722-723 A.D., issued a charter recording the transfer of Antarapallikā village near Dinnaputra in Surāştra. The donee was Bhaṭṭa Vāsudevabhūti, son of Dāmodarabhūti, and emigrant from Śrīvardhamānabhukti, and a resident of Liptikhaṇḍa.[65] Both these places, as in the case of the others in the charters discussed above, are still to be identified. But if Śrīvardhamānabhukti is the same as modern Burdwan or Vardhamana district of Bengal, then this would be one of the earliest available instances of Brāhmanical emigration known from Bengal. However, the identification is not established beyond doubt. Śrīvardhamānabhukti may have been the larger territorial unit within which was included Vardhamānapura or Wadhwan in Kathiawar. But this too cannot be stressed with certainty.

Jayabhaṭa IV was the last known of the early Gurjaras. The only date available for him, is the one provided by his Prince of Wales Museum Plates of *KS* 486/c. 735-736 A.D. By means of these Plates, Bhaṭṭa Āchchaḍa, son of Ādityanāga, whose original home was in the *āhāra* and pathaka of Lohikakşa,[66] which is as yet unidentified, received the village of Mannātha situated in the Bharukachchha *vişaya*. The grant has been edited by Mirashi, who locates Mannātha on the right bank of the Dhādhar. He points out, that it is the same as Magnath, about two miles south-east of Jambūsara and twenty-five miles north of Broach.

## C. 750 — 1030 A.D.

From about the middle of the eighth century, significant changes occurred in the political history of Northern India. The Maitrakas, early Gurjaras and Guhilas are no longer heard of. On the other hand, new dynasties like the Rāṣṭrakūṭas, Pālas, Gurjara-Pratihāras and the Paramāras came to power. In Orissa, a number of almost contemporary ruling houses made their appearance. For the sake of convenience, in this section, the records in which the Brāhmaṇas' original homes and places to which they migrated are identified, have been discussed region-wise, the order being Bengal, Rajasthan, Madhya Pradesh, Gujarat, Maharashtra, Orissa and the Kanara district. Bihar and Assam follow after this, as the two charters in which these regions occur as places of migration, belong to the eleventh century.

The Pālas of Bengal and Bihar at times extended their hold over other parts of North India. Dharmapāla, the second in this line, issued the Khalimpur Plates in his thirty-second regnal year. By this charter, the king made a grant of four villages—Krauñcaśvabhra in the Vyāghrataṭī-*maṇḍala* in Mahāntaprakāśa-*viṣaya* of Puṇḍravardhana-*bhukti* Māḍhāśāmmali village, bounded on the north by Gaṅginikā or dried up river bed, Pālitaka bounded on the east by the river Konṭhiyā and on the north by Gaṅginikā, and Gopippalī in the Āmraṣaṇḍika-*maṇḍala* of the Sthālikkaṭa-*viṣaya*. None of these villages has been identified. But Krauñcaśvabhra village is said to have been situated in Puṇḍravardhana-*bhukti*, which according to D.C. Sircar, is the same as North Bengal.[67] But he also points out, that certain border areas of Prāgjyotiṣa-Kāmarūpa, may have been annexed to Puṇḍravardhana-*bhukti* by Dharmapāla. The reason for this conjecture is, that Māḍhāśāmmali one of the villages included in the

Puṇḍravardhana-*bhukti*, and mentioned in this place, is regarded by some scholars, to be identical with, or to be situated near Mayūraśālmalī in Candrapuri-*viṣaya* in Prāgjyotiṣa-Kāmarūpa, as known from the Nidhanpur Plates of Bhāskaravarman. Moreover, as D.C. Sircar himself says, during the age of the Pālas and their contemporary rulers, considerable areas of East and South Bengal, were included in the *bhukti* called Puṇḍravardhana or Pauṇḍra. So the donated villages of the Khalimpur Plates lay in North Bengal, and possibly in the region bordering on Kāmarūpa. The beneficiaries of the grant were the god Nunna-Nārāyaṇa and some Lāṭa Brāhmaṇa priests,[68] and others who attended to the god. Obviously these Brāhmaṇas were inhabitants of the Lāṭa region, as can be seen from the epithet Lāṭa Brāhmaṇa given to them. Hence they had migrated from Lāṭa in Gujarat to Puṇḍravardhana-*bhukti* and must have received with others, four villages at a later date.

Gopāla II of the same family in his sixth regnal year, by his Jājilpārā grant, donated some lands to a Brāhmaṇa named Bhaṭṭaputra Yājñika Śrīdharaśarman, son of Śrīgarbha. He had emigrated from Muktāvastu and was residing in Sīha-*grāma*.[69] Muktāvastu has been identified with the Mūthāutha *bhaṭṭa-grāma* in Varendra-*maṇḍala* of the Talcher Plates of Gayāḍatuṅga,[70] and the Muktāvathi in Śrāvasti of the Kalibhanā Plates of the thirty-fourth regnal year of Somavaṁśi Mahābhavagupta I.[71] Muktāvastu perhaps was a locality like Kolāñca, Ṭakāri and Śrāvasti, which will be discussed later and which have been located by scholars sometimes in the Madhyadeśa region, sometimes in North Bengal and sometimes in Assam. The possibility is that in the present charter the second alternative is the more probable. Sīha-*grāma* where the donee was residing may be either modern Sihali or Sihole on the Gazole-Dinajpur road within Bansihari police station of Dinajpur district or Sahagrama within Parbatipur police station also in the Dinajpur district. While living in this village, Śrīdharaśarman received two *pallis* named Kāṣṭhagṝha and Mahārāja. They were situated in the village of Ānandapura and evidently denote two units of the village. Ānandapura itself was an *agrahāra* of Kuddalakhāta-*viṣaya* and Puṇḍravardhana-*bhukti*, the last place-name being the only one that can be identified, with North Bengal. Hence the Brāhmaṇa of the grant, possibly did not travel very far and although he left his home perhaps in a village in North Bengal, he merely moved to another, also in the same region.

Mahīpāla I who came later than Gopāla II and flourished towards the end of the tenth century, issued in his ninth regnal year, the Bangarh grant. It refers to the donee Kṛṣṇādityaśarman, son of Bhaṭṭaputra Madhusūdana, an emigrant from Hastipada-*grāma* and a resident of Cavaṭi-*grāma*.[72] He was given lands in Kuraṭapallikā-*grāma* in the Gokalikā-*maṇḍala* in the Koṭivarṣa-*viṣaya* in Puṇḍravardhana-*bhukti*. Hastipada-*grāma* where the donee had originally lived is sometimes identified with Hastigrāma of the Kalibhanā Plates of the sixth regnal year of Mahābhavagupta I,[73] which has been located by some as being near Vaiśāli or modern Basarh in the Muzaffarpur district of North Bihar. The identity of the sites of the village where the donee came to settle and the one that he received, has not yet been established. But Koṭivarṣa-*viṣaya* in which the donated village was situated, is regarded by D.C. Sircar, as being the same as the Dinajpur area of Puṇḍravardhana-*bhukti*. So the donee migrated perhaps from North Bihar, to the Dinajpur area of North Bengal.

Mūlarāja I, the founder of the Aṇhilvāḍa branch of the Cauḷukyas, by the Balera Plates of *V.S.* 1051/c. 994-995 A.D. granted a village to Dīrghācārya, son of Durlabhācārya, an emigrant from Kānyakubja[74] or Kanauj. The donated village Varaṇaka in Satyapura-*maṇḍala*, has been identified by Munshi Debi Prasad with the modern village of Balera in the Sanchor district of the erstwhile Jodhpur state. Sten Konow who edited the charter, does not agree with the location. On the basis of the boundaries of the village, Guṁdāuka or Gondau in the south, Metravāla or Mirpur in the north, Voḍha or Bodan in the west and Dhanāra or Dantwara in the east, he feels, that the village Varaṇaka in Sanchor lay further to the east. Dīrghācārya left Kanauj in U.P. and travelled westwards towards Rajasthan and there became the recipient of a village.

A fragmentary grant from Jodhpur, ascribed to one Siṁharāja, is dated in the *Vikrama* year 1054/c. 997 A.D. According to the editor, B.C. Chhabra, it cannot be said who this Siṁharāja really was. However he thinks, that the latter can be identified with the Cāhamāna king of this name. But Cāhamāna Siṁharāja is known to have been succeeded by his son, Vigraharāja II, whose Harṣa Inscription is dated *V.S.* 1030/c. 973 A.D.[75] His father Siṁharāja must have been ruling before this date, which puts him much earlier than *V.S.* 1054 the date of the above mentioned fragmentary grant. Hence Chhabra's view cannot be accepted. Siṁharāja of the inscription under review must have been a chief belonging to some family other than of the famous Cāhamāna Siṁharāja, ruling over some territory in Rajasthan. This fragmentary grant records, that a village in Satyapura-*pathaka* or Sanchor, was given to the Brāhmaṇa Upādhyāya Nannaka, son of Govinda. He had come from Bhillamāla.[76] Bhillamāla is identical with Bhinmal in the Jalore district of Jodhpur division, not far from Sanchor, near which lay the donated village.

Just as it is difficult to identify Siṁharāja, so it is to assign Vatsarāja of the Mahua Inscription, dated in the eighth century, to a particular dynasty. This Vatsarāja was not identical with the famous Gurjara-Pratihāra Vatsarāja. He may have been an independent or semi-independent ruler, the name of whose overlord is not mentioned. Ācārya Jinasena who completed his Jaina *Harivaṁśa* in Vardhamānapura or Wadhwan in Kathiawar, refers to one Vatsarāja, king of Avanti, ruling over eastern regions, in *Śaka* 705/c. 783-784 A.D. According to S. Sankaranarayanan and G. Bhattacharya, who have jointly edited the inscription, the author probably means the region to the east of Wadhwan. The traditional eastern division of India, comprising Aṅga, Vaṅga etc., is not the one indicated here. The latter area was at this time under the Pālas. Therefore the editors suggest that Vatsarāja may be identified with his namesake mentioned by Jinasena, probably ruling over the Avanti region.

The inscription is an eulogy, engraved on a temple in the Shivpuri district of Madhya Pradesh. The composer of the eulogy, Bhaṭṭa Iśāna, son of Bhaṭṭa Somāṅka, and younger brother of Bhaṭṭa Devasvāmin, hailed from Kāṇyakubja.[77] Thus either Iśāna himself, or his father had emigrated from Kanauj and had come to Madhya Pradesh, where Iśāna found employment.

The Paramāras consolidated themselves in the Malwa region, in about the first quarter of the ninth century. A Yādava charter from Devalili of the second half of the eleventh century, makes mention of a Brāhmaṇa whose ancestor Sillaṇa had emigrated from his home in Oyarī-*grāma* in Madhyadeśa,[78] to serve under Paramāra Vairisiṁha of Dhārā in Madhya Pradesh. Oyarī, the village where he had originally lived cannot be located. However, as regards the geographical extent of Madhyadeśa in which it stood, D. C. Sircar identifies it with the central part of Northern India and points out, that what was originally called Āryāvarta, was later named Madhyadeśa.[79] The early texts like the Mahābhāṣya and the *Baudhāyana Dharmasūtra,* define Āryāvarta, as the land to the east of Ādarśa, which according to K. K. Dasgupta,[80] is probably the same as Adarśana or Vinaśana in Sirhind in Patiala in the Punjab, where the river Sarasvatī is said to have disappeared into the ground, and to the west of Kālakavana near Allahabad. It was bounded on the north by the Himalayas and on the south by Pāriyātra or the western part of the Vindhyas along with the Aravalli range. Most of the texts give the same geographical limits for Madhyadeśa. However, there is some controversy as regards its eastern boundary. The *Kāvyamīmāṁsā* of Rājaśekhara, extends the eastern boundary as far as Vārāṇasī in U.P., while the Buddhist texts, the *Mahāvagga* and *Divyāvadāna* extend Majjhimadeśa, further to the east, one to include Kajaṅgala or Kankjole near the Rajmahal hills in Bihar and the other to include Puṇḍravardhana or North Bengal. Varāhamihira includes in Madhyadeśa, the rivers Sarasvatī and Yamunā, as well as Sāketa and Prayāga and makes Allahabad, the eastern boundary of Madhyadeśa. Hence as Dasgupta concludes, the upper and middle Gangetic basin, and the Yamunā-Chambal catchment area represented the heart of Madhyadeśa. Oyarī-*grāma* where Sillaṇa and his ancestors used to live, was situated in this region and from there he travelled in search of employment to the city of Dhārā in Madhya Pradesh.

Vākpati Muñja or Vākpati II of the Paramāra family, flourished in between c. 972 and 998 A.D. From Malwa he issued the Dharmapuri grant in *V.S.* 1031/c. 974 A.D. It records that a taḍāra named Pipparikā on the bank of the Narmadā, was granted to Vasantācārya, son of Dhanika Paṇḍita, who had emigrated from Ahichchhatra.[81] Ahichchhatra was an ancient town situated in the modern Bareilly district of U.P. Although the actual locality of the donated *taḍāra* is unknown, we are told that it stood on the bank of the Narmadā. So it must have been in Madhya Pradesh. And as the inscription mentions, the donee migrated southwards to Madhya Pradesh, from the Bareilly district of U.P. in the north.

Vākpati II also issued two sets of Gaonri Plates, one in *V.S.* 1038/c. 981 A.D. and the other in *V.S.* 1043/c. 986 A.D. The earlier charter records the grant of the village Vaṇikā in the Āvaraka-*bhoga* and Hūṇa-*maṇḍala*. Vaṇikā has been identified with Benka, fifteen miles north-west of Awar. Hūṇa-*maṇḍala* in which the donated village lay, may be the same as the northern part of the Malwa plateau. The *Śaktisaṅgama Tantra* (III. VII. 44) places Hūṇa-deśa to the south of Kāmagiri and to the north of Marudeśa, which according to D. C. Sircar[82], is practically the same area as suggested by the *Harṣacarita*, i.e. in the Punjab region. However, in this case, the first identification, that the Hūṇa-*maṇḍala* was the northern part of the Malwa plateau, seems to be more appropriate, as the donated village lay in that area.

The above mentioned village was made over collectively to twenty-six Brāhmaṇas in the *Vikrama* year 1038/c. 981 A.D. Some of them came from the Mālava area, but others from far and wide as far west as Gujarat and as far east as Bengal. One of the donees Bhāila, son of Hari emigrated from an unnamed place in Lāṭadeśa,[83] another Muṁjāla, son of Īśvara from Nāndipura in Lāṭadeśa, i.e. Nandod near Broach, and a third Nenaiyaka, son of Madhu from Kheṭaka[84] or Kaira, also in

Gujarat. Another donee Sarvānanda, son of Dīkṣita Lokānanda hailed from Kaṇopā, which has not been identified, but is said in the charter, to have been in Magadha,[85] that is South Bihar. Some of the donees came from different parts of Bengal. Donāka son of Gosaraṇa emigrated from Vilvagavāsa in Dakṣiṇa Rāḍha[86] (south-west Bengal). Bogra district in pre-1947 North Bengal was the original home of three donees, namely Śabara, son of Raṇāditya from Kulāñca, Madhumathana, son of Acala from Mitila-*pāṭaka* and Śaṅkara son of Devāditya from Dardurika.[87] Mitila-*pāṭaka* is identical with Mitail or Matialpara and Dardurikā is the same as Dadra in the Panchbibi thana, all being situated in the Bogra district. Both Mitila-*pāṭaka* and Dardurikā lay within Sāvathikā-*deśa*, which has been described as indicating the tract corresponding to North Bogra and South Dinajpur in old Bengal.

As regards Sāvathikā-*deśa* or Śrāvasti, Kulāñca or Kolāñca and Tarkāri, there is some controversy among scholars as to whether they were in U.P. or North Bengal. According to D. C. Sircar,[88] the Hili-Balurghat region of North Bengal was called Śrāvasti. He says, that a large number of Brāhmaṇas of Śrāvasti in Kośala in Madhyadeśa, i.e. in the Set-Mahet region in the Gonda and Bahraich districts of U.P., specially of Tarkāri in that region, which is located in some records in Madhyadeśa, were settled in the Hili-Balurghat region of North Bengal. They named their new settlements after their old habitations in U.P. He further points out, that as known from the Bangaon Plates, issued in the seventeenth regnal year of Vigrahapāla III, the Brāhmaṇas of a place called Kroḍāñca, Kroḍāñja or Kolāñca, apparently situated in U.P., probably in the Śrāvasti area, were highly respected by the Brāhmaṇas of Mithilā. He feels, that the Maithila Brāhmaṇas could not have been so respectful towards the Brāhmaṇas of North Bengal. Moreover, according to tradition, the ancestors of the *Kulīna* Brāhmaṇas of Bengal, came from Kroḍāñja. A village called Krosañja is stated to have been situated in Śrāvasti in the Śubhaṅkarapāṭaka grant of Dharmapāla from Assam.[89] P. N. Bhattacharya[90] holds, that this Śrāvasti lay in the kingdom of Kāmarūpa. According to him Śrāvasti in Uttara Kośala, i.e.

the Ayodhya region, was an important centre of the Buddhists. As a result of the spread of Buddhism in that region, the Brāhmaṇas of Śrāvasti left their home and came to settle in Kāmarūpa. Later when Bengal became free from Buddhist influence, the Brāhmaṇas migrated from Assam and went to settle in Puṇḍravardhana. D.C. Sircar, however, identifies the Śrāvasti of the Śubhaṅkarapāṭaka grant, with the Hili-Balurghat region of North Bengal. Both P.N. Bhattacharya and D.C. Sircar agree, that the Brāhmaṇas having left their original habitat settled in Śrāvasti, which they named after their home that they had left behind. So we have various sites called Śrāvasti, and likewise Tarkāri or Ṭakāri, and Kolāñca, which in different charters are said to be sometimes in Madhyadeśa, sometimes in the Gonda and Bahraich districts of U.P., in Bengal and in Assam. Hence the donees of the Gaonri Plates, whose homes are said to have been in Sāvathikā-*deśa* may have emigrated, as K.N. Dikshit the editor says, from North Bengal, or they may have come to Madhya Pradesh from U.P. or even from Assam.

Ayaka in Madhyadeśa, and another unnamed village also in the same region,[91] were the ancestral homes of Mūlasthāna son of Brahmapaṇḍita, and Puruṣottama, son of Līhā. From there the two Brāhmaṇas migrated to the Paramāra kingdom. One of the donees Govindasvāmin, son of Devasvāmin came from Madhupālikā.[92] This has been identified with Majhowli, a village name common in U.P. Pauṇḍarika, which itself is not identified, but which as the inscription says, was in Uttarakula,[93] was the home of Vāmanasvāmin, son of Dīkṣita Hari. Uttarakula has been described by the editor, as some tract to the north of the Ganges, and Pauṇḍarika may have been a locality there.

Sihaṭa son of Mitrānanda, and Āmatta son of Guṇākara, had originally lived in Śravaṇabhadra.[94] K.N. Dikshit identifies Śravaṇabhadra with Sonabhadra near Kanauj. In the Mahudi Plates of Paramāra Bhoja of *V.S.* 1074/c. 1017 A.D., Śravaṇabhadra has been described as situated in Gauḍa-*deśa*.[95] According to D. C. Sircar, the Gauḍa, country originally seems to have comprised in a narrow sense, the present district of Murshidabad, together with the southern-most areas of the Malda district of Bengal. It was bounded on the north by the Padmā and in the south by the Burdwan or Vardhamāna district. The *Bhaviṣya Purāṇa* regards Gauḍa as only one of the seven *deśas* forming Puṇḍra-*deśa*. The localities that made up the Gauḍa country were the present Murshidabad district, with parts of Nadia, Burdwan and Hooghly districts of West Bengal. In about the seventh century A.D. the name Gauḍa began to be used generally to indicate the countries of Eastern India. Moreover, besides Gauḍa in Bengal, some other tracts in different parts of India, were also known by this name. One such Gauḍa was the modern Gonda district of U.P., in which Śrāvasti was situated. The name Gauḍa was also used in a general sense for the five countries of Northern India, Sārasvata or the Kurukshetra region, Kānyakubja or Kanauj, Gauḍa or Bengal, Mithilā or Bihar and Utkala or Orissa.[96] Hsuan Tsang refers to Harṣa's conquest of the five Indies, which as R.S. Tripathi explains, comprised the five regions mentioned above. Sihaṭa and Āmatta, who were originally inhabitants of Śravaṇabhadra, could have emigrated from Bengal, or any one of these five countries, to the donated village.

Hence the beneficiaries of Vākpati II's Gaonri Plates, came from both far and near to settle in the village of Benka near Ujjain.

Sarvānanda, one of these donees, was endowed with the village of Kaḍahichchhaka in Maddhuka-*bhukti* by the second set of Gaonri Plates of Vākpati II, dated *V.S.* 1043/c. 986 A.D. The village have been identified with Kaḍacha or Karcha, three miles to the north of Narwal and three miles to the north-west of Gaonri near Ujjain. Maddhuka-*bhukti* in which the village stood, is indicated by the Maha or Mhow cantonment near Indore, about forty miles from Narwal. So Sarvānanda who had come from Kaṇopā[97] in Magadha in South Bihar, while enjoying a village with twenty-five other Brāhmaṇas, since *V.S.* 1038/c. 981 A.D., was made the sole proprietor of another village, also in the same region in *V.S.* 1043/c. 986 A.D.

According to B.C. Chhabra, the editor of the Mandakila Tal Inscription of *V.S.* 1043/c. 986 A.D. it refers to the ruling king (*lokanṛpaḥ*) in verse three. The chief town of the said king is called Mālava in verse four. So Chhabra thinks that the reference is to Mālava and its capital of that time, Ujjayinī. The description of the town as given in the record is comparable to that given by poets like Kalidāsa. Moreover, the king referred to is Vākpati Muñja, c. 972-998 A.D. D.C. Sircar does not accept this view. He feels that the reference in the two verses, is to Lokarāja, who may have been a chief of the ancient Mālava clan, as coins of the Mālavas have been found in large numbers at Nagar, which he thinks is the same as the Mālava-*nagara* of the inscription, and lies in the Uniara *Tahsil* in the Tonk district of Rajasthan. However, as the date of the inscription, *V.S.* 1043/c. 986 A.D., falls within the reign-period of Vākpati II, the king mentioned here may be Vākpati II himself. The object of the inscription was to record the erection of a temple by a man named Nandana. The composer of the eulogy was the Brāhmaṇa Vimalamati, son of Durlabharāja. He was the grandson of a Brāhmaṇa, who was fifth in descent from the poet Bāṇabhaṭṭa and has been described as "an ornament of a place called Roheṭaka",[98] which may be the ancient Rauhitaka in Haryana, forty-three miles north-west of Delhi. If this hypothesis is accepted the ancestors of Vimalamati or even he himself, had emigrated from Haryana, and came to the town called Mālava in this inscription, either in Rajasthan or in Madhya Pradesh. It must be noted here that Bāṇabhaṭṭa's original home was never in Haryana.

The Betma grant of Bhojadeva, nephew of Vākpati II, dated *V.S.* 1076/c. 1019 A.D. refers to the Brāhmaṇa Paṇḍita Delha, son of Thaṭṭhasika, whose ancestors had emigrated from Viśālagrāma which is unidentified. However, he himself had come from Sthāṇvīśvara or[99] Thanesar in Haryana. He received the village of Nalataḍāga, included in Nyāyapadra-saptadaśaka, identified with Nal in the Kaira district of Gujarat. Hence we see that the donee came from Thanesar in Haryana to the Kaira district of Gujarat.

In *V.S.* 1079/c. 1022 A.D., Paramāra Bhoja issued the Depalpur grant. By this charter, the Brāhmaṇa Vacchala, son of Bhaṭṭa Sośvara, who had originally lived in Mānyakheṭa,[100] was granted land at Kirikaikā in the western *pathaka* of Ujjayinī. Mānyakheṭa has been identified by D. C. Sircar with Malkhed in the Gulbarga district of the former Hyderabad state, now in Karnataka. Kirikaikā, the village in which the donated lands lay, is Karki in the Depalpur *pargana*, nearly forty miles to the south-west of Ujjain, which is in the western region of Madhya Pradesh. So in this case, the donee moved from modern Karnataka to Madhya Pradesh, where he received some land.

In the early years of the seventh century, a family of Cāhamānas, was ruling as petty chiefs either in Śākambharī or Sambhar region of Jaipur or in Māhiṣmatī on the Narmadā. A member of the family Bhartṛvaḍḍha II was appointed by his overlord, the Gurjara-Pratihāra Nāgabhaṭa I, to rule in the Broach region as his feudatory after the decline of the Gurjaras of Broach. In *V.S.* 813/c. 756 A.D., Bhartṛvaḍḍha II issued the Hansot Plates. The writer of this charter, Bhaṭṭa, Kakka has been described as *Vālabhya*[101] i.e. an emigrant from Valabhī. He left his home and came to Broach where he found employment under Bhartṛvaḍḍha II.

Rāṣṭrakūṭa Indra III issued the Jambgaon grant in *Śaka* 836/c. 914-915 A.D. by which the village of Kurundaka and other villages and also the village of Tenna in the vicinity of Kammanija situated in Lāṭa-*deśa* were given to Brāhmaṇas. Of these villages, Tenna, is the same as modern Ten near Kamrej in the Nausari division of the former Baroda state. The donee was the Brāhmaṇa Siddhapabhaṭṭa son of Vennapabhaṭṭa, who was originally from Pāṭaliputra.[102] Although Pāṭaliputra is generally identified with Patna in Bihar, yet as D. C. Sircar points out, there is a Pāṭaliputra in the South Arcot district of Madras. The name Pāṭaliputra has been given to modern Cuddalore, probably by the Brāhmaṇas who migrated there from Pāṭaliputra in the north.[103] So in this case, migration may have taken place either from the east or from the south. However, the names of the two Brāhmaṇas Siddhapabhaṭṭa and

Vennapabhaṭṭa indicate, that they were South Indians. So the donee emigrated probably from Cuddalore and went to the Baroda region.

Another grant of the time of Indra III from Chinchani dated *Śaka* 848/c. 926-927 A.D. merely mentions, that an endowment was made consisting of a village Kaṇāḍuka and some land in Devīhara village, so that the income accruing from it could be utilized for the upkeep and maintenance of a *maṭhika* for the worship of the goddess Daśamī and for the feeding of nine people belonging to the *Pañca-Gauḍīya-mahāpariṣad* of Samyāna.[104] The latter is identical with Sanjan in the Thane district of Bombay. According to D.C. Sircar[105] the term *Gauḍīya* here has been used in the sense of North Indian Brāhmaṇas in general. In the south, the Brāhmaṇas are divided into five classes, collectively known as Pañca-Drāviḍa, on the basis of the linguistic sub-divisions of South India. Similarly in the north, as discussed earlier, they are divided into the five groups—Sārasvata, Kānyakubja, Gauḍa, Maithila and Utkala—together given the general name Gauḍa. He concludes, that the term Gauḍa in this case has been applied to North Indians generally. So the Brāhmaṇas who benefited by this charter, could have travelled to Thane near Bombay from any or all of the five countries. There they formed a *mahāpariṣad* or assembly and later received a grant.

Govinda IV another Rāṣṭrakūṭa ruler, by his Cambay Plates, dated *Śaka* 852/c. 930 A.D., granted the village of Kevañja lying near Kāvikā and situated in the Kheṭaka district of Lāṭadeśa, Kevañja and Kāvikā have not yet been located. But they were included within the district of Kaira in Gujarat. The donee was the Brāhmaṇa Nāgamārya son of Mahādevayya. At the time of the grant, he was living in the city of Mānyakheṭa or Malkhed, although originally he had been a resident of the holy place of Kāvikā,[106] near which lay the gift village Kevañja. So Nāgamārya who at one time had lived in a village in the Kaira district of Gujarat, went southwards to Malkhed in Mysore sometime before the date of the grant, probably in search of employment.

The Sāngli grant of Govinda IV issued in the *Śaka* year 855/c. 933 A.D. records, that Keśava Dīkṣiṭa son of Dāmodara Bhaṭṭa who had lived in Puṁḍravardhana, was given Lohāgrāma,[107] included in the Rāmapuri-700. Puṁḍravardhana or Puṇḍravardhana, is a general term comprising North Bengal. The location of the donated village Lohāgrāma and Rāmapuri-700 of which it was a unit, has not yet been determined. But village names with numbers were frequent in Maharashtra and Kanara in the ninth and tenth centuries. Rāṣṭrakūṭa records give names of villages and territorial units like Belgol-300, Banavāsi-12,000, Purigeri-300, Bagenad-70, Kinsukad-70[108] and others. From this it can be surmised, that the donated village may have been situated in Maharashtra over which the Rāṣṭrakūṭas held sway. Hence Keśava Dīkṣita emigrated from North Bengal and went all the way to South Maharashtra, where he was benefited by a grant of the Rāṣṭrakūṭa ruler.

Shortly after Govinda IV came Kṛṣṇa III. In *Śaka* 862/c. 940 A.D., he issued the Deoli Plates. By this grant a Brāhmaṇa named Rishiappa or Rishiyapayya,[109] received a village named Tālapuruṁṣaka. Some conjecture about the modern location of the donated village can be made. It was bounded on the south by the river Kanhanā which has been identified with a river bearing the same name, running from the north-west of Nagpur to the south-east, on the west, by the village of Mohama which is present Mohgaon, situated in the Chhindwara district, fifty miles to the north-west of Nagpur and on the north by Vadhīra which is Berdi near Nagpur. So the donated village was apparently in the vicinity of Nagpur. The charter does not mention the original home of the donee. But R.G. Bhandarkar the editor suggests, that as his name ends in "appa" or "apayya" — Rishiappa or Rishiyapayya — the donee was a southerner. Kṛṣṇa III soon after his accession in c. 939 A.D., had turned his attention to the south. He came into conflict with Parāntaka Cola on the pretext of reinstating on the throne his Bāṇa ally Vikramāditya III who had been deposed by Parāntaka.[110] As a result of this political disturbance, the Brāhmaṇa Rishiappa may have left his home in the south and migrated northwards to the vicinity of Nagpur in Maharashtra.

Akālavarṣa in *Śaka* 882/c. 960 A.D. issued the Kolhapur Copper Plates. This charter records a grant made in favour of Govindabhaṭṭa, son of Devabhaṭṭa. He had emigrated from Kureggrāma in Karahāṭa-*viṣaya*,[111] which is identified with present Koregaon in the Karhad-*taluka* of Maharashtra. The village that he received was Rikkaṭi-*grāma* included in Alatage-700 in Kuhuṇḍi-*viṣaya*. K.G. Kundangar who edited the plates, identifies Rikkaṭi with the modern village of Rukadi about five miles to the south-east of Alatage, which stands seventeen miles to the north-east of Kolhapur in Maharashtra. So Govindabhaṭṭa did not travel very far, but left his home in Koregaon to go southwards towards Kolhapur, where a village was bestowed on him.

Another Rāṣṭrakūṭa record, the Kolagallu Inscription of Khoṭṭiga, dated in *Śaka* 889/c. 967 A.D., contains an eulogy of the Brāhmaṇa Gadādhara, who was born in Taḍā-*grāma*[112] and was the "crest-jewel of the Gauḍa country", and the "illuminator of the Varendrī country." Taḍā-*grāma* has been identified with Tara, twelve miles to the south-east of Dinajpur in North Bengal. He came to Kolagallu, where he installed and consecrated images of gods. According to the editor of the inscription, L.N. Rao, Kolagallu is a railway station on the Guntakal-Hubli section of the Madras and Southern Maharatta Railway. So in this case, the Brāhmaṇa Gadādhara came from Bengal all the way to the south. The composer of this inscription was the poet Madhusūdana, who belonged to a family which had emigrated from Ṭarkāri.[113] This has been identified by L. N. Rao with Ṭakāri, sixteen miles north-west of Gaya. If the identification is correct, from Gaya he came to Kolagallu, perhaps in search of employment. However, scholars hold divided opinions, as to whether Madhusūdana was a Brāhmaṇa.[114] The probability is, that he was not one.

A collateral branch of the Rāṣṭrakūṭas acted as viceroys of Gujarat and Mālava. Candrāditya a *viṣayapati* under Karka II[115] of this family, issued the Hilol Plates of the year 470, corresponding to c. 788 A.D. as suggested by H. D. Sankalia, who edits the plates, and by D. C. Sircar.[116] Both of them ascribe the date to the Gupta-Valabhī era. These plates record a donation of two pieces of land, one in Pādāṭaka-*grāma* and the other in the south of Hilohila-*grāma*. The donee Bhaṭṭa Mātṛgaṇa, son of Mātrīśvara, had come from Sānanda-*sthāna*.[117] This *sthāna* is the same as Sanand, a railway station on the Ahmedabad-Viramgam line about twelve miles west of Ahmedabad and the headquarters of the *taluka* of the same name. As regards the two villages in which the donated lands lay, Hilohila is Hilol in the Dehgam-*taluka* of the Ahmedabad district. Sankalia thinks that the other village Pādāṭaka may be identical with modern Pahada or Pada near Raudavat, about a mile east of Hilol. So both—the donee's original home, and the donated lands were in the Ahmedabad region of Gujarat.

Govindarāja of the viceregal family, issued in *Śaka* 732/c. 810 A.D., the Prince of Wales Museum Plates. They record a grant of the village Usauṇaka in the Vāhāula-Caturāśīti to the Brāhmaṇa Bhobika, son of Bhaṭṭa Jaya, an emigrant from Gauḍa-*deśa*. He was at the time of the grant, residing at Charmmanihauha,[118] or Chamarwara. M.G. Dikshit, the editor of the plates, identifies the village Usauṇaka with Wasan, two miles north of Chamarwara half way between Vahora or Vahaula and Bhilodia in the former Baroda state of Gujarat. Hence the donee migrated from any one of the Gauḍas and came to the Baroda region in Gujarat where he later received a village.

Karkka Suvarṇavarṣa, also of the viceregal family of Gujarat, by his Baroda grant of the *Śaka* year 734/c. 812 A.D., bestowed the village of Vaḍapadraka included in the Aṁkoṭṭaka-84. D.C. Sircar[119] identifies them with Baroda and Akota, a suburb of Baroda, respectively. The donee Bhānu Bhaṭṭa, son of Somāditya, had come from Valabhī[120] and the village that he received also lay within Gujarat.

An incomplete grant of Sinda Ādityavarman, dated *Śaka* 887/c. 965-966 A.D., gives an instance of migration to Maharashtra. It records the grant of a village Kiṇihikā included in the larger village Paṅgarikā situated in Rāmatīrhikā-84. The village Kiṇihikā is the same as Kinhai situated on the south bank of the Indrāyaṇi, near Shelarwadi, about sixteen miles north by west of Poona. The donee was Navaśiva, son of

Candrabhaṭṭa who had come from the Madhyadeśa[121] region to the vicinity of Poona in Maharashtra.

The Kalas Budrukh Plates of Bhillamarāja III of *Śaka* 948/c. 1025 A.D., record the grant of Kalaśa village to a number of Brāhmaṇas. The chief among them Maṅamvanāyaka, son of Śrīvatsanāyaka, had emigrated from Takkārikā in Madhyadeśa.[122] The village of Kalaśa is identical with Kalas Budrukh in the Akola-*taluka* of Ahmadnagar district of Maharashtra. Ṭakkārikā in Madhyadeśa is the same as Ṭakāri, from where the donee went to the Ahmadnagar district of Maharashtra.

A branch of the Caulukyas established themselves in North Gujarat. Bhīmadeva I of this family in *V.S.* 1086/c. 1030 A.D., by his Muṁdaka grant donated merely a *hala* of land in Muṁdaka-*grāma* in Varddhi-*viṣaya* identified with Vadhiar or Vadhi in North Gujarat. The donee was Vāsudeva, son of Balabhadra an *udīcya* Brāhmaṇa.[123] D. C. Sircar points out, that Prāgjyotiṣa or modern Gauhati area of Assam and the adjoining region was originally known as *udīcya* territory.[124] However, as G. S. Gai, the editor of the Muṁdaka grant points out, the appellation indicates that the Brāhmaṇa had come from some place in North India.

Another grant of Bhīmadeva I, dated in the same year *V.S.* 1086/c. 1030 A.D., records that Mansūra village in Ghaḍahaḍikā-12 of Kachchha-*maṇḍala* was bestowed on Bhaṭṭāraka Ājapāla, son of Ācārya Maṅgalaśiva. He was an emigrant from Navaṇīsaka in Kachchha-*maṇḍala.*[125] Of all the places mentioned only Kachchha-maṇḍala can be identified. According to D. C. Sircar,[126] the word means "a region on the sea-coast", which has led different areas to be regarded as Kaccha. There is one Kaccha or Kacchapa identified with Cachar in Assam or Coochbehar. Kaccha may also indicate the district around Bhṛgukachchha or Broach near the mouth of the Narmadā. Again it may indicate Cutch to the north-west of Gujarat. In this case, the last mentioned area is meant, as the Caulukyas held sway over Kutch or Cutch. Bhaṭṭāraka Ājapāla therefore left his home in Navaṇīsaka and migrated to another village, both of them being situated in the same region.

From about the middle of the eighth century, several dynasties made their appearance in different parts of Orissa. However, neither their chronology and the boundaries of their principalities, nor their exact status and mutual relationship can be ascertained.

The Bhauma-Karas exercised authority over Balasore, Cuttack, Puri, Hindol, Angul, Dhenkanal, Talcher and the northern Ganjam district. In later years they ruled over portions of these districts simultaneously with the Somavaṁśis of Kośala. Daṇḍimahādevī, daughter of Śubhakara V of this family, issued the Santiragama charter in the tenth century. It refers to Bhaṭṭa Mākyadeva, son of Jālladeva, an inhabitant of Dharmapāṭṭi, who had emigrated from Ṭakāri,[127] located by the editor D.C. Sircar, in the Set-Mahet region of U.P. The Brāhmaṇa received Santīra-*grāma* and another locality called Komyosaṅga, situated within Tamura-*viṣaya* in Dakṣiṇa Tosala. The donated villages have not been identified. But Dakṣiṇa Tosala in which they were included, according to D.C. Sircar,[128] comprised the Ganjam-Puri-Cuttack area. So Mākyadeva went from U.P. to Dakṣiṇa Tosala in Orissa.

Daṇḍimahādevī was succeeded by her step-mother Vakulamahādevī, a queen of Śubhakara V. A grant issued by her also dated in the tenth century records that the Brāhmaṇa Mihadhīchāya, son of Nīlakaṇṭha, who was a resident of Kanteḍa-*grāma*, and an emigrant from Śāvastha-deśa,[129] received the village Chhoḍātavutsā attached to the Uregoḍḍā-*Khaṇḍa*, situated in the Aśravaṇakatikā-*viṣaya* in Uttara Tosala. Śāvastha-*deśa* has not been identified by the editor P.R. Srinivasan. It probably refers to Śrāvasti in U.P. The modern names of the donated village and the *viṣaya* in which it lay are not known. But they were situated in the Uttara Tosala country. As D.C. Sircar explains,[130] the ancient Utkala country in the Balasore region, was roughly known as Uttara Tosala, to which the Brāhmaṇa came all the way from U.P.

Dharmamahādevī, who flourished in the middle of the tenth century, and was a queen of Śāntikara III, ruled after Vakulamahādavi. She figures as the donor of the Taltalai Plates. By this charter, the village Taratabi or Taltalai situated in Talamura-*viṣaya* or Talmul, about seven miles from the sub-divisional headquarters of Angul in the Cuttack district, was made the subject of a grant. The latter was made in favour of the donee Śrī Padmanābha, son of Gadādhara, who was a resident of Koṁsalā or Kaṁsarā in the Hindol state, three miles from Taltalai. He, however, hailed originally from Kolāñca.[131] C. Das and K. C. Panigrahi who jointly edited the plates merely mention, that Kolāñca was in Northern India, without locating its site. However, like Ṭakāri and Śāvastha-*deśa* of the two previous charters, Kolāñca too was probably in U.P., from where padmanābha came to settle in Orissa.

The Śulkis ruled over Talcher and the Dhenkanal area, at first probably as feudatories of the Karas, but later as independent rulers. The records of this family are not dated in any well-known era. But they are referred on palaeographic grounds, to about the ninth and tenth centuries.

The Dhenkanal grant of Jayastambha records, that the village Candrapura in Konkula-*khaṇḍa*, connected with the Goilla district in Kodāloka-*maṇḍala*, was granted to the donee Vāvana, son of Khambha. He had emigrated from Kolāñca[132] which may be located in U.P. though the editor H.P. Sastri, did not suggest its identification. Candrapura the donated village is the same as Kuala in the former Dhenkanal state. So the donee migrated from U.P. to the Dhenkanal state in Orissa.

Another grant from Dhenkanal, that of Kulastambha, refers to the Brāhmaṇa Bhaṭṭa Bṛhaspati, son of Bhaṭṭa Ravi. His ancestral home was in the village of Nidhati which is unidentified, but is known to have been situated within Madhyadeśa.[133] From here Bṛhaspati emigrated and came to Orissa, where he received from Kulastambha, a village named Jhaḍabāda in Goilla-*viṣaya* which formed a part of the former Dhenkanal state.

Almost a contemporary of the Śulkis and Karas, was the family of the Tuṅgas. In the beginning they were probably feudatory chiefs under the Karas, and later assumed independence. They held sway over Yamagarta, and ruled over parts of former Talcher, Pallahara and Keonjhar states.

Vinītatuṅga II issued the Talcher Plates recording grant of land jointly to two Brāhmaṇas. One of them Bhaṭṭaputra Naraka, son of Sādhāraṇa had come from Puṇḍravardhana and was at the time of the grant, living in Royarā.[134] With his co-donee, he was given the village of Maddhamaṇḍa. The donated village has not yet been identified, but Royarā to which the donee came from North Bengal, was situated on the borders of the old Sonpur state.

The Asiatic Society's Plates of Gayāḍatuṅga, on the basis of their script, may be assigned to the tenth or eleventh century. They mention a number of Brāhmaṇa donees. The original home of only the first named, Bhaṭṭaputra Dādo, son of Govinda, has been mentioned in the charter. He is said to have been an inhabitant of Ahichchhatra in U.P. Having emigrated from there, he was residing in Kuruva-*bhaṭṭagrāma*, a village in Oḍra-*viṣaya*.[135] According to D. C. Sircar, Oḍra-*viṣaya* was a name applied at the time to the whole of coastal Orissa, and ultimately to the entire Oriyā speaking area.[136] All the donees received one village, Toro-*grāma* in the Veṇḍuṁga-*viṣaya*, identified with Thorakota and Balanga in Yamagarta-*maṇḍala* or Jamgadia in Angul in the former Pallahara state. Hence Bhaṭṭaputra Dādo and perhaps the other Brāhmaṇas (all of whom belonged to one *gotra*), of the charter left their homes in Ahichchhatra and came to the coastal region of Orissa, sometime before they received the village.

By his Talcher Plates, Gayāḍatuṅga made a grant of Vāmāitāllo-*grāma* in Tuṁkera-*viṣaya*. Although the village remains unidentified, Tuṁkerā-*viṣaya* is the same as Tonkour in Pallahara. They were situated in Yamagarta-*maṇḍala* in Angul in the old Pallahara state. There were three beneficiaries of the charter. Vāsudeva, son of Lallaḍa and his son Rāmadeva were emigrants from Sāvathi and residents of Yamagarta-*maṇḍala*.[137] D.C. Sircar, editor of the charter, locates this Sāvathi in the area around Baigram in the Bogra district of old North Bengal. It was from here that the two Brāhmaṇas went to Jamgadia. The third donee Devaśarman, son of Pauṁa, was residing in Sāvira-*bhaṭṭa-grāma*, which although unidentified, was situated in Oḍra-*viṣaya* or coastal Orissa. He had, however, come from Mūthāutha-*bhaṭṭa-grāma* in Varendra-*maṇḍala*,[138] or North Bengal. Hence all three Brāhmaṇas left their homes in North Bengal, and came to settle in different parts of Orissa, later receiving jointly, a village from Gayāḍatuṇga.

The Bhañjas were contemporaries of the Karas and Tuṅgas. They ruled over the northern portion of the Ganjam district for about three hundred years. Most of their grants are undated. Those that are dated, use epochs and eras, which have not yet been equated with the Christian era and have been referred by various scholars to a period ranging from about the tenth or eleventh to the fourteenth or fifteenth centuries. The charters have been mostly discovered in the former states of Mayūrbhañja, Sonpur, Baud, Dasapalla and the northern portion of the Ganjam district.

The Keśari Plates of Śatrubhañja record, that Bhaṭṭaputra Daṇḍapāṇi, son of Cakrapāṇi, had emigrated from the Madhyadeśa region.[139] He received the village of Syallāmāyi in Urtti-*viṣaya*. The village is not identified. But Urtti-*viṣaya* in which it lay, was in Khiching in Mayūrbhañja.

The Singharā Plates of Raṇabhañja, refer to the donee Bhaṭṭa Vohe, son of Bhaṭṭa Śaṅkha. He at the time of the grant, was living in Gandhaṭāpāri, although originally he had come from Bhadrapalāśī in Magadha.[140] These places are not identified. However, there is a river Palāśini which D.C. Sircar thinks, is the same as Paras, a tributary of the Koel in the Chotanagpur district of South Bihar.[141] It may be that Bhadrapalāśī said to have been in Magadha, was situated on the bank of the Palāśini or Paras. Bhaṭṭa Vohe received the village of Singharā on the bank of the Bāgh river, forming the boundary between the former Sonpur and Baud states. At present it is in the old Baud state. Hence the Brāhmaṇa left his home in a village in South Bihar, and came to the Baud region in Orissa.

The undated Baud grant of Raṇabhañja, records the grant of the village Amvasari in the Sivara-*khaṇḍa* neighbourhood, in the Dakṣiṇapalli sub-division of Khiñjali-*maṇḍala*, identified with the former Keonjhar state in Mayūrbhañja. The donee was Devahara, son of Kācila. He was a resident of

Mahiṣipadraka and had emigrated from Madhyadeśa,[142] from where he went towards Mayūrbhañja in Orissa.

By the Tasapaikera charter of his thirteenth year, Raṇabhañja made a grant of the village of Tasapaikera in Uttarapalli on the Mahānadī river in Orissa. The donee Śrī Śrīdhara, son of Vāpula, had originally been living in the Brāhamaṇa village of Bhaṭṭa Nirola,[143] identified with Nirla in the Aska-*taluka* of the Ganjam district. At the time of the grant, however, he was living in Kamari probably in the Sambalpur district.

Another grant of Raṇabhañja is dated in his twenty-sixth year. By this charter, a grant was made of the village of Vāllāśṛṅga in the Khātiā-*viṣaya*. The village has been identified with modern Balasinga, about two miles from Baud and situated at the confluence of the Mahānadī and Salanki or Salki in the Baud state.[144] The beneficiary was Bhaṭṭaputra Dāmodara, surnamed Bhūṣaṇa, son of Bhaṭṭabhūṣaṇa who had come from the Bhaṭṭa village of Khaḍuvāpalī in Madhyadeśa.[145] So Dāmodara came to the vicinity of Baud, where he was given a village and which his son Chhaḍoka received after his death.

In his fiftieth year, Raṇabhañja issued the Aidā Plates or Orissa Museum Plates. These record the grant of Vārigāmā-*grāma* on the bank of the Mora river, attached to Roirā-*viṣaya*. The last place-name, the only one to have been located so far, is modern Royara. The Brāhmaṇa who received the village was Bhaṭṭaputra Paṇḍita Varada, son of Bhaṭṭa Śavara. He resided in Tarigrāma, but had originally come from Tālahṛtakī-*grāma* in Varendrī-*maṇḍala*.[146] The two villages have not been identified. But Tālahṛtakī-*grāma* was in North Bengal, from where the Brāhmaṇa went to the Sonpur region of Orissa.

Another Baud grant of Raṇabhañja dated in his fifty-eighth year, records, that the village Turullā in Tullaśṛṅga-*viṣaya* both of which are unidentified, was given to Bhaṭṭa Śubhadāma, son of Vṛṣabhadāma. At the time of the grant, he was living in Bhaṭṭa Tadalā in Oḍra-*viṣaya*. But his ancestral home was in Ṭakāri in Śrāvasti.[147] A. Banerji, who edited this Baud grant, locates this Ṭakāri in Madhyadeśa. From there Śubhadāma came to coastal Orissa, sometime before Raṇabhañja bestowed the village on him.

Kanakabhañja issued a grant also from Baud. By this charter, he benefited the Brāhmaṇa Harivaṁśa, son of Dhanapati. He had come from Hastigrāma in Madhyadeśa.[148] He was given two *pāṭakas* of land in Jamarāpura and Sihipura Vāhulāveṇḍaka. These are not identified. But the Tela *nadī* which formed their boundary to the north, is the same as the Tel river forming the boundary between the former Baud and Sonpur states. Hence Harivaṁśa came from a village in Madhyadeśa, like so many others, to the Baud-Sonpur region of Orissa.

Narendrabhañja issued two sets of Ādipur Plates. By one of them, Devadevadāma, son of Bhaṭṭa Vaḍḍhakādāma, hailing from *Bhaṭṭagrāma* Āllavida in Oḍra-*viṣaya*, was given a village.[149] Although the Brāhmaṇa's native village has not been identified, it lay somewhere in the coastal region of Orissa. He received Śarapadraka-*grāma* or modern Soras near Khiching or Saradaha in Karanjia *pargana*. Kerakera-*viṣaya* in which it was situated, is still the name of a village in Ghoshdapir, in Ādipur *pargana*, about twelve miles to the south-south-east of Khiching. Hence, unlike the other immigrants to Orissa who have been discussed above, Devadevadāma of this charter confined his journey within Orissa and moved merely from a village in the coastal region, to one near Khiching.

Jayabhañja in his third year, by his Antirigam Plates, gave the village Reṅgarḍā in Khiñjalīyagaḍa-*viṣaya* to the donee Jagaddhara who was an emigrant from Ṭakāri in Madhyadeśa, and a resident of Paṭavāḍa-pāṭa in Koṇḍarāvaṅga-*viṣaya* of Dakṣiṇa Tosala.[150] Reṅgarḍā, the donated village, has not been identified. But according to T.C. Rath who edits the charter, Khiñjalīyagaḍa-*viṣaya* in which it lay, signifies the former name of Gumsur. B.C. Mazumdar identifies it with modern Kimedi, in the north-west of the Ganjam district. But according to Rai Bahadur Hiralal, it indicates the former Keonjhar state.[151] So the Brāhmaṇa Jagaddhara emigrated from Ṭakāri and came to settle in a village in the Ganjam-Puri-Cuttack region, comprising Dakṣiṇa Tosala. While he was living there, he received a village either in Gumsur or in the ganjam area, or in the former Keonjhar state.

Vidyādharabhañja, issued a grant from Ganjam, bestowing the village Mūla Māchāḍa in Māchāḍa-*khaṇḍa-viṣaya*. The village and the *viṣaya* have been identified by Hiralal, with Machgaon in the Cuttack district. But according to H.C. Ray,[152] Krishnamacharlu's identification of Māchāḍa with Majhigam in Behrampur (Madras), is more appropriate. The beneficiary of the charter was Bhaṭṭa Purandara, coming from Manmāṇā near Varedbhi in Taḍisama-*viṣaya*.[153] Hiralal identifies these places with Mandara and Tadasinga in the Gumsur-*taluka*. In this case too, the migration was probably confined within Orissa itself.

The Antirigam grant of Yaśabhañja, refers to the astrologer Jagadharaśarman, son of Vidyādhara. An emigrant from Vapabhūmi or Boppangi in Tihāra-*viṣaya*[154] or Tikkarapada in the Gumsur-*taluka*, Jagadhara at the time of the grant was living in Paṭṭavādapaṭaka in Koṇṭarāvaṅgu-*viṣaya*. These are identical with Patatupuram and Kotayagada in the Chatrapura-*taluka*. He received the village Komyāṇa, the same as modern Konomona also in the Chatrapura-*taluka* of the Ganjam district. It was situated in Vodā-*viṣaya*, i.e. Boddapatti, three miles from Konomona. Hence emigrating from a village in the Gumsur-*taluka*, the astrologer came to Chatrapura-*taluka*, near which he was later to be endowed with a village.

Neṭṭabhañja of the Bhañja family, issued the Juraḍa grant, in which the Brāhmaṇa Pātra-Śrī Vāppanna, son of Bhaṭṭa Guheśvara, from Gaṅgavāḍi,[155] figures as the donee. Gaṅgavāḍi, the region over which the Gaṅgas ruled, denotes the territories around Mahendragiri in the Ganjam district. He received Jurāḍā-*grāma* in the Gaḍa-*viṣaya* of Khiñjali-*maṇḍala*, identified with Jarada, a village in the Kodola-*taluka* also in the Ganjam district. Hence both the donee's original home, and the village that was made over to him, were in the same geographical region.

Neṭṭabhañja also issued the Russellkonda Plates. These were written by a Brāhmaṇa named *Vandya* Devabhadra.[156] D. C. Sircar, who edited the plates points out, that this is reminiscent of the Vandyopādhyāyas, a *kulīna* class among the Rāḍhīya Brāhmaṇas of Bengal. Hence it is possible, that

Devabhadra had originally lived in Bengal, from where he came to Orissa, looking for employment.

The records of the early members of the Somavaṁśi dynasty, have been found in the Sambalpur tract, in the eastern part of the South Kośala country. They cannot be assigned to any date earlier than the tenth century. Of all the dynasties of Orissa, it is during the rule of this family, that we find the largest number of clear cases of migration.

Mahābhavagupta I in his third year, issued the Vakratentalī charter. It records the grant of the village of Vakratentalī in Lupattarā-*khaṇḍa* identified with modern Bantentuli, sixteen miles west of Sonpur town, and Lepta, six miles south-east of Bolangir in the old Patna state.[157] The donee was Bhaṭṭaputra Jātarūpa, son of Śrīvachchha. At the time of the grant he was residing in Meraṇḍā or Menda, seventeen miles west of Sonpur. But his original home had been in the village of Vallikandara in Rāḍha.[158] Although the village itself is unidentified, it was situated in West Bengal, from where Bhaṭṭaputra Jātarūpa migrated to Orissa.[159]

One of the charters issued in the sixth regnal year of Mahābhavagupta I, was the Kalibhanā Copper Plate. It mentions the Brāhmaṇa Govinda, son of Koṇḍa. He was an emigrant from Hastipada and a resident of Jambūgrāma.[160] Hastipada according to D.C. Sircar and P.C. Rath who jointly edited the plate, reminds them of Hastigrāma near Vaiśāli, i.e. modern Basarh near Muzaffarpur in North Bihar. This perhaps suggests, that Hastipada may be identical with Hastigrāma. Jambūgrāma where the donee resided, was also the donated village, lying within Potā-*viṣaya*. It is the same as Jamgaon, a village contiguous to Kalibhanā in the old Patna state in the Sambalpur tract in Orissa. Potā-*viṣaya* according to Hiralal,[161] is identical with Povā-*viṣaya* or Pow, eight miles north-east of Bolangir in the old Sonpur state. So the donee seems to have migrated from a village in North Bihar, to another in the Bolangir region of Orissa.

In the same year, Mahābhavagupta I by his Patna Plates, granted the village of Vakaveḍḍā in the Oṅga-taṭa-*viṣaya* to four Brāhmaṇas Oṅga-taṭa *viṣaya* is the district on the bank of the Oṅga, a small river joining the Mahānadī in Sonpur. According to Hiralal,[162] Vakaveḍḍā is probably Bakti, fifteen miles north or Bolangir and four miles south of Oṅga river. But B.C. Mazumdar[163] identifies Vakaveḍḍā, with Bakebira, close to Salebhata police station on the river Oṅga.

One of the donees Koṇḍadeva, son of Rāmaśarman had migrated from Kaliṅga and was a resident of Pampāsarasī.[164] Kaliṅga is the same as Mukhalingam in modern Andhra Pradesh. Koṇḍadeva left his home here and went to live at Pampāsarasī. If Pampāsarasī is the same as Pampā, then according to D.C. Sircar, it is identical with Hampi[165] in the Bellary district of Mysore state. There is, however, a town called Pampapura in Vidhyachala, five miles to the west of Mirzapur in U.P.[166] D.C. Sircar's identification, however, seems to be more likely and Koṇḍadeva probably settled down in Hampi in the Bellary district, later receiving a grant in Orissa. Whereas Koṇḍadeva had come to settle in Pampāsarasī, another donee of the charter, Dāmaka, son of Aivuli had migrated from Pampāsarasī and was residing in Loiśṛṅgā,[167] identified with Loisinga in the Patna state, eleven miles north of Bolangir. The third donee whose name is missing, but who was the son of Nārapagaṇḍa, was at the time of the grant, living in Khaṇḍakṣetra, although originally his home had been in Oḍyaśṛṅga[168] or Odsinga in the former state of Athamallik near Sonpur. Vāsudeva son of Hṛṣikeśa, the last of the immigrant Brāhmaṇas had come from Koṅkaledda, identified with Koknara in the Bora Sambhar Zamindari of Sambalpur district, four miles from Narasinghanath. From there he migrated and took up residence in Lipatuṅga[169] or Lepta near Bolangir. So while two of the donees of the Patna Plates came from outside, one from Kaliṅga in modern Andhra Pradesh, and the other from Hampi in the Mysore state, the other two came from within Orissa, and were jointly to enjoy a village in the vicinity of Bolangir.

In his eighth regnal year, Mahābhavagupta I issued the Nagpur Museum Plates, which refer to the grant of Satalama village, attached to Kaśaloda-*viṣaya*. These have been located and are identical with modern Satalama and Kusarada, te miles north-west of Satalama in the Baragarh-*tahsil* of Sambalpur district. The donee Bhaṭṭaputra Sānthakara was a resident of Murujuṅga-*grāma*, having emigrated from Puruṣamaṇḍapa villages in Oḍra-*deśa*.[170] The two villages are not identified. However, Puruṣamaṇḍapa village being situated in Oḍra-*deśa*, lay somewhere in the coastal region of Orissa. Hence in this case too, the Brāhmaṇa donee was originally an inhabitant of Orissa itself, and later received a village in the same region, although in a different locality.

The Mahākosala Historical Society's Plates issued by the same king in his eleventh year, mention the gift of the village Liñjira in Prithaurā-*bhukti*. L. P. Pandeya who has edited the charter, has identified Liñjira with a village of the same name, close to Baramakela in the old Sarangarh state. Prithaurā-*bhukti* is Pithora in the Padampur tract, about forty-five miles to the north-west from Sambalpur town and about twenty miles from Liñjira. The recipient of the village was the Brāhmaṇa-Bhaṭṭa, son of Cakradhara. Having migrated from the village of Madhura in Madhyadeśa he had come to live in Ullakheṭa[171] the location of which is as yet unknown. While residing there, he was benefited by a grant of the Somavaṁśi ruler, receiving a village in the former Sarangarh state.

By a set of grants issued from Cuttack, Mahābhavagupta I in his thirty-first regnal year, handed over four villages to Bhaṭṭa Mahattama Sādhāraṇa. He was the son of Bhaṭṭa Śobhana, an emigrant from Ṭakāri, probably in U.P. He at first settled in Turvunā in Kośala.[172] Turvunā is unidentified. However, Kośala in which it lay, during the period under review, was divided into two parts. One according to D.C. Sircar,[173] was Uttara Kośala or the region around Ayodhya, with its capital at Śrāvasti. Dakṣiṇa Kośala or Kośala proper, comprised the Raipur-Bilaipur-Sambalpur regions of Madhya Pradesh. The eastern part of Dakşiṇa Kośala was formed by the Patna-Sonpur region in the upper valley of the Mahānadī, over which the Somavaṁśis are known to have been ruling. So having emigrated from a locality in U.P., Bhaṭṭa Sādhāraṇa came to a village in the Raipur-Bilaspur-Sambalpur region.

Later Mahābhavagupta I endowed him with four villages, Raṇḍā and Alāṇḍalā in the Povā-*viṣaya* in Kośaladeśa, Arkigrāma in Tulumva-*khaṇḍa* and Tūleṇḍā in Sandāna-*viṣaya*. Raṇḍā and Alāṇḍalā are identical with Renda, six miles from Bolangir and Alanda, three miles east of Bolangir. Arkigrāma has not yet been identified. But Tulumva-*khaṇḍa* in which it was situated, is modern Turun on the Mahānadī, twenty-seven miles south of Sambalpur. Tūleṇḍā in Sandāna-*viṣaya* is Tulunda near Povā or Pow and Sonda, eleven miles east of Sonpur.

Mahābhavagupta I in his thirty-fourth year, issued another set of Kalibhanā Plates. It deals with the grant of Konnayillā-*grama* in Ṭokkārā-*viṣaya* to the Brāhmaṇa Devu, son of Gāṅgeya, an emigrant from Muktāvathi-*grāma* in Śrāvasti,[174] and a resident of Anjiṇi-*grāma*. Muktāvathi in Śrāvasti can be identified with Muktāvastu and may be located in North Bengal. Although the modern equivalent of Konnayillā-*grāma* has not yet been found, yet Ṭokkārā-*viṣaya* in which it lay, is the same as Tukra, about fourteen miles east of the town of Bangarh in Orissa.

Mahābhavagupta I was succeeded by his son Mahāśivagupta I Yayāti, who as D.C. Sircar holds, ruled in the second half of the tenth century, c. 970-1,000 A.D. Like his father, he too made gifts of land mostly in Kośala, or more specifically in Dakṣiṇa Kośala to immigrant Brāhmaṇas.

In his third year, Mahāśivagupta I issued the Mārañja-Murā charter. It records the grant of the two villages Mārañja and Murā, situated within the Santovardā-*khaṇḍa* of *Sambaravāḍi-maṇḍala*, within the Bhrāṇḍa-*viṣaya* in the Kośala country. Of all these names only the Kośala country can be identified. The donee was Bhaṭṭaputra Yaśakara, son of Śāntikara, an emigrant from Hastigrāma in Madhyadeśa,[175] located near Vaiśāli in North Bihar.

B.C. Mazumdar, the editor of the above-mentioned charter, locates Hastigrāma in the tract covered by the northern portion of the district of Balasore and the sub-division of Contai. His argument is, that the other charters of the Trikaliṅga Guptas, show grants of lands in Kośala, to Brāhmaṇas having the family name "Kara", like the donee of this charter, coming from Oḍra-*deśa*. Besides the Oriyā Brāhmaṇas living in the Contai sub-division, call themselves inhabitants of Madhyadeśa, which according to him, is the region between Bengal and Orissa. He also states that it was not merely from Kanauj, once called Madhyadeśa, that Brāhmaṇas came directly to be settled in Kośala and to be associated with the Oriyā speaking Brāhmaṇas there.

It is rather difficult to accept these views. The geographical limits of Madhyadeśa, as known from the texts, never include either Bengal or Orissa. So Mazumdar's location of Madhyadeśa is not correct. At the same time, the land-grant charters provide several instances of Brāhmaṇas emigrating from various centres in Madhyadeśa, e.g. Nidhati, Madhura and so on, and coming to Kośala in Orissa. Moreover, just because the Oriyā Brāhmaṇas of the Contai sub-division call themselves inhabitants of Madhyadeśa, it does not necessarily follow that the donee of this charter also came from Contai. The grant itself states, that he had originally lived in a particular village in Madhyadeśa. Hence he definitely migrated from the region known as Madhyadeśa, to the Kośala country in Orissa.

By a Cuttack grant issued in his ninth regnal year, Mahāśivagupta I donated Cāndagrāma in Marada-*viṣaya* in Dakṣiṇa Tosala, to the Brāhmaṇa Śaṅkhapāṇi, son of Dinakara. Although the village itself remains unidentified, it lay in the Ganjam-Puri-Cuttack area comprising Dakṣiṇa Tosala It may, however, be pointed out, that Fleet while translating the passages of the plates, writes Dakṣiṇa Kośala, instead of Tosala. Dakṣiṇa Kośala or the Raipur-Bilaspur-Sambalpur region, lay to the north-west of the area indicated by Dakṣiṇa Tosala. It may be, that as the Somavaṁśis are known to have ruled in Dakṣiṇa Kośala, Fleet changed the names relying on the possibility of Tosala being a mistake for Kośala. Anyway, as the original text of the charter itself mentions Tosala, the donated village lay in the Ganjam-Puri-Cuttack area.

At the time of the grant, Śaṅkhapāṇi was living in Śilābhañjapāṭi in Oḍra-*deśa*, having formerly emigrated from Śrīvalla-*grāma* in Madhyadeśa.[176] It must be noted, that where the *gotra* of the donee is mentioned, the grant reads "*Ṭakkārapūrva-Bhāradvāja-gotrāya*". According to Fleet, the Brāhmaṇa belonged to a branch of the Bharadvāja *gotra*, and was previously settled at Ṭakkāra or Ṭakkārikā in Madhyadeśa. The village from which he came is not identified. However it is possible that it lay near Ṭakāri or in the Set-Mahet region of U.P. So Śaṅkhapāṇi who had left his home in Madhyadeśa, was already living in coastal Orissa, sometime before Mahāśivagupta I granted a village to him.

In his twenty-fourth and twenty-eighth regnal years, Mahāśivagupta I issued two sets of Patna grants, benefiting the Brāhmaṇa Bhaṭṭa Mahodadhi, son of Siddheśvara, who was an emigrant from Śrāvasti-*maṇḍala*, and a resident of Antaradi in Lāvaḍā-*viṣaya*.[177] Lāvaḍā is Lebda, forty-eight miles south-west of Bolangir in the former Patna state. Śrāvasti-*maṇḍala* where the donee originally lived, represents the locality of Śrāvasti in U.P. By the earlier grant, he received the village of Ḍelā-ḍelī or Helā-helī and four years later, he was given the village of Luttarumā. These villages themselves are as yet unidentified. They were, however, both situated in Telātaṭṭa-*viṣaya* in Kośala-*deśa*. It has been located as the country on the bank of the Tel, a tributary of the Mahānadī in Kośala-*deśa*. So Mahodadhi the donee, left his home in Śrāvasti and went to the Bolangir region, and while living there, received two villages, not very far away.

Mahāśivagupta I Yayāti, was succeeded by his son Mahābhavagupta II, who according to D.C. Sircar, ruled about the beginning of the eleventh century, c. 1000-1015 A.D. In his third year, he issued the Cuttack grant. The donee was Rāṇaka, Rāchcho son of Bhaṭṭa Vaśiṣṭha, a resident of Singoāgrāma or Singar in Devibhoga-*viṣaya* or Deobhog, in the extreme south of Raipur district. He had emigrated from Kāsilli *bhaṭṭagrāma* in Śrāvasti-*maṇḍala*[178] located in U.P. He was granted Gauḍasimiṇilligrāma in the Kośala-Sākhaṅgadyanhā-*viṣaya*. Although this village has not been identified, we are told, that it lay in the Kośala country.

Another charter the Kudopali grant of Mahābhavagupta II, issued in his thirteenth year, refers to Bhaṭṭaputra Nārāyaṇa, an emigrant from Hastipada.[179] He received the village of Loisarā in the Giḍāṇḍā-*maṇḍala*. Loisarā is identical with a village of the same name in the Baragarh-*tahsil* of Sambalpur district, sixteen miles south-west of Sambalpur town. As regards Giḍāṇḍā, according to Hiralal,[180] it should be Siḍāṇḍā and he identifies it with Saranda in the Baragarh-*tahsil*, eleven miles south-west of Sambalpur town. So in this case, the Brāhmaṇa's original home might have been in North Bihar, and he came to Sambalpur district of Orissa, where he received a grant.

Kīrttirājadeva of the Eastern Gaṅga family, by his Phulsara Copper Plate, bestowed upon Bāpanna, son of Guheśvara, who had come from Gaṅgavāḍi,[181] territories around Mahendragiri in the Ganjam district. The Brāhmaṇa was given Khīṇvaḍa-*grāma* in Varttanī-*viṣaya*. S.N. Rajaguru, who edited the plate, identified the village with the present Kharida village in Athagada estate. Varttanī-*viṣaya* forms a part of the present Athagada estate and comprises a portion of the adjacent Soreda-*taluka*.

Three Brāhmaṇas, emigrants from Bengal, are known from the Cheedivalasa Plates of Eastern Gaṅga Devendravarman, dated in the *Gaṅga*-year 397/c. 893-894 A.D. They were Ādityabhaṭṭa, Yajñubhaṭṭa, and Khaṇḍidevabhaṭṭa, described as *Vaṅgajebhya,*[182] i.e. original inhabitants of Bengal. Having migrated, they were living in Sividi or modern Seedi or Cheedi, which lay within Kandalivāda village, and which they were later to receive.

A minor dynasty, that of the Nandas, was ruling in the Gondama region of Orissa, which may be the entire hilly tract, extending from Bonai and Bamra in the north upto Jeypore in the Visakhapatnam district in the south. The Baripada Museum Plates of Devānanda of this family, and probably assignable to the ninth century, refer to the donee Bhaṭṭa Brahmadhara, son of Śaktidhara. He had emigrated from Puṇḍravardhana or North Bengal and was residing in Jambama Nārāyaṇapura,[183] which is unidentified. He received the village of Lambeva, in the Potoḍā-*viṣaya* in Airāvaṭṭa-*maṇḍala*. These have been identified by K. C. Panigrahi who edited the plates, with Limbu in the old Narasinghapur state, Potal in the old Hindol state, and Ratagarh in the Banki police station of Cuttack district, respectively.

Two other villages, both unidentified, but lying within Airāvaṭṭa-*maṇḍala*, were donated by Devānanda. By his Jurerpur Plates, he benefited the Brāhmaṇa Kuladevapāla-bhaṭṭa, son of Devapāla. Like Brahmadhara of the Baripada Plates, Kuladevapāla had come from Bengal. But the latter came from Rāḍha,[184] or south-west Bengal. From there he went to Ratagarh and was given Palāmūnāgrāma in Kahāśṛṅga-*visaya* in the Airāvaṭṭa-*maṇḍala*. Three Brāhmaṇas, Sakrahūti, Mahindrahūti Dīkṣita and Vāsuhūti Dīkṣita who had emigrated from Hastipada,[185] figure as the donees of another grant of Devānanda. They were to share jointly Tamvāvaragrāma in Sarāvakhaṇḍa-*viṣaya* of the Airāvaṭṭa-*maṇḍala*. So the donees of all the charters of Devānandadeva, came from outside Orissa, and travelling from Bengal and Bihar, they came to the Cuttack district of Orissa, where they were given villages in the vicinity of Ratagarh.

Kulika Vipracandra, a feudatory assigned on palaeographic grounds of the script of his charters to the first half of the eleventh century, was ruling over a small territory, in the North Kanara district of Karnatak, comprising the Kūrmmadeva-*viṣaya* and Gokarṇa-*viṣaya*. He issued a charter, by which Bhaṭaputra Ugranandī son of Vīranandī, an emigrant from *Bhaṭṭagrāma* or a Brāhmaṇa village in Varendrī,[186] or North Bengal, received the village Vajapātti in Gokarṇa-*viṣaya*. The donated village is not identified. But according to D.C. Sircar, there are two places called Gokarṇa.[187] There is a village called Gokarṇa, on the Bāgmatī in Nepal. The other Gokarṇa and the one relevant to this charter has been located in the Karwar (North Kanara) district of Karnataka. Hence the donee migrated from a village in North Bengal and, went possibly to the Kanara district of Karnataka.

Kulika Vīra Pracaṇḍadeva, probably of the same royal family, by his Hindol Plates, gave the village of Vaḍapāṭi in the *viṣaya* of Kūrmmadeva, to three Brāhmaṇas, Bhaṭṭaputra Duvanandī, Thiranandī and Bhaganandī, who were the sons of Bhaṭṭaputra Ravinandī. Like Ugranandī of the previous charter, they too had come from *Bhaṭṭagrāma* in Varendrī.[188] So the donees migrating from a predominantly Brāhmaṇa village in North Bengal, came to South India and were given a village in the Karwar (North Kanara) district of Karnataka.

A grant of Saurāditya, dated *V.S.* 1077/c. 1020 A.D. refers to Bhaṭṭa Yaśāditya, son of Bhaṭṭa Vāṭṭho. He was a resident of Usīya-*grāma*, but his family had originally lived in a place called Chhela.[189] Chhela has been identified with Chailaha of Motihari police station or Chilabhar of Bettiah-thana in North Bihar. He received Vanapallī-grāma situated in Vyālisi-*viṣaya* within the Daradagandakī-*maṇḍala*. Vanapallī village is the same as Bangaon in Bagaha thana. According to D.C. Sircar, who edited the plates, Daradagandakī-*maṇḍala* in which it lay, was apparently situated on the banks of the Gandaka. This name is applied to three rivers, the greater Gandaka which runs through Gorakhpur, Champaran, Muzaffarpur, Saran and Patna districts, and joins the Ganges at Patna, the lesser Gandaka running through Gorakhpur and Saran districts and falling into the Gogrā, and the little Gandaka which runs through the Saran district and Tirhut an joins the Bāgmatī. So the Daradagandakī-*maṇḍala* probably comprised the areas in North Bihar through which the Gandaka flows, and the border regions of U.P. Hence the Brāhmaṇa Yaśāditya, having migrated from a village in North Bihar, did not go far, but was endowed with a village probably lying in the same region.

In the early years of the eleventh century, the kings of Kāmarūpa, whose names ended in Pāla, were ruling in Assam. Indrapāla of this family, issued the Guakuci Plates. Devadeva, son of Vāsudeva, whose ancestors lived in the village of Vaināma in Sāvathi,[190] received some land in the division called Paṇḍari in the Mandi-*viṣaya* to the north of Lauhitya. According to P. N. Bhattacharya,[191] the Rangiya station on the old Eastern Bengal railway within Mawzar Pargana is called Panduri. Sāvathi in which lay the Vaināma village, where the ancestors of Devadeva lived, has not been identified. It may have been Śrāvasti, situated on the boundary of Gonda Bahroich in U.P. or North Bengal, from where the donee migrated to Assam.

**Unidentified places or areas connected with immigrant Brāhmaṇas**

Apart from all these charters, wherein both the original homes and the areas to which the Brāhmaṇas migrated are identified, there are a number of others in which the location of only their former places of habitation is known.

In the first quarter of the ninth century, a new dynasty, that of the Candellas, was founded in the modern village of Khajuraho in the Chhatarpur district of Madhya Pradesh. In a grant of Dhaṅgadeva of this family, of *V.S.* 1055/c. 998 A.D., there is reference to a Brāhmaṇa Rudra Śrī Yaśodhara, son of Rudra Jayakumāra. He had emigrated from Tarkkārikā and was a resident of Dūrvvāharā-*grāma*.[192] Kielhorn who has edited the charter does not identify Tarkkārikā. It was, however, the same as Ṭakāri, perhaps in U.P. From there the Brāhmaṇa moved and received the village of Yullī in Ūṣaravāha, which has not yet been identified.

Paramāra Bhoja issued the Mahudi Plates in *V.S.* 1074/c. 1017 A.D. It refers to the donee Mārkaṇḍaśarman, son of Bhaṭṭa Śrīpati, who had emigrated from Śravaṇabhadra in Gauḍa-*deśa*.[193] Although Śravaṇabhadra has not been located, Gauḍadeśa, is that part of West Bengal which lies to the north of Burdwan and south of the Padmā. The donated village was Dugāryī-*grāma* in the Bhūmigṛha-paścima-dvipaṁcāśatka which is as yet unidentified.

A number of charters from Orissa record grants of villages whose sites are uncertain. Dharmamahādevī, the Bhauma-Kara queen, by her Angula Copper Plate, benefited Śrīdhara-bhaṭṭa, son of Vitebhaṭṭa, who had come from Kolañca.[194] He received some land in Deśaṇa-*grāma*, which has not yet been identified.

In the same way, Śulki Jayastambha, in a grant from Dhenkanal, made an endowment of the village of Kameśirsa in the Tagakula district. The donee was the Brāhmaṇa Dhirivva-raṅgati Śarman Citra Dīkṣita, son of Cāsaṅgaturda Citra Dīkṣita, an emigrant from Hastipada[195] in North Bihar. However, the village which he was granted, cannot be identified.

Vinītatuṅga II by his Talcher Plates, granted the village of Maddhamaṇḍa to two Brāhmaṇas. The village is unidentified. But one of the donees, Bhaṭṭaputra Naraka, came from Puṇḍravardhana, and at the time of the grant was living in Royarā,[196] on the border of the old Sonpur state.

Śatrubhañja of the Bhañja family, issued a charter from Dasapalla. In it the reference is to an emigrant from Khaḍuvāvallī in Madhyadeśa. He was the Brāhmaṇa Ājapāla, son of Nīlakaṇṭha, who having left his home in Madhyadeśa came to live in an unidentified village named Santoṣamādhava[197] Koṅkairā, the donated village in Ramalava-*viṣaya* has also not been identified.

In his twenty-fourth regnal year, Raṇabhañja issued a grant from Dasapalla. The village Hastileṇḍā in the Tullasidgā district with the five quarters, that formed the subject of the grant has not been identified. The beneficiary was Padmākara, son of Prabhākara, a resident of Burullā village. His ancestral home was in Pecipāṭaka, probably a village in Varendrī-*maṇḍala*,[198] from where he came to Orissa.

A Baud grant of Raṇabhañja dated in his fifty-eighth year, mentions the Brāhmaṇa Śubhadāma, son of Vṛṣabhadāma, an emigrant from Ṭakāri in Sāvathideśa or Śrāvasti probably in U.P. At the time of the grant he was living in the village of Tadalā in Oḍra-*viṣaya*[199] or coastal Orissa. He received Turallā-*grāma* in Tullaśṛṅga-*viṣaya*, neither of which has yet been identified.

Another Brāhmaṇa Bhaṭṭaputra Tiku, son of Madhusudaṇa, had come from Śāluvigrāma in Madhyadeśa. He is described as the donee of the Gaintala Plates of the eleventh year of Mahābhavagupta I. Having emigrated, he first settled down in Lapusoḍḍāgrāma[200] in Kośaladeśa. But neither the village Ṛṣigrāma that he received, nor Nimunā-*viṣaya* in which it stood, has been identified.

The Eastern Gaṅga ruler Devendravarman III in the *Gaṅga* year 308/c. 804-806 A.D., issued the Indian Museum Plates. They refer to the grant of the village of Purujvanā in Bukudravaka in Lohadhaṅgara. None of these places has been located. The donee Govindaśarman, son of Bhaṭṭa Nārāyaṇa, has been described as being a resident of a place in Uttara Rāḍha,[201] i.e. the northern part of south-west Bengal. Although the village that he received has not yet been definitely located, it must have been in the Ganjam district over which the Eastern Gaṅgas had ruled.

At times, the area to which a Brāhmaṇa migrated, or where he received a village is identified, but not the exact location of the place where he or his ancestors had originally lived. This is true of a number of grants.

In the last quarter of the tenth century, when the weak Pāla empire was steadily declining, a number of independent or semi-independent dynasties became stronger in Bengal. One of these were the Kambojas who ruled over West Bengal and possibly portions of North Bengal. Nayapāla of this family, issued the Irda Copper Plates, assigned by the editor N.G. Majumdar on palaeographic grounds, to the latter part of the tenth century. They record the grant of the village Bṛhat Chhattivannā, adjoining Kaṇṭi, Sammāsha and Bāḍakhaṇḍa, within the Daṇḍabhukti-*maṇḍala*, belonging to Vardhamāna-bhukti. Chattivannā has been identified with modern Chhatna in the Bankura district of Bengal. There is a locality named Chhatina on the bank of the Suvarṇarekhā between Belyabera and Nayabashan, which may be the Chhattivannā of the inscription. Vardhamāna-*bhukti* in which the donated village was included, comprised the major part of Burdwan district of West Bengal, as well as Daṇḍabhukti at one time. So the village was situated in West Bengal. The grant was made to Aśvattha-śarman, son of Anukulamiśra, born in Droṇa and an emigrant from Kuṇṭīra[202] neither of which has been identified.

The Siyadoni Inscription has been assigned to the period of Gurjara-Pratihāra Devapāla, who ruled for a year c. 948-949 A.D. In the second part of this inscription, we are told, that a certain king of Mahodaya, granted the town Rāyakka to some Brāhmaṇas, who later on came to be called Rāyakka-bhaṭṭas. One of the descendants of these Brāhmaṇas named Vaśiṣṭha came to Siyadoni,[203] where his son Dāmodara founded the temple of Murārī and endowed it with funds for worship of the deity. The town Rāyakka has not been identified. Siyadoni, where Vaśiṣṭha came and settled down has been located about ten miles north-north-west of Lalitpur near Jhansi at Siron Khurd in Madhya Pradesh. However, it is difficult to say from where Vaśiṣṭha actually originated.

In the Gaonri Plates of Paramāra Vākpati II of *V.S.* 1038/c. 981 A.D., which have been discussed above, the original places of habitation of most of the donee Brāhmaṇas are known. But in a few cases like that of Lohina, who came from Kāvaḍa *bhaṭṭagrāma*, Candrāditya from Cauramba and Ātuka from Umvarācara,[204] the ancestral homes have not been identified.

The Ujjain grant of Paramāra Bhoja, dated *V.S.* 1078/c. 1021 A.D. records the grant of the village Vīrāṇaka, situated within the limits of the division or the country to the west of Nāgadraha. According to N. J. Kirtane, the editor, this was in Ujjain. The beneficiary of the grant was Dhanapati Bhaṭṭa, son of Bhaṭṭa Govinda, an emigrant from Śrīvādā near Vellavalla, both of which are unidentified and a resident of Rādha Sursaṅga Karṇāta.[205] B. N. Sharma[206] thinks, that this is identical with Karnata in South India. But in the absence of proof, this cannot be definitely accepted. So the donee's places of emigration and residence, both though known, remain unidentified.

By his Banswara grant of the *Vikrama* year 1076/c. 1019 A.D., a hundred *nivartanas* of land at Vaṭapadraka included in the Ghāghradora-*bhoga* of Sthālī-*maṇḍala*, were granted to the Brāhmaṇa Bhāila. He was the son of Vāmana, whose ancestors had emigrated from Chinchanagara,[207] which is not identified. So it is not known from where the donee came to the Gujarat region, where some land in the village of Vaṭapadraka, located in modern Baroda district was handed over to him.

The Bhadresar Plates of Cauḷukya Bhīmadeva I of *V.S.* 1117/c. 1060 A.D., record that the village of Jabhaganā in the Kachchha-*maṇḍala*, was given to Govimdāsa, son of Dāmodara. The village though unlocated, was situated in the Cutch region. The Brāhmaṇa's family had lived in Prasannapura,[208] from where he emigrated and the identity of which is as yet unknown.

Like these Brāhmaṇas, a number of others who received lands in Orissa, came from places which are unidentified. Śāntikara of the Bhauma-Kara family, donated Kākura-*grāma* in the Talcher-*viṣaya* in Yamagarta-*maṇḍala* by a copper plate from Angul. The site of the village has not yet been traced, although it lay in the geographical unit corresponding to modern Talcher and jamgadia in Angul in the former Pallahara state. The donee Vāmanasvāmiśarman, son of Padmanābha, came from Ilāpada,[209] which, however, has not been identified.

Daṇḍimahādevī of the above-mentioned dynasty, issued a charter benefiting the Brāhmaṇa Pratihāra Dhavala son of Vāśu, an emigrant from Viṅgināṭaka.[210] He was given Villa village in Varaḍākhaṇḍa-*viṣaya* in Koṅgoda-*maṇḍala*, which has been placed by Cunningham in the Ganjam district, and by Fergusson, between Cuttack and Aska in the Ganjam district. However, the ancestral home of the donee has not yet been identified.

A grant of Śulki Raṇastambha refers to the donation of Jārā village in the district of Jārā in the Rāḍha-*maṇḍala*. It seems apparent that the village is identical with modern Jara in the Hooghly district of West Bengal. The donee was Paucuka, son of Hari, an emigrant from Telliṅgabhaṭṭagrāma in Rāḍha-*maṇḍala*.[211] According to the editor H.P. Sastri, the donee who belonged to the Kaśyapa *gotra* and was a student of the *Yajurveda*, was not a Rāḍhīya Brāhmaṇa, as among the latter, only the *Sāmaveda* was studied. Moreover, of the fifteen villages from which the Brāhmaṇas of the Kaśyapa *gotra* among the Rāḍhīs derive their village name, Telliṅgabhaṭṭa is not one. H.P. Sastri may be right in his view, that the donee was not a Rāḍhīya Brāhmaṇa. Both his name and the name of the village from which he came, seem to belong to South India. Yet the fact cannot be dismissed, that the charter itself states, that the village was in Rāḍha-*maṇḍala*. There is no other Rāḍha in India, except the one in south-west Bengal. Hence the identity and location of the donee's original home remain rather uncertain.

Vinītatuṅga II issued the Khargaprasad Plates, recording the grant of Khāmbhāra village in Lavanatāicha-*khaṇḍa-kṣetra*. The village is not identified. But Lavanatāicha-*khaṇḍa* in which it lay was probably near Yamagarta-*maṇḍala* or Jamgadia, as residents of Yamgarta-*maṇḍala* are addressed at the time of issuing the grant. The donee was Bhaṭṭa Iśāna, son of Ānanda, who hailed from Poḍhi and resided in Koṭamala,[212] neither of which has yet been identified.

The same is the case with two grants of Śatrubhañja. His Sonpur Plates give the name of Bhaṭṭaputra Kṛṣṇa, son of Ākhaṇḍala, who had come from Ālāpagrāma,[213] which is unidentified. He received Milupāḍi-*khaṇḍa-kṣetra* in Royarā-*viṣaya*.

Likewise, the exact location of Śrīkheda from where Bhaṭṭaputra Bappi, son of Keśi emigrated, is not known, although it is stated to be in Dakṣiṇāpatha. Having emigrated he was living in Oḍijoṅga,[214] and received a village from Śatrubhañja. This was Komvavāḍā-*grāma* in Vodā-*khaṇḍa-viṣaya* or Boddapatti, three miles from Konomona, in the Chatrapura-*taluka* of the Ganjam district.

In his fifty-fourth year, Raṇabhañja by a grant from Baud, gave to an unnamed Brāhmaṇa, whose father was Vāsudeva, the village of Konatinthi in the Khātiyā-*viṣaya* of Khiñjali-*maṇḍala*. Konatinthi is the same as Kontuani, about two miles south of Baud and it lay in Keonjhar in Mayūrbhañja in Orissa. The recipient of the charter, having emigrated from Apilomuleri, was a resident of Amvāsarasarā[215] neither of which can be traced.

Narendrabhañja in set of Ādipur Plates made a grant of the village Vṛhat Sārāi in Urtti-*viṣaya* in Khijjinga. These are identical with Sorai near Urti, twelve miles to the north-west of Khijjinga or Khiching on the right bank of the Vaitaraṇī, about ninety miles to the west of Baripada. The donee Śītaladevaśarman, was an emigrant from Tilapudraka,[216] the location of which is unknown.

Mahābhavagupta I, in his sixth regnal year, issued the Patna Museum Plates, wherein two Brāhmaṇa brothers Keśava and Apya, sons of Dāddī are referred to as emigrants from Kommāpira which is unidentified. They were living in Loiśṛṅga[217] or Loisinga near Bolangir. While residing there, they received the nearby Pāsitalā-*grāma* or Pointala, two miles east of Bolangir, in Potā-*viṣaya*.

Mahāśivagupta I, son of Mahābhavagupta, in his fourth year, by his Orissa State Museum Plates granted Kuḍukulokhaṇḍa Kṣetra in the Gaṇḍitama-*viṣaya* in Uḍradeśa. These places have not been identified. According to P.R. Srinivasan who edited the charter, Uḍradeśa in which the village lay, was the region comprising the modern districts of Puri and Cuttack. However, Uḍradeśa and Oḍra-*deśa* may well refer to the same region of coastal Orissa. The recipient was Śrī Kāko resident of Yaśakaṭaka, and an emigrant from Śrāvasthālekhaḍīya-*grāma*, which has not been located.[218] Although the editor takes Yaśakaṭaka to mean Cuttack, the name may refer to the king's temporary camp. To this place Śrī Kāko had come, probably in search of a better fortune.

Four years later, Mahāśivagupta I issued the Patna Museum Plates, benefiting Śrī Kāmadeva, son of Narasiṁha. Having emigrated from an unidentified place called Mādhvīla, the Brāhmaṇa was living in Jalajaḍḍa or Jallajodo near Talagaja in Kośala.[219] Later he received the village of Talakajja or modern Talagaja, ten miles south-east of Bolangir in Sanūlā-*viṣaya* or Soinnula in the Patna state in the same geographical region of Kośaladeśa.

Puṇḍarīkaśarman, son of Nārāyaṇaśarman, appears as the donee of the Nibinnā grant of the fifteenth year of the abovementioned ruler. An emigrant from Bhaṭaparoli, a village which has not yet been located, he was living in Maramenḍā in the Kośala country.[220] He received from the king, the village Nibiṇḍā or modern Nibinna in the Sonpur state in the Ganuṭapāta-*maṇḍala* or Ghantapara near Nibinna in Kośaladeśa.

In the early part of the eleventh century, Kramāditya, an independent king was ruling probably in Bihar He issued a copper plate dated *V.S.* 1081/c. 1024-1025 A.D. By this charter, Bhaṭṭa Puruṣottamadeva, son of Bhaṭṭa Upātto, an emigrant from Kesātyi[221] which is not identified. received the village

Siṁvala in the Suvarṇakhaṇḍa-*viṣaya*. Although the modern names of these places are unknown, Suvarnakhaṇḍa-*viṣaya* may probably have been the area through which the Suvarṇarekhā flows, i.e. in the Chotanagpur region of Bihar. According to V.V. Mirashi who edited the grant, Suvarṇakhaṇḍa may have been a part of Suvarṇabhūmi, which was perhaps the ancient name of Singbhum. Hence the Brāhmaṇa Puruṣottamadeva, received a village, located probably in Bihar.

A number of other charters from Orissa, give place-names, among which those referring to the original homes of immigrant Brāhmaṇas and the places to which they had migrated and the donated villages, have not yet been identified.

The Puri Plates of Kulastambha, record the grant of a village Paḍāra, attached to Goilo-*khaṇḍa* to Bhaṭṭaputra Velluka, son of Ānanti, and emigrant from Āviddhā.[222] By his Talcher Plates, Kulastambha granted to Bhaṭṭa Viśvarūpa who had come from Maṅgalavilā,[223] the village Singa in Paścima-*khaṇḍa* Pūrva-*viṣaya*. Jayastambha by a grant from Dhenkanal, donated some land in the village Llolapura in the Kodāka-*maṇḍala* to Ṛṣivaka son of Cāndavachcha, an emigrant from Mutāvaṣu.[224] Another charter of the same ruler, also issued from Dhenkanal, records the grant of an unnamed village in Tahakula division in Kagavimulāktamaśiṅga. The recipient Govvarahūtiśarmā Citradīkṣita, son of Seṅgatada Citradīkṣita, had come from a place called Dastipada.[225] None of the areas mentioned above has yet been located.

The second donee of the Talcher Plates of Vinītatuṅga II, which have already been discussed, was Lakhādita, son of Ujola, an emigrant from Mṛthāvastu.[226] With his co-donee he was given the village of Maddhamaṇḍa. Neither his home, nor the donated village has till now been identified.

Another set of Talcher Plates, issued by Gayāḍatuṅga, records the grant of Svalpa-Kompai village in the Khembāi-*viṣaya* to Bhaṭṭa Bhāinadeva, son of Gokuladeva. His family had resided at Śrīchchhātra[227] from where he emigrated. But as in some other charters, in this too none of the places can be traced on a modern map.

Neṭṭabhañja, by a set of plates, granted two villages Rāig-rāma and Seḍagrāma near Nānā-*khaṇḍa-viṣaya*. The donee was Bhaṭṭa Dāuli, son of Bhaṭṭa Siḍa. He was a resident of Kolakhali, but his family originally came from Vātalaviḍima.[228]

All these places are as yet unidentified. In these seven records, the exact location of the areas where the Brāhmaṇas received lands and villages or the places where they at first settled down is unknown. Yet they definitely migrated to Orissa, as they are found benefiting by the land-grants made by the ruling houses of Orissa. However, no idea can be formed about the original homes that these Brāhmaṇas had left behind. As a result, the value of these charters as workable instances of mirgration, becomes diminished.

### C. 1030 A.D. onwards

In this section a few such cases are included in which there is a possibility of the donees having migrated to the area of the grant, sometime between c.1030 and 1050 A.D. Also those charters have been taken into account, in which the ancestors of migrant Brāhmaṇas are mentioned, who can be placed round about c. 1030 A.D.

Kāmarūpa in the eleventh century was being ruled by a family of kings whose names ended in Pāla. The Silimpur Stone Inscription, which on the basis of its script, is ascribed to the second and third quarters of the eleventh century, mentions Kāmarūpa-*nṛpati* Jayapāladeva. He is said to have offered a gift of nine hundred gold coins and land yielding an income of a thousand measures of rice, to a Brāhmaṇa Prahāsa, who, however, refused to accept them. Prahāsa belonged to a family renowned for its scholarship. Seven generations of his ancestors are mentioned. Originally they had lived in Tarkāri within Śrāvasti and later in Bālagrāma in Varendrī in Puṇḍravardhana-*bhukti*.[229] Bālagrāma in Varendrī is in North Bengal. As regards Tarkāri, in this case it was also situated in North Bengal, as the inscription describes its location by saying, that it was separated from Bālagrāma, only my Sakaṭi, which may be the name of a river. Even in Bālagrāma, these Brāhmaṇas did not live for long, but moved to a neighbouring village Śīyamva (ba), also in Bengal, where Prahāsa himself was probably living. Śīyamva(ba) was in the vicinity of Silimpur, in the Bogra district of North Bengal. So the ancestors of Prahāsa were involved in a double migration, first from a locality in Śrāvasti to a village and again to another, although the entire movement was confined within Bengal.

Vigrahapāla III of the Pāla dynasty perhaps a contemporary of Jayapāla of Kāmarūpa in his twelfth regnal year, issued the Amgachi grant. By this, he donated half of Brāhmaṇī-*grāma* in Koṭivarṣa-*viṣaya* in Puṇḍravardhana-*bhukti*. The recipient was Khoduladevaśarman, son of Arkkadeva, and grandson of Padmāvanadeva. One of these, having emigrated from Kroḍañci or Kolāñca, was living in Chhattrāgrāma in Matsyāvāsa,[230] sometime before the date of the grant. Later Khoduladevaśarman received from the Pāla ruler, some land in a village of North Bengal.

In the seventeenth year of Vigrahapāla III, a Brāhmaṇa officer named Ghaṇṭīśa, by means of the Bangaon Plates, granted a plot of land in Tīrabhukti to another Brāhmaṇa Ghāṇṭukaśarman. The donee was the son of Tuṅga and grandson of Yogasvāmin. Although at that time he was living in Iṭṭāhāka, the family had originally come from Kolāñca.[231] As regards Ghaṇṭīśa, the donor, the record mentions, that his great-grandmother, was the grand-daughter of one Kāccha, who came to Tīrabhukti from Kroḍāñca.[232] Tīrabhukti is the modern Tirhut division in North Bihar. D.C. Sircar who edited the plates feels, that Kroḍāñca or Kolāñca from where the ancestors of both the donor and donee came, can be placed in the Set-Mahet region of U.P.

Karṇa Kalacuri issued in the *Cedi* year 793/c. 1042 A.D., the Benares Plates by which he granted the village Srusī within Kāśī-*bhūmi* to the learned Viśvarūpa, son of Nārāyaṇa and grandson of Vāmana. His ancestors had come from the village of Vesāla.[233] Kielhorn who edited the plates feels, that Vesāla may be the Pāli form of the word Vaiśāli, i.e. modern Basarh, in Muzaffarpur district of North Bihar. Although Susī the donated village has not been identified, it was included within

Kāśī-*bhūmi*, which is the same as modern Benares. So the ancestors of Viśvarūpa migrated from a village in North Bihar, and came to the vicinity of Benares in U.P.

In the middle of the ninth century, two Śīlāhāra families began to rule as feudatories of the Rāṣṭrakūṭas, in northern and southern Konkon. Śīlāhāra Nāgārjuna of the northern Konkan branch in *Śaka* 961/c. 1039 A.D., issued the Thana Plates. By this charter, he made a grant to Mādhava Paṇḍita, son of Gokarṇṇa Paṇḍita, who had migrated from Hastigrāma in Madhyadeśa.[234] The grant consisted of the village of Muṁj-avalī in the Koriyalā-12, on the Bombay-Poona line of the Central Railway. So Mādhava Paṇḍita's father having emigrated from a village in Madhyadeśa, settled somewhere in northern Maharashtra.

Another set of Thana Plates, issued by Mummuṇirāja of the same family in *Śaka* 970/c. 1048-1049 A.D., records two grants to two groups of donees, consisting of revenues and other income from some villages. Among all these, there was only one immigrant donee Daddapaiya, son of Brahma-nāyaka. He had emigrated from the Madhyadeśa region[235] and settled in the Bassein area of Maharashtra.

Some Brāhmaṇas appear as donees of another grant of Śītāhāra Mummuṇirāja, dated *Śaka* 971/c. 1049 A.D. The donated village Kichchita in the Mandarāja district, has not yet been located. Among the donees were three[236] whose ancestors had emigrated from elsewhere. One was Koko Paṇḍita, son of Piṭāmaha, whose ancestors came from Gauḍa, which may be located in Bengal or may be one of the countries forming Pañca-Gauḍa. Another family represented by Yajña Dīkṣita and his son Devadhara Dīkṣita who was the donee, had lived in Muṁjasthāna in Madhyadeśa. The ancestors of Dāmodara, son of Sūdana Dīkṣita were originally inhabitants of Bhṛgu-kachchha or Broach in Lāṭa-*deśa*. So from different parts of North India, Brāhmaṇas came to the Maharashtra region and were endowed with a village whose identification is yet unknown to us.

By the Belwa Plates of his eleventh regnal year, Vigraha-pāla III, granted parts of a village called Lovanikāma, lying within Phāṇitavīthī-*viṣaya* of Puṇḍravardhana-*bhukti* to Jayānandadevaśarman, son of Śrīpatideva and grandson of Hṛṣikeśadeva. Some ancestors of the donee had emigrated from a village called Vaheḍā[237] which has not yet been identified, and were living in Vellāvagrāma.

The Sungal C.P. Inscription of Vidagdhadeva dated in the eleventh century A.D., records the grant of one bhū of land called Serī and of half a bhū of land called Lavāla in the village of Sumaṅgala in the Tāvasaka district. The donee was Srī Naduka, son of Dedduka and grandson of Devanna who had emigrated from Kurukṣetra. He belonged to the Kaśyapa gotra and was a student of the Vājasaneya Śākhā. The grant was made as an agrahāra, with the right to grass, fruit trees, water courses, channels and fallow lands. Together with the privileges of non-payment of taxes, non-interference by royal officers and of inalienabilily, the donee could also keep servants, cowherds and cultivators. (Sircar, D.C. SELECT INSCRIPTIONS, Vol. II. pp. 427-428, II 11-26).

According to J. Ph. Vogel, (ANTIQUITIES OF CHAMBA STATE PART I, P. 101), Vidagdha's reign may have coincided with the period of invasion of Northern India by Sultan Mahmūd. So it is possible, that the disturbed political situation of the time, encouraged this family to emigrate from their ancestral home in the Kurukṣetra region. They moved albeit a short distance, and were given lands in Sungala, now in the Chamba district of Himachal Pradesh.

Inscriptions apart, literature too provides us with several examples of migration.

The lives of some poets, authors, grammarians and dramatists, rather their wanderings from one place to another, show that they left their ancestral homes to settle elsewhere. The author of the *Kirātārjunīyam*, Bhāravi who flourished in the later half of the sixth century, himself lived in the court of Kubja Viṣṇuvardhana of the Eastern Cāḷukya family of Piṣṭapura in the Godavari district. His forefathers had originally been inhabitants of Ānandapura in Gujarat and had migrated from there to Nāsikya, i.e. in Maharashtra. Later Bhāravi being invited by Pallava Siṁhaviṣṇu of Kāñcī, went to live at his court,[238] and there became a friend of the prince Mahendravikrama.

The author of the *Harṣacarita*, Bāṇabhaṭṭa, a contemporary of Harṣavardhana of Kanauj, lived in the first half of the seventh century. Bāṇa's home was at Prītikūṭa near the bank of the Hiraṇyavāha or Śoṇa,[239] which rises in the Vindhya hills and flows through the Daṇḍaka forest. V.S. Agrawal[240] agrees with this view. He, however, points out, that according to K. Upadhyaya, Prītikūṭa is modern Piyur in the Shahabad district of Bihar. But Bāṇa himself mentions, that his home was near the river Śoṇa, which ran through the Daṇḍakāraṇya. It is true, that the precise extent of Daṇḍakāraṇya is far from certain. It seems to have been a general name, comprising all forests from the Yamunā to the Krishnā. Guha who helped Bharata to cross the Ganges, has been described in the *Rāmāyaṇa*, as being well acquainted with the Daṇḍakāraṇya, which may have stretched right up to the Ganges. Hemādri in his digest (in *Vratakhaṇḍa* section) says, that Devagiri or modern Daulatabad was in Seuṇadeśa on the confines of Daṇḍakāraṇya (vide Bombay Gazetteer, Part II, p.231): Kane too has held, that the original home of Bāṇa was in Daṇḍakaraṇya and not near Buxar. Agrawal also feels, that as Bāṇa himself describes the Soṇa as lying near Candraparvata, the latter must have been situated in that part of the Vindhya hills from where the Śoṇa rises. So Bāṇa's ancestral home was probably in the region of Madhya Pradesh near the source of the river Śoṇa. From there he went to live in the court of Harṣavardhana at Kanauj.

Bhavabhūti, author of the *Mālatī-Mādhava, Mahāvīracarita* and *Uttararāmacarita* has been assigned by V.V. Mirashi and P.V. Kane to the eighth century. The *Mahāvīracarita*[241] and *Mālatī-Mādhava*[242] state that he had been born in Padmapura in Dakṣiṇāpatha or the Deccan. According to the later text Padmapura is located in Vidarbha or modern Berar. Some scholars identify Padmapura with Padmāvatī or Padam Pawaya near Narwar. D.C. Sircar and others do not agree with this view. They prefer to locate Padmapura in Vidarbha as stated in the prelude to the *Mālatī-Mādhava*. It may be pointed out that in the footnotes of his edition of the *Mālatī-Mādhava*, Bhandarkar mentions that some manuscripts omit the word Vidarbheṣu from the text.[243]

Kalhaṇa in his *Rājataranginī* mentions, that Bhavabhūti was the court-poet of Yaśovarman of Kanauj.[244] Hence from Berar in Maharashtra, Bhavabhūti migrated to Kanauj in U.P.

The *Rājataraṅgiṇī* also refers to the rhetorician Vāmana. Stein assigns him to the eighth century. He was a minister of Jayāpīḍa of Kashmir.[245] Later on Vāmana went to the court of Rāṣṭrakūṭa Govinda III[246] leaving his home in the extreme north of India and coming southward to Maharashtra.

Rājaśekhara, the author of the *Karpūramañjarī* lived about c. 900 A.D. He belonged to a Yāyāvara Brāhmaṇa family of Maharashtra. This is indicated by a statement in the *Bālarāmāyaṇa*[247] that his great-grandfather Akālajalaḍa, was *Mahārāṣṭracūḍāmaṇi* or a crest-jewel of Maharashtra. Sten Konow[248] adds, that in the colophon to the Benares edition of his *Karpūramañjarī*, the poet applies this epithet to himself. V.V. Mirashi[249] too agrees, that Rājaśekhara styled himself personally as the ornament of the Maharashtra country. All this emphasises the fact that he originated from Maharashtra and either he or his ancestors migrated from there. In his plays, Rājaśekhara is found to occupy the position of a court-poet at Kanauj. He was the *guru* of Gurjara Pratihāra Mahendrapāla I c. 885-908 A.D., as mentioned in his *Karpūramañjarī*.[250] His contacts with Kanauj continued in the time of Vināyaka I Mahīpāla. Rājaśekhara also had some connection with the Cedi princes. His name is mentioned in the Bilhari Inscription and he was probably a contemporary of Śaṁkaragaṇa.[251]

Another author Abhinanda, flourished in the first half of the tenth century. In his *Kādambarīkathāsāra*, he states, that his ancestors had been originally inhabitants of Gauḍadeśa from where they migrated to Kashmir.[252]

Indurāja or Pratihārendurāja, in the middle of the tenth century, wrote a commentary on the *Kāvyālaṁkāra* of Udbhaṭa. Indurāja added the word *Konkana* to his name, showing that he was originally from the Konkan region. He migrated from there to Kashmir.[253]

Lakṣmīdhara the poet, lived in the first half of the eleventh century. Originally, an inhabitant of Bhaṭṭa Kośala in Gauḍa, he went to Mālava in Madhya Pradesh and lived in the court of Paramāra Bhoja.[254]

Bilhaṇa, the author of the *Vikramāṅkadevacarita* flourished in the second half of the eleventh century. His ancestors belonged to a sect of Madhyadeśa Brāhmaṇas, and had originally lived in Madhyadeśa. From there they migrated to Kashmir. Bilhaṇa himself was born at Koṇamukha near Pravarapura in Kashmir.[255] He left Kashmir in the reign of King Kalaśa.[256] Visiting Mathurā, Kānyakubja, Prayāga, Vārāṇasī and the royal courts at Ḍāhala and Aṇhilvāḍa, he finally came to Southern India, to the court of Cāḷukya Vikramāditya VI Tribhuvanamalla (c. 1076-1127 A.D.), and there received the title of *Vidyāpati*. Kalhaṇa describes how he was honoured by the Cāḷukya king. So Bilhaṇa's travels took him on a long journey from the north, finally bringing him to the Deccan.

Alberuni in the first chapter of his work on India,[257] refers to migrations, when he describes how the victories of Mahmūd, had made the Hindus "like atoms of dust scattered in all directions." With their sciences and their knowledge they fled to Kashmir, Benares and other places. Besides Alberuni makes repeated references to Kashmiri authors and mentions Kashmiri scholars among his informants, if not among his actual teachers. His references to a local Kashmir festival,[258] the anecdote about the propagation of *Śiṣyahitāvritti* in Kashmir,[259] and to a statement contained in an almanac for the *Śaka* year 951/c. 1029-1030 A.D., which had come from Kashmir,[260] as well as his detailed knowledge of the topography of Kashmir, all point according to Stein,[261] to personal contact with Kashmiri scholars. It is doubtful whether Alberuni himself, had ever visited Kashmir. Hence it is possible, that he depended for a considerable part of his information on the *paṇḍitas* who had emigrated from Kashmir.

Sanskrit stories of the period contain some references to migration of Brāhmaṇas. The *Daśakumāracarita* of Daṇḍin who flourished in the period between c. 635-700 A.D., mentions a Brāhmaṇa Mātaṅga who used to live in the Vindhya forest. Later, obeying a divine order, he entered the Daṇḍaka forest and became king of Pātāla.[262] Pātāla here obviously refers to some place in the Daṇḍaka forest, where Mātaṅga went in search of adventure. Some other Brāhmaṇas sons and grandsons of the ministers of Rājahaṁsa king of Magadha, also left their homes in Magadha to settle elsewhere. Kāmapāla, a son of Dharmapāla, who went from Magadha to Vārāṇasī,[263] Pramati, son of Sumati, who settled down in Śrāvasti[264] and Mitragupta, grandson of Dharmapāla, who is found in the city of Suhma, called Dāmalipta,[265] can be enumerated among such immigrant Brāhmaṇas. Dāmalipta is also called Tāmralipta, which according to D.C. Sircar, is sometimes mentioned in literature, as a part of Suhma, sometimes as an independent state and sometimes as a part of Vaṅga.[266] In this case, probably the first is meant.

Like the *Daśakumāracarita*, the *Kathāsaritasāgara* of Somadeva, contains similar instances. One Putraka who had lived in Chinchani in the Deccan left his home and entered the Vindhya forest and finally came to Pāṭaliputra.[267] The Brāhmaṇa Śrīdarśana went from Trigarta—The region between the rivers Ravi and Sutlej—to Mālava.[268] Vikramapura (in modern Bangladesh) was the home of Vīravara, who also went to Mālava.[269] From the Deccan, came Pralambabāhu, migrating to Kauśāmbī in U.P., seeking employment under Naravāhanadatta, son of Udayana king of Vatsa.[270] Some other Brāhmaṇas were driven away by famine. For instance Govindasvāmin who was living on the banks of the Yamunā, left his home and settled in Benares.[271] Yaśaskara emigrated from Śobhāvatī in the territory of Kaliṅga and went to the city of Viśālā.[272]

It is true, that the testimony of these stories is not as reliable as the information supplied by inscriptions and by texts like the *Rājataraṅgiṇī* or by Alberuni's *India*. Yet it can safely be surmised, that migration as a feature of human life, must have been well-known to people of those days. References to them could otherwise have hardly found a place in these tales.

## Conclusion

From a study of the instances of migration discussed, some conclusions can be drawn. During the approximately three hundred years, from c. 475-750 A.D., when most migrations are known to us from the region of Gujarat, movement was confined to short distances. The majority of the Maitraka charters show, that Brāhmaṇas moved within Gujarat. Remarkably, however, even in later years, i.e. from c. 750-1030 A.D. when long distance migrations became more usual, e.g. when Brāhmaṇas travelled from villages in Bengal to places as far south as the Kanara district of Karnataka, most of the Brāhmaṇas of Gujarat did not leave Gujarat. In marked contrast, were Brāhmaṇas who went from different parts of Madhyadeśa to villages in Bengal and Orissa in the east, and others who came from Bengal to northern Maharashtra in the Deccan.

Coming to the places from where the Brāhmaṇas emigrated, and those to which they went, familiarity of surroundings, may have been largely responsible for the movement from towns to towns and villages to villages. In most of the Maitraka charters, Brāhmaṇas leaving towns, proceeded not towards villages, but towards important cities like Kaira or even the capital town of Valabhī. Most of the Brāhmaṇas who came to settle in Bihar, Bengal and Orissa, emigrated from villages and took up fresh residence in other villages.

Some, perhaps the more adventurous among the immigrant Brāhmaṇas, left towns to settle in villages. The grants of the Gurjaras, and a few of the Somavaṁśis of Orissa, reveal this trend. This phenomenon, however, is difficult to explain.

As for the factors responsible for the pattern of migration in Gujarat—i.e. the movement from towns to towns—in the early centuries of the period under survey, we may cite the cases of Viṣṇumitra, who went from Ānarttapura to Kheṭaka, Nārāyaṇamitra, who migrated to Kheṭaka from Ānandapura and Magopadatta, who leaving Ānandapura came to Valabhī. These may be explained in two ways. A town always offers greater opportunities, as far as earning a livelihood is concerned. Brāhmaṇas who were leaving their ancestral homes, perhaps due to economic reasons, would therefore naturally come to towns, rather than to villages. Besides, since the early centuries of the Christian era, Gujarat had many trading centres and ports, which added to the attraction of the towns and contained within themselves, the promise of wealth and fortune.

It was the possibility of coming to the notice of the ruling family that brought migrating Brāhmaṇas from villages to towns. It has already been described that the Brāhmaṇas Nāgamārya, Sillaṇa and Kāladeśī Devu, followed this pattern. Leaving their ancestral villages, they migrated to towns and subsequently received grants from Rāṣṭrakūṭa Govinda IV, Paramāra Vairisiṁha and Somavaṁśi Mahābhavagupta I respectively.

It was on this varied pattern, that Brāhmaṇas in Northern India, migrated from one part of the country to another. The reasons why they moved, and how they fared in the lands to which they went, will now be assessed.

## *Appendix I*

Number of inscriptions giving place-names (connected with migrant donee Brāhmaṇas) which have been identified.

| | c. 475-606 A.D. | c. 606-647 A.D. | c. 647-750 A.D. | c. 750-1030 A.D. | c. 1030 A.D. onwards (ancestors of donees) |
|---|---|---|---|---|---|
| Identified places of emigration only | 2 | 1 | 1 | 10 | 1 |
| Donated village or villages identified with certainty | 1 | 4 | 8 | 18 | 1 |
| Both or all places of emigration, residence and/or immigration identified | 2 | 5 | 12 | 67 | 5 |

## Appendix II

Number of inscriptions giving place-names (connected with migrant donee Brāhmaṇas) which are not yet identified.

| | c. 475-606 A.D. | c. 606-647 A.D. | c. 647-750 A.D. | c. 750-1030 A.D. | c. 1030 A.D. onwards (ancestors of donees) |
|---|---|---|---|---|---|
| Unidentified places of emigration only | 1 | 4 | 8 | 18 | 1 |
| Donated village or villages not identified. | 2 | 1 | 1 | 10 | 1 |
| Both or all unidentified places of emigration, residence and/or immigration | x | x | x | 7 | x |

## Appendix III

Total number of inscriptions connected with migrant Brāhmaṇas.

| | c. 475-606 A.D. | c. 606-647 A.D. | c. 647-750 A.D. | c. 750-1030 A.D. | c. 1030 A.D. onwards (ancestors of donees) |
|---|---|---|---|---|---|
| | 5 | 9 | 21 | 104 | 8 |

# *Appendix IV*

## The Hindu Śāhis

Alberuni in his *India* writes about the Hindu Śāhis or Sāhiyas who were ruling in Afghanistan and the Punjab before the invasion of Sultan Mahmūd. They belonged to the family founded by Kallār, the Brāhmaṇa Vazīr who had imprisoned his master Lagatūrmān, the last of the Turki Śāhis of Afghanistan and had usurped the throne (*India* edited by Sachau, 1964, Vol. II, Chap. XLIX, p. 13). Round about c. 1021 A.D., when the Śāhis were completely routed by Sultan Mahmūd, they began to emigrate and sought refuge in Kashmir. The *Rājataraṅgiṇī* too refers to this. The ruling Loharas of Kashmir were their relatives by marriage. Kalhaṇa mentions a number of Śāhi princes, Rudrapāla, Diddapāla, Utpala and Anaṅgapāla, who in the time of King Ananta (c. 1028-1063 A.D.), and Bijja, Pittharāja and Pāja, who in the time of Ananta's son Kalaśa (c. 1063-1089 A.D.), exercised considerable influence in the court of Kashmir (*RT*, VII, verse 144-149 and 273-274). They also received large sums of money, Diddapāla drawing eighty thousand *dināras* daily and Rudrapāla, one and a half lakhs of the same currency. As Kalhaṇa puts it, they exhausted the revenues of the kingdom (*RT* VII, verse 144).

There is, however, some controversy about the caste of the Śāhis. While Alberuni believes that they were Brāhmaṇas, scholars like Y. Mishra, (*The Hindu Sahis of Afghanistan and the Punjab*, p.3 f), and others are of the opinion, that they were Kṣatriyas.

**References**

1. Huntingdon, E., in *EB* XV, p. 463.
2. *ESS*, IX-X, p. 426.
3. Roux, G., *Ancient Iraq*, p. 186.
4. Chandra, S., *Dependence and Disillusionment*, p. 110.
5. *EB*., op. cit., p. 471.
6. *Ibid.*
7. *ESS*, op. cit., VII-VIII, p. 646.
8. Childe, G.V., *What Happened In History*, pp. 248 and 274.
9. There is some controversy regarding the date of this king. A. Ghosh assigns him to the last quarter of the seventh century, and V.V. Mirashi to the seventh decade of the sixth. D.C. Sircar on the other hand, on palaeographic grounds holds, that Tīvara's rule covered about a decade to the third quarter of the sixth century.
10. *EI* XXXIV, p. 116, 11.24-26 (text).
11. Sankalia, H.D., *SHCGEG*, p. 63.
12. As mentioned by H.P. Sastri in *SHCGEG*, p. 68, fn. 2.
13. Sircar, D.C., *SGAMI*, p. 209.
14. *IA* VII, p. 72, 11.4-5 (text).
15. Sircar, D.C., *SGAMI*, p. 207.
16. The Christian equivalent of *saṁvat* 286 should have been c. 605-606 A.D. Hence this grant belongs not to the middle of the sixth century, but to the early years of the seventh.
17. *EI* XI, p. 179, 1.19 (text).
18. *IA*, I, pp. 14-18.
19. Majumdar, R.C., *HB I* p. 197.
20. Sankalia, H.D., *op. cit.*, p. 200
21. *CII* IV, p. 41, 1.21 (text).
22. Sircar, D.C., in *CA*, p. 195.
23. *CII* IV, p. 62, 1.35 (text).
24. *Ibid.* 11.40-41 (text).
25. *Ibid.* IV, p. 77, 1.16 (text); p. 80, 1.14 (text).

26. *JBBRAS, N.S.*I., p. 70, 1.32 (text).
27. Sircar, D.C., *SGAMI,* p. 208.
28. *EI* VIII, p. 193, 1.40 (text).
29. *Ibid.* XXXV, p. 286, 11.34-35 (text).
30. *JBBRAS, N.S.*I, p. 30, 11.21-22 (text).
31. *EI* XXVII, p. 40, 1.22 (text).
32. *JBBRAS, NS.*I., p. 55, 1.33 (text).
33. *IA* XV, p. 187.
34. Sankalia, H.D., *op. cit.*, p. 62.
35. *EI* VIII, p. 193, 1.38 (text).
36. *Ibid.* p. 198, 1.41 (text).
37. *Ibid.* XXXIV, p. 170.
38. *Ibid.* p. 172, 1.12 (text).
39. D.C. Sircar points out, that it is difficult to say, whether Purapaṭṭa is a geographical name, or whether it has been used in the sense of *paṭṭa-viṣaya* or metropolitan district around the *pura* or the capital.
40. According to D.C. Sircar, the early Guhilas of Mewar ruled in the Udaipur division, while the copper-plates of the Guhilas of Kiṣkindhapura, have all been discovered at Dungarpur, to the south of Udaipur. Hence this Kiṣkindhapur cannot be the same as Kekind in the old Jodhpur state, to the north-west of Udaipur. On the other hand, he identifies it with Kiṣkindha which is a ruined city in the vicinity of Kalyanpura in the Bhomat district of Udaipur, bordering on the Dungarpur region, and which is the Kiṣkindha of the Dhulev Plates of Bheṭṭi of the Guhila family.
41. *IA* VII, p. 73, 11.15-16 (text). For identification of Desor, see *SHCGEG,* p. 68.
42. Sankalia, H.D., *op.cit.*, p. 71.
43. It is remarkable that the donee of this charter and his father, have the same names as the donee of the previous one and father of the latter. Moreover they belonged to the Śārkarāksi *gotra* and were students of the *Ṛgveda*. Besides, in both the charters they are said to be emigrants from Anarttapura. Also in the second charter, the donee is said to be residing in Kheṭaka, where he had received

the earlier grant. So it is possible that Khāragrāha II made a further grant of land to the donee of the charter of Dharasena IV, and the Brāhmaṇas of the later grant were identical with those of the earlier one.

44. *IA* VII, p. 79, ll.14-15 (text).
45. *JBBRAS, N.S.*I., p. 72, ll.48-49 (text).
46. *Ibid.* p. 74, l.47 (text).
47. Majumdar, R.C., in *CA*, p. 148.
48. *EI* IV, p. 80, l.53 (text).
49. *IA* XI, p. 309, l.20 (text).
50. *CII* IV, p. 86, l.19 (text).
51. *Ibid.* IV, p. 141, l.37 (text).
52. *EI* XXV, p. 30, ll.13-14 (text).
53. Sircar, D.C., *SGAMI*, p. 207.
54. *EI* XXVII, pp. 200-201, ll.18-19 (text).
55. Dasgupta, K.K., *TLB*, pp. 60-61, 69.
56. *EI* XXVII, p. 200, l.18 (text).
57. *Ibid.* XXVI, p. 67, l.11 (text).
58. *Ibid.* XXXIV, p. 121, l.10 (text).
59. *IA* XV, p. 340, l.41 (text).
60. *EI* I, p. 88, l.42 (text).
61. *IA* V, p. 212, ll.22-23 (text).
62. *JBBRAS, N.S.*I., p. 73, l.46 (text).
63. *EI* XXI, p. 210, l.48 (text).
64. *Ibid.* XXII, p. 119, l.46 (text).
65. *JBBRAS*, XI, p. 344, l.26 (text).
66. *CII* IV, p. 106, l.35 (text).
67. Sircar, D.C., *SGAMI*, p. 276.
68. *EI* IV, p. 250, l.51 (text).
69. *JASB* XVII, p. 144, l.36 (text).
70. *EI* XXXIV, p. 96.
71. *IHQ* XX, p. 245; *IO* IV, p. 151.
72. *EI* XIV, pp. 327-328, ll.48-49 (text).
73. *IHQ* XX, p. 238; *IO* IV, p. 100.
74. *EI* X, p. 78, l.10 (text).
75. Sharma, D., *Early Chauhan Dynasties*, p. 34.
76. *EI* XXXVI, p. 46, l.5 (text).
77. *Ibid.* XXXVII, p. 55, l.4 (text).

78. *Ibid.* pp. 81-82, ll.17-18 (text).
79. Sircar, D.C., *SGAMI*, p. 213, fn. 3.
80. Dasgupta K.K., *op.cit.*, p. 13, fn. 3.
81. *IA* VI, p. 52, ll.20-21 (text).
82. Sircar, D.C., *SGAMI*, p. 108.
83. *EI* XXIII, p. 110, l.36 (text).
84. *Ibid.* p. 110, l.32 (text).
85. *Ibid.* p.109, l.14 (text).
86. *Ibid.* l.21 (text).
87. *Ibid.* p. 109, l.19 (text) for Kulāñca; *Ibid*, p. 110, l.30 (text) for Mitila-*pāṭaka*, *Ibid*, p. 110, l.29 (text) for Dardurikā.
88. Sircar, D.C., *SGAMI*, pp. 297-298.
89. *KS.*, p. 155, l.38 (text).
90. *KS.*, pp. 164-166.
91. *EI* XXIII, p. 109, l.15; p. 110, l.26 (text).
92. *Ibid.* p. 110, l.27 (text).
93. *Ibid.* p. 109, l.24 (text).
94. *Ibid.* p. 110, ll.28 and 34 (text).
95. *Ibid.* XXXIII, p. 218, l.13 (text).
96. Sircar, D.C., *SGAMI*, pp. 121-125 and 129.
97. *EI* XXIII, p. 113, ll.17-18 (text).
98. *Ibid.* XXXIV, p. 84, l.33, verse 35 (text).
99. *EI* XVIII, p. 323, l.12 (text).
100. *IHQ* VIII, p. 312, l.14 (text).
101. *EI* XII, p. 203, ll.32-33 (text).
102. *Ibid.* IX, p. 36, ll.48-49 (text).
103. Sircar, D.C., *SGAMI*, p. 211, p. 297 fn. 4.
104. *EI* XXXII, p. 53, ll.29-30 (text).
105. Sircar, D.C., *SGAMI*, pp. 128-129.
106. *EI* VII, p. 40, ll.50-51 (text).
107. *IA* XII, p. 251, ll.46-47 (text).
108. Altekar, A.S., *RAT*, pp. 77, 112.
109. *EI* V, p. 196, l.53 (text).
110. Altekar, A.S., *RAT*, p. 116.
111. *JBBRAS*, *N.S.* X, p. 28, l.58 (text).
112. *EI* XXI, p. 264, ll.40-41 (text).
113. *Ibid.* p. 265, l.70 (text).

114. The lines that describe the poet's lineage are: Śrīkarmārakulāḥvayadvija varagrāmastu (grāmāttu) Tarkārito niṣkramya kramanirmalassamabhavatta.... (*Ibid. p. 265,* 11.69-71). L.N. Rao translates these lines thus "a family immigrated from Tarkāri, the village of the excellent twice-born karmāra community, and became pure in successive generations." But the term *Śrīkarmārakula*, refers to a family of blacksmiths, who could obviously not be Brāhmaṇas. So an alternative translation of these lines could be that he belonged to a family of blacksmiths, who lived in Tarkāri, the best of the villages settled by Brāhmaṇas. If Madhusūdana belonged to this *Karmārakula,* he could not have been a Brāhmaṇa.

115. There is some controversy as regards the overlord of Candrāditya. Sankalia prefers to identify him with a Karka or Kakka of the Rāṣṭrakūṭa family of Central India. He feels, that to identify Kakka of this record of c. 788 A.D. with Kakka of the Antroli-Chharoli Plates of c. 757 A.D. (*IA* XXXI, p. 334), would be to give him too long a period of rule. But D.C. Sircar believes that Karka of Central India, was the father of Rāṣṭrakūṭa Prabala of the Pathari Inscription of c. 861 A.D. (*EI* IX, p. 248 ff). He finds it doubtful that Karka could have ruled at a date three quarters of a century earlier than the date of his son's record. Besides, kings with long reign periods are known, e.g. Dharmapāla c. 770-815 A.D., Candella Dhaṅga c. 954-1002 A.D. and Paramāra Bhoja, c. 1000-1055 A.D. Hence a span of thirty-one years between the Antroli-Chharoli Plates and the Hilol Plates is not too much. Moreover Candrāditya's overlord Kakka having semi-independent titles *Mahāsāmantādhipati Paramarājādhirāja Parameśvara*, is no other than Kakka II of the Gujarat branch, as he probably assumed semi-independence after the death of Dantidurga. On the other hand, there is no evidence to show that Karka of Central India was an imperial or semi-independent ruler. Hence D.C. Sircar correctly identifies Kakka of the Hilol Plates with either Kakka II of the Antroli-Chharoli Plates, or

with a descendant of the latter. This identification seems more probable than that of Sankalia.

116. *EI* XXXIV p. 219.
117. *Ibid.* p. 217, 1.4 (text).
118. *Ibid.* XXVI, p. 253, 11.31-32 (text).
119. Sircar, D.C., *SGAMI,* p. 256.
120. *IA* XII, p. 160, 11.44-45 (text); *JASB, NS,* VIII, p. 297, 1.35 (text).
121. *EI* XXV, p. 170, 1.27 (text).
122. *IA* XVII, p. 121, 11.35-36 (text).
123. *EI* XXXVII, p. 36, 1.6 (text).
124. Sircar, D.C., *SGAMI,* p. 37, fn. 7.
125. *IA* VI, p. 193, 11.6-7 (text).
126. Sircar, D.C., *SGAMI,* pp. 111-112.
127. *EI* XXIX, p. 89, 11.34-35 (text).
128. Sircar, D.C., *SGAMI*, p. 174.
129. *EI* XXXVI, p. 312, 11.36-37 (text).
130. Sircar, D.C., *SGAMI,* p. 174.
131. *IHQ* XXI, p. 220, 1.35 (text).
132. *JBORS* II, p. 407, 11.14-15 (text).
133. *Ibid.* p. 403, 11.26-27 (text).
134. *EI* XXXVIII, p. 131, 11.18 and 20 (text).
135. *Ibid.* XXXIV, pp. 102-103, 11.19-20 (text).
136. Sircar, D.C., *SGAMI,* p. 175.
137. *EI* XXXIV, p. 100, 11.27-28 (text).
138. *Ibid.* p. 99, 11.23-24 (text).
139. *EI* XXV, p. 163, 1.16 (text).
140. *JBORS* VI, p. 484, 11.12-13 (text).
141. Sircar, D.C., *SGAMI,* p. 62.
142. *JBORS* XX, p. 152, 1.29 (text).
143. *Ibid.* II, p. 174, 11.12-13 (text).
144. *EI* XVIII, p. 300.
145. *Ibid.* XII, p. 327, 11.25-26 (text).
146. *Ibid.* XXXVII, pp. 261-262, 11.22-23 (text); *OHRJ* XI, p. 158, 11 23-24 (text).
147. IHQ X, p. 477,- 11.20-21 (text).
148. *Ibid.* IX, p. 764, 1.20 (text).
149. *EI* XXV, p. 160, 11.20-21 (text)

150. *Ibid.* XIX, p. 44, 11.14-16 (text).
151. *Ibid.* XVIII, p. 288.
152. Ray, H.C., *DHNI,* I, p. 429 fn. 1.
153. *EI* XVIII, p. 297, 11.19-20 (text).
154. *Ibid.* p. 299, 11.23-25 (text).
155. *Ibid.* XXIV, p. 19, 1.14 (text).
156. *Ibid.* XXVIII, p. 263, 1.40 (text).
157. Ray, H.C., *DHNI* I, p. 397, fn. 1-2.
158. *EI* XI, p. 94, 11.12-13 (text), *IO* IV, p. 96, 11.12-13 (text).
159. As regards the place of emigration of the donee it has been read in *EI* XI, p. 94, as *Rādhāphaṁvallikandara-vinirgatāya*. But Ajay Mitra Shastri in an article entitled "Notes on the Kaüvatal and Vakratentalī charters" in *Studies in Indian Epigraphy*, Vol. III, differs from this. According to him what has been read as *phaṁ* is in reality, *yāṁ*, and the expression in question should therefore be read as *Rādhāyāṁ Vallikandara-vinirgatāya.* It would follow from this, that the donee came from a village known as Vallikandara in Rāḍha.
160. *IHQ* XX, p. 242, 1.20 (text); *IO* IV, p. 102, 1.20 (text).
161. *DHNI* I, p. 399, fn. 2.
162. *EI* XI, p. 198.
163. *Ibid.* p. 101.
164. *Ibid.* III, p. 342, 11.17-18 (text).
165. Sircar, D.C., *SGAMI*, p. 308.
166. Dey, N.L., *Geographical Dictionary of Ancient and Mediaeval India,* p. 144.
167. *EI* III, p. 342, 11.11-12 (text); *IO* IV, pp. 106-107, 11.11-12 (text).
168. *Ibid.* 1.13, *Ibid.* p. 107, 1.13 (text).
169. *Ibid.* 1.15; *Ibid.* 1.15 (text).
170. *EI* VIII, p. 141, 11.16-17 (text); *IO* IV, p. 120, 11.16-17 (text).
171. *Ibid.* XXII, p. 137, 11.11-12 (text); *IO* IV, p. 213, 11.11-12 (text).
172. *Ibid.* III, p. 348, 1.11 (text); *IO* IV, p. 140, 1.11 (text).
173. Sircar, D.C., *SGAMI,* pp. 168, 261, 270, 335.
174. *IHQ* XX, pp. 247-248, 11.11-12 and 14 (text); *IO* IV,

p. 153, 11.11-12 and 14 (text).

175. *JBORS* II, p. 54, 1.1 (text); IO IV, p. 220, 1.25 (text).
176. EI III, p. 353, 11.32-33 (text); *IO* IV, p. 179, 11.32-33 (text).
177. *JASB, N.S.*I., p. 18, 11.34-35 (text) and p. 21, 11.38-39 (text); *IO* IV, p. 192, 11.34-35 (text) and p. 198, 11.38-39 (text).
178. *EI* III, p. 357, 11.38-39 (text); *IO* IV, p. 208, 11.38-39 (text).
179. *Ibid.* IV, p. 258, 1.15 (text); *IO* IV, p. 239, 1.15 (text).
180. *DHNI* I, p. 407, fn. 6.
181. *JAHRS* III, p. 40, 1.18 (text).
182. *Ibid.* II, p. 150, 1.21 (text).
183. *EI* XXVI, p. 79, 11.28-29 (text).
184. *Ibid.* XXVII, p. 30, 1.28 (text).
185. *OHRJ* XV, p. 120, 1.30 (text).
186. *EI* XXXVIII, p. 65, 11.14-15 (text).
187. Sircar, D.C., *SGAMI*, pp. 106, 111.
188. *OHRJ* XII, p. 7, 11.14-15 (text).
189. *EI* XXXV, p. 135, 1.23 (text).
190. *KS*, p. 137, 1.41 (text).
191. *Ibid* p. 131f.
192. *IA* XVI, p. 203, 1.9 (text).
193. *EI* XXXIII, p. 218, 11.13-14 (text).
194. *JASB* XVII, p. 249, 1.22 (text).
195. *Ibid.* XXVII, p. 323, 1.23 (text).
196. *EI* XXXVIII, p. 131, 11.18 and 20 (text).
197. *EI* XXIX, p. 193, 11.20-21 (text); *OHRJ* I, p. 212, 11.20-21 (text).
198. *JBORS* VI, p. 271, 11.26-27 (text).
199. *IHQ* X, p. 477, 11.20-21 (text).
200. *OHRJ* XI, p. 195, 11.17-18 (text); *IO* IV, pp. 125-126, 11.17-18 (text).
201. *EI* XXIII, p. 77, 1.17 (text).
202. *Ibid.* XXII, p. 156, 1.27 (text).
203. *Ibid.* I, p. 178, 11.40-41 (text).
204. *Ibid.* XXIII, p. 109, 11.17, 18, 25 (text).
205. *IA* VI, p. 54, 11.2-3 (text).

206. Sharma, B.N., *SCHNI*, p. 16.
207. *IA* XLI, p. 202, 11.17-18 (text).
208. *EI* XXXVII, p. 39, 1.11 (text).
209. *OHRJ* XIII, p. 2, 1.12 (text).
210. *EI* VI, p. 139, 1.32 (text).
211. *JBORS*, IV, p. 171, 11.18-19 (text).
212. *EI* XXXVIII, p. 127, 1.23 (text).
213. *Ibid*. XI, p. 100, 1.26 (text).
214. *OHRJ* IV, p. 75, 11.17-18 (text).
215. *EI* XII, p. 324, 1.20 (text).
216. *Ibid*. XXV, p. 156, 1.19 (text).
217. *JASB, N.S*.I., p. 13, 11.12-13 (text); *IO* IV, p. 113, 11.12-13 (text).
218. *EI* XXXVIII, p. 189, 11.24-25 (text); *IO* IV, p. 161, 11.24-25 (text).
219. *JASB, N.S*.I., p. 14, 11.9-10 (text); *IO* IV, p. 168, 11.9-10 (text).
220. *EI* XI, p. 100, 1.26 (text); *IO* IV, p. 186, 11.15-16 (text).
221. *JBRS* LI, p. 57, 11.7-8 (text).
222. *EI* XXIX, p. 169, 11.31-32 (text).
223. *Ibid*. XII, p. 158, 11.18-19 (text).
224. *JBORS*, II, p. 410, 1.15 (text).
225. *Ibid*. p. 415, 1.23 (text).
226. *EI* XXXVIII, p. 131, 1.20 (text).
227. *Ibid*. XXXIV, p. 95, 1.18 (text).
228. *Ibid*. XXVIII, p. 282, 11.18-19 (text).
229. *EI* XIII, p. 290, 11.2-4 (text).
230. *Ibid*. XV, p. 298, 1.39 (text).
231. *Ibid*. XXIX, p. 56, 1.39 (text).
232. *Ibid*. p. 57, 1.49 (text).
233. *Ibid*. II, p. 309, 1.38 (text).
234. *Ibid*. XXXVII, p. 254, 1.60 (text).
235. *Ibid*. XXXVIII, p. 157, 11.97-98 (text).
236. *Ibid*. XXV, p. 61, 11.61-62, 64 (text).
237. *Ibid*. XXIX, p. 12, 1.42 (text).
238. Krishnamachariar, M., *HCSL*, pp. 147-148.
239. *Harṣacarita* (ed.), Kane (1965), I, p. 8, 11.12-17.
240. Agrawal, V.S., *Harṣacarita, EK Sanskrikita Adhyayana*, p. 18.

241. *Mahāvīracarita*, (ed.), Todar Mall, (1928), I, p. 2, 11.5-6.
242. *Mālatī-Mādhava*, (ed.), M.R. Telang and W.S. Paniskar (1905), p. 7, 11.1-2.
243. cf. p. 11 (1905).
244. *RT* IV, verse 144.
245. *Ibid.* verse 497.
246. Krishnamachariar, M., *op. cit.*, p. 734.
247. *Bālarāmāyaṇa*, i. 13, p. 9.1 as quoted by Sten Konow in Rājaśekhara's *Karpūramañjarī*, p. 180.
248. Konow, S., and Lanman, C.R., *Rājaśekhara's Karpūra-mañjarī*, pp. 180-181.
249. Mirashi, V.V., *Bhavabhūti, His Date, Life and Works*, p. 379.
250. *Karpūramañjarī*, (ed.), S. Konow and C.R. Lanman, (1963), i. 5.
251. Konow, S. and Lanman, C.R., *op. cit.*, pp. 181-182.
252. Krishnamachariar, M., *op. cit.*, p. 163.
253. *Ibid.* p. 741.
254. *IC*, I, pp. 703-704.
255. Dasgupta, S.N. and De, S.K., *HSL* I, pp. 350-351.
256. *RT* VII, verses 935-937.
257. *Alberuni's India*, (ed.), Sachau, (1964), Vol. I, Chap. I, p. 22.
258. *Ibid.* Vol. II, chap. LXXVI, p. 178.
259. *Ibid.* Vol. I, chap. XIII, pp. 135-136.
260. *Ibid.* chap. XLV, p. 391.
261. Stein, M.A., *Kalhaṇa's Rājataraṅgiṇī*, Vol.II, pp.359-360.
262. *Daśakumāracarita*, (ed.), Kale, (1966), II, 24-28.
263. *Ibid.* IV, 125.
264. *Ibid.* V, 143.
265. *Ibid.* VI, 149.
266. Sircar, D.C., *SGAMI*, p. 246.
267. *Ocean of Stories*, (ed.), Penzer, (1968), Vol. I, chap. III, IB, pp. 21-24.
268. *Ibid.* Vol. VI, chap. LXXIII, 163 E, p. 102.
269. *Ibid.* Vol. IV, chap. LIII, 70, p. 173.
270. *Ibid.*, 69, p. 173.
271. *Ibid.* Vol. II, chap. XXV, 29 C, p. 196.
272. *Ibid.* Vol. VIII, chap. C I IV, p. 2.

Chapter II

# Causes of Migration

It has been stated in the previous chapter that Brāhmaṇas in considerable numbers were on the move throughout the period c. 475-1030 A.D. It is remarkable, however, that the contemporary inscriptions are silent as regards the factors which prompted these migrations.

The only positive cause for migration can be found in the tradition preserved in the *Kulajis* and *Kulapañjikās*, of the Rāḍhīya and Vārendra Brāhmaṇas of Bengal. The story, contained in the *Kulaji* texts, maintains, that there was a king Ādiśūra of Bengal, who requested the king of Kanauj or Kolāñca, to send him five learned Brāhmaṇas, who knew the *Vedas* and Vedic sacrifices. The reason was the dearth of such Brāhmaṇas in Bengal. When the king of Kanauj refused, Ādiśūra sent against him seven hundred Brāhmaṇas of Bengal, seated on bulls, as he knew that his adversary would not take up arms against Brāhmaṇas riding on bulls. As expected, the king desisted from war and sent the five Brāhmaṇas as requested by Ādiśūra. In Bengal, these five Brāhmaṇas performed a sacrifice and then returned to Kanauj. But at home, their relatives treated them as degraded Brāhmaṇas, as they had made a journey to Bengal, and asked them to perform penances. At this, they with their wives and servants returned to Bengal, where the king granted them five villages to live in. The Rāḍhīya and Vārendra Brāhmaṇas of Bengal are described as the descendants of these five Brāhmaṇas. The seven hundred Brāhmaṇas who had gone to fight for Ādiśūra came to be known as Saptaśati.

While some modern scholars accept the story, others refuse to believe in its authenticity. N. Vasu,[2] the champion of the *Kulaji* texts, suggests, that Ādiśūra was not the name of any particular individual. The authors of the *Kulajis*, bestowed this name as an honour on those Hindu kings, who at different times, before the advent of the Muslims, devoted themselves to the improvement of Hindu society. It was for one of these kings, that five Brāhmaṇas came to perform a sacrifice. N. Vasu gives two sets of dates for the coming of the Brāhmaṇas. While the Rāḍhīya *Kulaji* texts date the advent of the Brāhmaṇas in *Śaka* 668/c. 746 A.D. both Vācaspatimiśra and the Vārendra *Kulapañjis* ascribe this event to *Śaka* 654/c. 732 A.D. These Brāhmaṇas—Kṣitīśa, Medhātithi Vītarāga, Sudhānidhi and Saubhari—belonged to five different *gotras* and became the forefathers of the Rāḍhīya and Vārendra Brāhmaṇas. The king who enlisted their services was the first Ādiśūra. On the basis of the *Rāḍhīya Kulamañjarī*, N. Vasu places him in *Śaka* 654/c. 732 A.D. He was probably the earliest among the Śūra rulers, to become the master of Pañca Gauḍa. N. Vasu also accepts the view given in the Kāyastha *Kulaji* texts of Uttara Rāḍha, identifying Ādiśūra with Bhoja of Kānyakubja, who by winning back and safeguarding his ancestral dominions, came to be known as Ādivarāha. At the same time, he makes Mādhava, father of Ādiśūra, a contemporary of Yaśovarman, and says, that it was under the influence of the latter, that Mādhava among others, was encouraged to spread the Vedic religion in the Gauḍa-*maṇḍala*.

N. Vasu's account has been challenged by a number of scholars. The identification of Ādiśūra with the Gurjara-Pratihāra ruler Bhoja, cannot be justified, as Bhoja ascended the throne in the second quarter of the ninth century and Ādiśūra according to N. Vasu, lived in the eighth. On the other hand, the date of Ādiśūra, *Śaka* 654/c. 732 A.D., makes him a contemporary of Yaśovarman of Kanauj, whose reign may be placed between c. 700 and 740 A.D.[3] N. Vasu holds, that Ādiśūra was so called, because he established his authority over Pañca Gauḍa. But R.D. Banerji[4] points out, that it is difficult to accept this as a historical fact. During the time of

Yaśovarman, no ruler of Bengal had acquired control over Kanauj, which comprised one of the five countries within Pañca Gauḍa. Hence the identity of Ādiśūra, on the basis of the views of N. Vasu, remains rather uncertain.

R. Chanda,[5] does not doubt the existence of Ādiśūra, although he suggests a different date for him. He quotes the legends prevalent among the Vārendras, which make Vallālasena, a descendant of Ādiśūra on his mother's side. He believes in the most popular view regarding the identity of Ādiśūra. Writing in 1910, he gives the date of Ādiśūra, eight hundred and fifty years before 1910, in c. 1060 A.D. He places Ādiśūra, thirty-four or thirty-five generations before the time when he was writing, and ascribing twenty-five years to each generation, calculates, that Ādiśūra lived in the second and third quarters of the eleventh century. This according to him, is in keeping with the view, that the encestors of Vallālasena may have come to Bengal with the Karṇāṭa prince Vikramāditya Cāḷukya, during his expedition against Bengal and Assam, sometime before c. 1068 A.D. Moreover, there is reference to Raṇaśūra of Dakṣiṇa Rāḍha in the Tirumalai Rock Inscription, dated c. 1024 A.D. of Rājendra Coḷa. R. Chanda suggests, that Ādiśūra could well have been a son or a grandson of Raṇaśūra.

R. Chanda, however, doubts the historicity of the story, that Ādiśūra had the five Brāhmaṇas brought from Kanauj. The Bhubaneśvara *praśasti* of Bhaṭṭa Bhavadeva, gives a detailed account of the latter's ancestry. He belonged to the Sāvarṇa *gotra* and his forefathers lived in Siddhala in Rāḍha. R. Chanda places the first mentioned member of Bhavadeva's family, in the last quarter of the tenth century A.D. He had received Hastinībhiṭṭa village, probably from Mahīpāla I of the Pāla dynasty. According to R. Chanda, Vācaspati the composer of the *praśasti*, describes the Brāhmaṇas of the Sāvarṇa *gotra* living in Siddhala in such a way, that they seem to have been living there since time immemorial. He feels, that had the story of these Brāhmaṇas being descendants of the five Brāhmaṇas brought by Ādiśūra, been current at the time of the composition of the *praśasti*, Vācaspati would have definitely mentioned it, as one of them must have been an ancestor of

Bhavadeva. The fact that Vācaspati does not do so, fails to provide, in his view, a historical basis for the story of Ādiśūra and the five Brāhmaṇas.

P. Niyogi is one of the scholars, who do not accept the account of the *Kulapañjikās*, regarding Ādiśūra. She, however, does not give any evidence to substantiate her views, but merely states that the historical value of the *Kulapañjikās* has not been proved.[6] Like P. Niyogi, B.N. Sharma too, gives the bare outline of the Ādiśūra story, and only mentions, that it is difficult to say, how far this tradition is correct.[7]

But D.C. Sircar[8] explains in detail why the Ādiśūra legend is totally unreliable. The different genealogies of Ādiśūra, the variety in the sacrifices for the performance of which, the Brāhmaṇas were brought by the king, the different capitals attributed to him, and the date of the coming of the five Brāhmaṇas, ranging from *Śaka* 654 to *Śaka* 999, have been pointed out by him. Moreover he says, that the reference to the *Śaka* era in the stories of Ādiśūra, shows that they were fabricated after the *Śaka* era became popular in Bengal, about the twelfth century A.D., long after Ādiśūra is supposed to have flourished, either in the eighth or in the eleventh century.

D.C. Sircar also gives some additional evidence which goes against both N. Vasu's and R. Chanda's identification of Ādiśūra. According to him, a Śūra royal family in ancient Bengal is known. But no genuine ruler named Ādiśūra is found in the Bengal sources. The only Ādiśūra known to the history of East India is a petty chief who is mentioned by Vācaspatimiśra of Mithilā in his *Nyāyakaṇikā*, in the passage: *nija-bhuja-vīryam-āsthāya-śūrān-Ādiśūra-jayati*. Vācaspatimiśra composed his *Nyāyasūci* in *V.S.* 898/c. 841 A.D. Hence Ādiśūra his contemporary, must have flourished in the middle of the ninth century. D.C. Sircar holds, that he was a petty chief of North Bihar, who may have been a vassal of the Pālas of Bengal and Bihar. Legends may have grown around his name for his activities in connection with the settling in his dominions, of certain Brāhmaṇa families coming from Kolāñca.

At the same time, D.C. Sircar refuses to accept the tradition, that the Brāhmaṇas who came from Kānyakubja or

Kolāñca to Bengal, at the invitation of Ādiśūra, in *Śaka* 654/c. 732 A.D., were the ancestors of the *Kulīna* Brāhmaṇas of Bengal. On the other hand, he points out, that the institution of Kūlinism may have been partially borrowed by Bengal from Mithilā. The Maithila Brahmanical *mūlagrāma* is the place where the family originally lived. One of its *gāṁis* Gaṅgaulī, is according to him, the same as the Bengali Brahmanical *Kulīna* cognomen Gāṅgaulī or Gaṅg-opādhyāya. Brāhmaṇas from the village Gaṅgaulī, probably migrated to Bengal, and keeping their *gāṁi* and adding to it the title of *upādhyāya*, came to be called Gaṅgopādhyāya. Hence D.C. Sircar believes, that it was not the Brāhmaṇas who came from Kānyakubja to Bengal, but those who came from Mithilā, who may have brought the institution of Kulinism, with themselves to Bengal. He also adds, that this shows, that the social division of high class Bengal Brāhmaṇas into Rāḍhīya and Vārendra, and the attempt to locate the Rāḍhīya and Vārendra *gāṁis* respectively in Rāḍha and Vārendra, are unsound.

As regards the origin of the *gāṁi*, while the Rāḍhīya *Kulajis* attribute its introduction to Kṣitiśūra, grandson of Ādiśūra, the Vārendra *Kulajis* make Vallālasena responsible for it.[9] According to R.C. Majumdar,[10] it was well known in the twelfth and thirteenth centuries in Bengal. But as D.C. Sircar points out, the word *Bṛhac-Caṭṭa*, occurs in the Faridpur Copper-plate of the sixth century A.D.[11] D.C. Sircar agrees with Pargiter, that *Caṭṭa* is apparently the same as the modern Caṭṭopādhyāya, a cognomen of the *Kulīna* Brāhmaṇas of Bengal. He also cites the Russellkonda Plates of Neṭṭabhañja, in which a Brāhmaṇa of Bengal, is found to have borne the name Vandya Devabhadra.[12] He feels, that it is possible, that the word Vandya may have had some connection with the growth of the cognomen Vandy-opādhyāya among the Rāḍhīya Brāhmaṇas of the *Kulīna* class. On the basis of all this evidence, the *Kulaji* tradition making Kṣitiśūra or Vallālasena the founders of the *gāṁi* system, can hardly be regarded as plausible.

Like D.C. Sircar, R.C. Majumdar too, does not accept the Ādiśūra legend as historic and authentic. He points out, that sometimes Ādiśūra is said to be the ruler of Bengal and Orissa, while other authorities add Aṅga, Kaliṅga, Karṇāṭa, Kerala, Kāmarūpa, Saurāṣṭra, Magadha, Mālava and Gurjara to his dominions. His capital is located by some scholars in Gauḍa, and by others in Vikramapura. The texts are not unanimous about whether the Brāhmaṇas were brought from Kāśī or from Kānyakubja. The coming of the Brāhmaṇas too, has been variously dated in *Śaka* 654, 675, 804, 854, 864, 914, 954, 999.[13] R.C. Majumdar also enumerates the different sacrificial ceremonies for which the Brāhmaṇas were invited, as mentioned in the various *Kulaji* texts—the *Cāndrāyaṇa-vrata, Agnihotrīya-yajña, Putreṣṭi-yajña* and *Vājapeya* sacrifices. He gives three sets of names for the five Brāhmaṇas. Vācaspati and the compilers of the Rāḍhīya *Kulajis*, name them as Bhaṭṭa Nārāyaṇa, Dakṣa, Chhāndaḍa, Harṣa, and Vedagarbha. The Vārendra texts enumerate them to be Nārāyaṇa, Suṣeṇa, Dharādhara, Gautama and Parāśara. On the other hand, according to Eḍumiśra, Harimiśra, Devīvara and other well-known *Kulācāryas*, the Brāhmaṇas were Kṣitīśa, Vītarāga, Sudhānidhi, Tithimedha or Medhātithi and Saubhari.[14]

R.C. Majumdar at the same time, gives some fresh evidence[15] to disprove the idea inherent in the *Kulajis*, that there were no learned Brāhmaṇas in Bengal before the eleventh century when Ādiśūra is supposed to have been living. The accounts of the two great Brāhmaṇa families mentioned in the Bādāl Pillar Inscription and the Bhubaneśvara *praśasti* of Bhaṭṭa Bhavadeva, prove the existence of learned Brāhmaṇas in Bengal in the eighth, ninth and tenth centuries A.D. If, however, Ādiśūra was living in the eighth century which is the earliest date ascribed to him, it is surprising, that the two Brāhmaṇa families make no mention to an ancestor, who must have been one of the five brought to Bengal by Ādiśūra from Kanauj.

As far as the institution of Kulinism is concerned, R.C. Majumdar points out, that there is no corroborative epigraphic evidence for attributing its beginning to Kṣitiśūra and Vallālasena in the Rāḍhīya and Vārendra *Kulapañjikās*. If the rank of a *Kulīna* was bestowed on the basis of personal merit, as it was supposed to have been done, he finds it strange, that eminent Brāhmaṇas like Kedāramiśra, Bhavadeva, Aniruddha Bhaṭṭa who was Vallālasena's own *guru* and Halāyudha were not given this honour, and the only persons who received it, were those who were unknown outside the *Kulaji* texts.[16]

Inscriptions show the existence of a considerable number of Brāhmaṇas in Bengal, before the eighth century A.D. As early as the time of Kumāragupta I, the Dhanaidaha Copper Plate, dated c. 433 A.D., refers to the grant of a *kulyavāpa* of land to Varāhasvāmin, a Sāmavedin Brāhmaṇa of North Bengal (*EI* XVII, p. 345 f). The Kalaikuri grant, dated *GE* 120/c. 440 A.D. acquaints us with grant of land to three Brāhmaṇa students of the Vājasaneya school, possibly in the Rajshahi district (B.C. Sen, *Some Historical Aspects of the Inscriptions of Bengal*, p. xii). The donee Bhaṭṭa Brahmavīrasvāmin in the Mallia Plate of the sixth century A.D., was a *Sāmavedin* Brāhmaṇa of the *Chhāndogya Śākhā*, (*EI* XVIII, 60 f), and he was given a village in the Murshidabad district. None of these as well as other Brāhmaṇa donees mentioned in inscriptions in between the fifth and sixth centuries, are known to have migrated to Bengal. Moreover, inscriptions of the Pāla period tell us that Brāhmaṇas migrated to Bengal from Lāṭa, Madhyadeśa, Kolāñca, Ṭakāri, Muktāvastu and other places. When seen in this light, the story of the *Kulajis*, that the descendants of the five Brāhmaṇas brought to Bengal, multiplied to millions, while those who were already living there and who later migrated from other places, practically vanished without leaving any trace, seems to be rather absurd. And this, according to R.C. Majumdar, is the most potent argument against the *Kulaji* story.[17]

A point to be noted is, that in the *Kulaji* texts, Kolāñca and Kānyakubja are both regarded as identical. This, however, cannot be accepted, as they are definitely two different place-names. The equivalents for Kānyakubja are counted by R.S. Tripathi. These are, Kanyakubja, Mahodaya or Mahodayā, Gādhipura or Gādhinagara, Kuśasthala, Kuśika and Kusumpura or as Hsūan Tsang calls it Keu-su-mo-pu-lo.[18] But nowhere is

Kolāñca mentioned as an equivalent for Kānyakubja.

The mutually contradictory versions of the Ādiśūra story, the lack of epigraphic evidence to corroborate it, the possibly earlier origin of the *gāṁi* system, and the importation of Kulinism, probably from Mithilā, all point to the unreliable nature of the *Kulaji* tradition. As regards the existence and identity of Ādiśūra, although only one Ādiśūra who is mentioned by D.C. Sircar, is known from history, yet the fact that a king of this name may have lived at some other time, can not be totally denied. He may or may not have been a member of the Śūra family ruling in West Bengal in the eleventh century. It is the legends that have grown around him, that are rather absurd. As R.C. Majumdar[19] observes, a consideration of all available facts lead to the conclusion, that the story owes its origin to an attempt in the fifteenth and sixteenth centuries, to trace the beginnings of the social divisions which existed at that time, to the early period to which the Hindus naturally looked back as their golden age. The considerable time that elapsed between the proposed date of Ādiśūra, and the beginning of the legends that became attached to his name, impel us to disbelieve the authenticity of the story. According to R.C. Majumdar, the Bengalis of the fifteenth and sixteenth centuries, depended for the reconstruction of social history, partly on family stories, partly on current traditions and largely on a vivid imagination. This in his view, explains the genesis of the varying accounts of the *Kulajis*. The story of Ādiśūra therefore, is a concocted tale with few elements of truth in it, and the idea that it postulates, of migration of Brāhmaṇas to Bengal, at an invitation from the king, cannot be accepted.

Some scholars believe, though this is not supported by the inscriptions and texts of the period under study, that Brāhmaṇas were invited to come and settle in the court of a king or feudal chief. P. Niyogi explains, that Brāhmaṇas of Bengal, had gradually built up a solid reputation, which sometimes spread beyond the borders of Bengal.[20] The obvious implication is, that they were invited by rulers of other regions to come to their kingdoms. It may be pointed out here, that there are instances of invitations extended to renowned sages and priests by kings in ancient times. The *Rāmāyaṇa*[21] tells us about Ṛṣyaśṛṅga, whom Daśaratha invited to perform the *aśvamedha* sacrifice, whereby he could be blessed with sons. In later years, there is evidence of a learned Brāhmaṇa named Hiraṇyadāma, being invited from India, by Jayavarman II of Kambuja, to perform some *Tāntrik* rites.[22] However, no such instance is noticeable in the period between c. 475-1030 A.D. The king's desire to increase his religious merit, and that of his parents, is stated in the majority of charters, as the purpose of a grant. In some cases, the performance of the five great sacrifices, is clearly mentioned as the reason for which a Brāhmaṇa receives the donation. Yet nowhere has anything been specifically stated either about a Brāhmaṇa or a *purohita* being requested to come from elsewhere and perform a great sacrifice, or about a Brāhmaṇa renowned for his scholarship, being invited to grace the court of a king.

It may be argued, that there may have been an invitation in the case of the collective land grants, e.g. the Navalakhi Plates of Śīlāditya I of *GS* 286/c. 545-546 (?), 605-606 A.D. By this charter, Śīlāditya I benefited forty-four migrant Brāhmaṇas, probably in the Baroda region. At the time when Śīlāditya I was ruling, the Maitrakas were gradually consolidating their power. As a result, the grant of one village to so many migrant Brāhmaṇas may have been prompted by a desire to colonize new areas. Introducing Brāhmaṇas there, may have been the first step in this direction. By the Bonda Plates of Mahāśiva Tīvara, of the latter half of the sixth and early half of the seventh century, and the Gaonri Plates of Paramāra Vākpati II of *V.S.* 1038/c. 981 A.D., villages were collectively given to twenty-five or twenty-six Brāhmaṇas at a time. Among the donees, some had emigrated from other regions. But in all probability, these migrations had taken place some time before the date of the grant, and the Brāhmaṇas were already living somewhere in the vicinity of the donated villages. Thinking it expedient for some reason or the other, the kings later granted to them villages, perhaps requesting them to settle there. The location of the donated lands in these cases, points to political, rather than any other motive, as being responsible for such invitations. Mahāśiva Tīvara granted the two localities of Bondaka and Avaḍika. He is known to have founded a principality in South Kośala, comprising the Raipur-Bilaspur-Sambalpur regions of Madhya Pradesh. The two localities where the Brāhmaṇas were settled, lay within this region, in the Raigarh district of Madhya Pradesh. This, and the fact, that the grant was made in the fifth regnal year of Tīvara, shortly after his accession, show that the purpose behind the settlement of twenty-five Brāhmaṇas,was the protection and consolidation of a newly acquired territory, as the Brāhmaṇas could be utilized to exert moral pressure on the people and ensure their loyalty to the king. In the same way, Vākpati II settled twenty-six Brāhmaṇas in the Hūṇa-*maṇḍala*, identified with the northern part of the Malwa plateau. Probably Hūṇa-*maṇḍala* formed the boundary of his kingdom, and he felt that it would be easier to defend it, if he settled a large number of Brāhmaṇas there.[23] The social position of the Brāhmaṇas, could guarantee their safety from the attacks of neighbouring kings, and their presence in the border regions, would to a certain extent, safeguard the frontiers of the kingdom. Hence in such cases, where Brāhmaṇas were asked to settle in newly acquired territories, or on border lands, it was more an exploitation of their socio-religious status for diplomatic purposes on the part of the king, rather than regard for their learning or spiritual piety that prompted such invitations. Anyway, the invitation, if there was any, was made after the Brāhmaṇas had already migrated. Definitely, the migration did not take place as a result of the invitation. So some other factors must have been responsible for the movement of Brāhmaṇas throughout the period.

A number of inscriptions refer to emigrations from Bengal. It is to be noted, that most of these occurred during the years which marked the growing weakness and instability of the Pāla empire. Keeping this in mind, it would not perhaps be wrong to suggest, that the political condition of the Pāla kingdom, may have had something to do with the abandonment of their homes, by Brāhmaṇas who moved to settle elsewhere.

The rule of the successors of Devapāla, who died in c.850 A.D. was marked by a gradual process of decline and disintegration, which reduced the Pālas to the position of an insignificant political power in Northern India towards the close of the ninth century. Devapāla was succeeded by his son Śūrapāla. D.C. Sircar on the basis of the Mirzapur Inscription, ascribes to him a reign period from c.850-858 A.D. He might have been ousted by Vigrahapāla I (c. 858-860 A.D.), son of Devapāla's cousin Jayapāla.[24] Moreover, the fact, that a record of Rāṣṭrakūṭa Amoghavarṣa I of c. 866 A.D., refers to the kingdoms of Anga, Vaṅga and Magadha, instead of to Bengal as a whole, also supports the theory of internal disruptions. Neither Vigrahapāla I, nor his son and successor Nārāyaṇapāla I c.860-917 A.D. (according to D.C. Sircar's calculation), had any military victory to his credit. On the other hand, the Rāṣṭrakūṭas made occasional military raids into the Pāla kingdom and Mihira Bhoja, the Gurjara-Pratihāra monarch too, carried out a successful expedition against them. It is also possible, that the Pālas had to face a formidable confederacy, probably organised by Bhoja, consisting of Guṇāmbhodhideva, the Kalacuri king of Gorakhpur, Kalacuri Kokalla I of Ḍāhala, and Guhilot Guhila II.[25] Mahendrapāla I, son of Bhoja followed in his father's footsteps and annexed Magadha and even northern Bengal from the Pālas, as proved by his inscriptions found in the Patna and Gaya districts of South Bihar, and at Paharpur in the Rajshahi district of North Bengal. The Pālas, however, regained their hold over Magadha and North Bengal, before the death of Nārāyaṇapāla I. Yet in the time of his successors, Rājyapāla, c. 908-940 A.D., Gopāla II, c. 940-960 A.D. and Vigrahapāla II, c. 960-988 A.D., (according to R.C. Majumdar), the strength of the Pālas was again seriously threatened. The two principalities of Assam and Orissa, which had once been subjugated by Devapāla, and the imperial ambitions of the Kalacuri kings, Yuvarāja c. 915-945 A.D., and Lakṣmaṇarāja II, c. 945-970 A.D., and of the Candellas Yaśovarman. c. 925-954 A.D., and Dhaṅga, c. 954-1002 A.D., all combined to further weaken the Pāla kingdom. As in the time of Nārāyaṇapāla I, again in the middle of the tenth century, North Bengal was lost to the Pālas. A Kamboja chief, probably taking advantage of their weakened condition, set up an independent principality, ultimately comprising western and northern Bengal. East and South Bengal also broke away from the Pālas, and were ruled by the Candras. Pāla, rule in the last decade of the tenth century, was confined only to Aṅga and Magadha. The Pāla fortunes revived temporarily during the time of Mahīpāla I (c. 988-1038 A.D.), who won back northern and eastern Bengal, and some other parts of his ancestral dominions. Yet he too had to face the invasion of Rājendra Coḷa, in the course of the latter's northern expedition, which lasted from c. 1021 to 1023 A.D., and that of Kalacuri Gāṅgeyadeva. During the reign of Nayapāla, c. 1038-1055 A.D., son and successor of Mahīpāla I, Gāṅgeyadeva's son Karṇa, continued his attacks on the Pāla territories. Meanwhile, the Somavaṁśis of Orissa invaded Bengal in the middle of the eleventh century, and eastern Bengal again passed out of Pāla hands. So by this time the Pāla monarch was almost a phantom. While he had lost his hold over eastern, western and southern Bengal, in Magadha too his power was reduced to a mere shadow.

This political instability of the Pāla empire must have been responsible to some extent, for compelling emigration from Bengal, A natural desire for security and a more settled life, might have prompted several Brāhmaṇa families to leave the disturbed region. Quite a number of them moved towards Orissa. Kuladevapālabhaṭṭa of the Jurerpur Plates of Devānanda and Govindaśarman of the Plates of Devendravarman III of the *Gaṅga* year 308/c. 804-806 A.D. left their homes in Rāḍha. Others like Bhaṭṭa Brahmadhara, the donee of the Baripada Plates of Devānandadeva, Padmākara of the Dasapalla grant of Raṇabhañja, Paṇḍita Varada who was the beneficiary of the Aidā Plates of the same ruler, Bhaṭṭaputra Naraka of the Talcher Plates of Vinītatuṅga II and Bhaṭṭa Devaśarman, of the second set of Talcher Plates of Gayāḍatuṅga and the Kāladeśī Devu, known from the Kalibhanā Plates of the thirty-fourth year of Mahābhavagupta I, had all been living in various settlements in Varendrī and Puṇḍravardhana in North Bengal. Three Brāhmaṇas Ādityabhaṭṭa, Yajñubhaṭṭa and Khaṇḍidevabhaṭṭa, described as *Vaṅgajebhya*, and *Vandya* Devabhadra, the writer of the Russellkonda Plates of Neṭṭabhañja, were also residents of Bengal. All these Brāhmaṇas migrated to Orissa where under the Bhañjas, Tuṅgas, Somavaṁśis, Nandas and Eastern Gaṅgas, they received grants or found employment. They were settled in villages, in the Baud and Dasapalla regions, in Pallahara, Dakṣiṇa Kośala, Airāvaṭṭa-*maṇḍala* and in the Ganjam district. The kingdom of the Rāṣṭrakūṭas attracted Keśava Dīkṣita of the Sāngli Plates of Govinda IV and Gadādhara of the Kolagallu Inscription, who like most of the emigrants, came from North Bengal. Four Brāhmaṇas, Ugranandī, Duvanandī, Thiranandī and Bhaganandī, also from Varendrī, went further to the south, to the Kanara district of Karnataka, where they were bestowed with villages by the kulikas Vipracandra and Vīra Pracaṇḍadeva.

These perhaps, are only some, besides the many others, whose names have not been recorded, and who left the Pāla kingdom during the troubled period that followed the death of Devapāla. It is remarkable, that most of the Brāhmaṇas had been original inhabitants of North Bengal. This region, except on two occasions, once towards the close of the ninth century, when it was annexed by Gurjara-Pratihāra Mahendrapāla,[26] and again in the middle of the tenth century, when a Kamboja chief set up an independent principality, ultimately including western and northern Bengal,[27] had remained under Pāla control. It may be suggested, that the disturbances in other parts of Bengal, were serious enough to threaten even those living under Pāla protection in North Bengal, so that a fair number of them preferred to leave their original homes within the Pāla territory and moved to new areas.

Other parts of Northern India too, fell a prey to rival imperial aspirations of powerful kings, as well as to internal dissensions and weaknesses. This fact can help to explain migration from such disturbed areas, which can be traced back to the seventh century.

At the beginning of the eighth century, the Parlakimedi Plates issued in the *Gaṅga* year 204/c. 700 A.D. by the Eastern Gaṅga king Anantavarman, refer to a Brāhmaṇa Viṣṇusomācārya, an emigrant from a village in Kāmarūpa, to the Ganjam district. The history of Kāmarūpa after the death of Bhāskaravarman, in the middle of the seventh century, is rather uncertain. The dynasty of Śālastambha which immediately succeeded Bhāskaravarman, has left behind neither literary nor epigraphic records. It is from references to them in the inscriptions of the later kings of Assam that something is known about them[28] From this it seems, that Kāmarūpa may have been in a state of political confusion, in the days following the death of Bhāskaravarman, and before the family of Prālambha gained control. The migration of Viṣṇusomācārya may have occurred during the period.

The Mahua Inscription of Vatsarāja, of the eighth century, is an eulogy composed by Bhaṭṭa Iśāna. Either he or his father had come from Kānyakubja to Mahua in Madhya Pradesh. It was from about the latter half of the eighth century, that Kanauj began to attract the attention of the contending imperial powers, the Pālas, the Gurjara-Pratihāras and the Rāṣṭrakūṭas. Dharmapāla, c.770-815 A.D., and Gurjara-Pratihāra Vatsarāja (not the Vatsarāja of the Mahua Inscription) both intending to acquire control over Kanauj, came into conflict in the Gaṅgā-Yamunā Doab. However, Rāṣṭrakūṭa Dhruva intervened and defeated first Vatsarāja and then Dharmapāla.[29] It is possible, that it was during this disturbed time, when the Doab region was threatened by all three powers that the Brāhmaṇa Iśāna or his father emigrated from Kanauj, and went to live in modern Madhya Pradesh under Vatsarāja, who was an independent or semi-independent king, ruling over Avanti.

The quarrels of ruling families, and their efforts to increase their sphere of influence at the expense of their neighbours, might have been responsible for driving away a Brāhmaṇa from the far south of Mysore to Maharashtra. The Deoli Plates of Rāṣṭrakūṭa Kṛṣṇa III of *Śaka* 862/c. 940 A.D., refer to a grant of land made in the vicinity of Nagpur to a Brāhmaṇa

Rishiyappaya, who had probably emigrated from the south. Although Kṛṣṇa III ascended the throne at the end of c. 939 A.D., he had been responsible for the administration of the Rāṣṭrakūṭa kingdom, during the brief reign of his father Amoghavarṣa III. It was during his father's life-time, that Kṛṣṇa sent a successful invasion into Gaṅgavāḍi, against its king Rājamalla, with the intention of deposing him and placing on the throne Rājamalla's younger brother Būtuga, who was married to Kṛṣṇa's sister.[30] It may be, that Rishiyappaya had been living in Gaṅgavāḍi, i.e. in Karnataka, at the time of this Rāṣṭrakūṭa expedition. The uncertain political situation in Gaṅgavāḍi resulting in the deposition of one brother and the accession of another to the throne, as well as the Rāṣṭrakūṭa invasion, may have forced him to realize the possible danger to Gaṅgavāḍi in the future, not only from the Rāṣṭrakūṭas, but other southern powers as well. Moreover, Kṛṣṇa III's expedition against Parāntaka Cola after his accession, aimed at the reinstating of Vikramāditya III-Kṛṣṇa's Bāṇa ally-on the throne, might have added a further incentive. Hence the Brāhmaṇa left his home and migrated to the kingdom of the Rāṣṭrakūṭas, who at that time ruled over a considerably large area, and were undoubtedly the most powerful force in the Deccan and perhaps more capable of providing greater security and stability. It may be mentioned here, that two emigrations from Gaṅgavāḍi to Orissa, recorded in the Juraḍa grant of Neṭṭabhañja and the Phulsara Copper Plate of Kīrttirājadeva, may also have been caused by the political situation discussed above.

If the strength of the Rāṣṭrakūṭas had brought Brāhmaṇas to their kingdom, their weakness in the years following the death of Kṛṣṇa III in c. 967 A.D., possibly resulted in the emigration of Brāhmaṇas from their territories. Kṛṣṇa III had been succeeded by his brother Khoṭṭiga. During the reign of the latter, Paramāra Sīyaka, eager to avenge his earlier defeat at the hands of Kṛṣṇa III, attacked the Rāṣṭrakūṭa dominions in c. 972 A.D., defeated the Rāṣṭrakūṭas and plundered their capital.[31] The Rāṣṭrakūṭa empire did not long survive this misfortune and soon completely collapsed. It is likely that this decline in the fortunes of the Rāṣṭrakūṭas, led to the migration of the two Brāhmaṇas, one from Nāndipura in Lāṭadeśa, i.e. Nandod near Broach, and the other from Kheṭaka or Kaira, mentioned in the Gaonri Plates of Paramāra Vākpati II of *V.S.* 1039/c. 981 A.D. The successful expedition of Sīyaka, whose family was slowly consolidating itself and rising to power at this time, must have provided an incentive to the Brāhmaṇas to migrate to the Paramāra kingdom, then under Sīyaka's son, Vākpati II.

Internal dissensions within a kingdom also caused the flight of Brāhmaṇas. Perhaps this explains why the Brāhmaṇa Vacchala emigrated from his home in Mānyakheṭa or Malkhed and went to Ujjayinī, as stated in the Depalpur grant of Paramāra Bhoja of *V.S.* 1079/c. 1022 A.D. Mānyakheṭa at this time was under Jayasiṁha II Cāḷukya of Kalyāṇī. The references in an inscription to a revolt by his generals and vassals, and to a plot to murder the king, point to internal troubles within Jayasiṁha's kingdom. Moreover, sometime before c. 1019 A.D., he had to face the combined force of three powerful kings, Kalacuri Gāṅgeyadeva, Paramāra Bhoja and Rājendra Coḷa, who formed a confederacy and made simultaneous attacks on the Deccan. Jayasiṁha could ultimately repulse them by c. 1024 A.D. But before that he had been defeated by Rājendra Coḷa, and Paramāra Bhoja had annexed one of his possessions viz. northern Konkan to his territories.[32] It is understandable that in this disturbed state of affairs, anyone would feel insecure. So the Brāhmaṇa Vacchala decided to emigrate. He could have migrated to the kingdom of the Coḷas. Instead he went to Ujjain. Rājarāja Coḷa, father of Rājendra, earlier during the reign of Jayasiṁha's uncle Satyāśraya, had invaded the kingdom of the latter, killed Brāhmaṇas and forcibly married off Brāhmaṇa girls to men of other castes.[33] These events perhaps prevented Vacchala from moving to the Coḷa kingdom. On the other hand, Ujjain under Bhojadeva, was an ancient religious centre. Moreover, Bhoja was a powerful king and a patron of Brāhmaṇas. At the same time it was easier to go to Ujjain from Malkhed, than to the Jabalpur area where Gāṅgeyadeva was ruling. To reach Jabalpur, Vacchala would have had to pass through Paramāra territory. So he left his home in the Deccan and travelled north to Ujjain, urged by a desire for greater security.

Just as aggressive imperialism forced Brāhmaṇas to migrate northwards to North Maharashtra and Madhya Pradesh, in the same way, they were compelled to leave North India and come to the west. The Prince of Wales Museum Plates of Govindarāja, issued in *Śaka* 732/c. 810 A.D., refer to a Brāhmaṇa Bhobika who had migrated from the Gauḍa country to Baroda. More than a century later, a *Pañca-Gauḍīya-mahāpariṣad* of Samyāna or Thane is mentioned in a grant of Rāṣṭrakūṭa Indra III in *Śaka* 848/c. 926-927 A.D. Gauḍa in those days comprised a geographical region covering a large section of Northern India and the Brāhmaṇas of the two charters mentioned above, may have migrated from anywhere within its limits. Kanauj which symbolized supreme power in Northern India, had become the bone of contention between the Pālas, Gurjara-Pratihāras and Rāṣṭrakūṭas. Earlier, Rāṣṭrakūṭa Dhruva had led an expedition into Northern India. His example was followed by his son Govinda III in the last decade of the eighth century. He marched into Northern India via Bhopal and Jhansi in Madhya Pradesh and defeated Gurjara-Pratihāra Nāgabhaṭa II. At the same time Dharmapāla of Bengal and Cakrāyudha the puppet ruler on the throne of Kanauj both offered him submission. Probably by c. 800 A.D., the northern expedition was over and Govinda III returned to his own kingdom. His grandson Kṛṣṇa II, c. 878-914 A.D., following in his grandfather's footsteps, led a campaign against Gurjara-Pratihāra Bhoja. Although the latter gained some initial success, he was finally defeated by Kṛṣṇa II at Ujjain and lost Malwa to the Rāṣṭrakūṭas. In the next reign Indra III who came to the throne in c. 914 A.D., soon after his accession, declared war against Gurjara-Pratihāra Mahīpāla, also known as Vināyakapāla II, sometime between c. 915 and 918 A.D. Taking the Bhopal-Jhansi-Kalpi route, he crossed the Yamunā marched upon Kanauj, and captured it, while Mahīpāla fled for his life, and Indra III returned home.[34]

So time and time again, the Rāṣṭrakūṭas penetrated into Northern India and after upsetting the balance of power, although temporarily, returned victorious to the Deccan. At the same time, in North India, the Pālas and Gurjara-Pratihāras were struggling among themselves for political supremacy. It is possible, that in such a situation, Bhobika and the members of the *Pañca-Gauḍīa-mahāpariṣad*, thought it safer to emigrate from North India. They went in one case, to the Baroda region of Gujarat, held by the viceregal Rāṣṭrakūṭa family, and in the other to Thane under the imperial Rāṣṭrakūṭas themselves. Moreover the Rāṣṭrakūṭas proved themselves to be the better, even in their encounters with their southern neighbours. Govinda III in the early years of the ninth century, achieved success against Vijayāditya II of Veṅgī and also defeated the combined Pallava, Pāṇḍya, Kerala and Gaṅga forces before c. 802 A.D. Kṛṣṇa II in spite of an initial setback, ultimately won a decisive victory over Cāḷukya Vijayāditya III and Bhīma of Veṅgī. All these factors might have helped the Brāhmaṇas to make their decision and their choice of settlement fell obviously on the Rāṣṭrakūṭa dominions.

The Madhyadeśa occurs frequently in the records of the period, as an area of emigration. Madhyadeśa and certain places situated in it, e.g. Madhura, Nidhati, Khaḍuvāpalī, Maṁjasthāna and others, which have as yet not been located or identified, are mentioned as places from which Brāhmaṇas moved to settle elsewhere. It is interesting to note, that records which refer to emigrations from Madhyadeśa, a region comprising the upper and middle Gangetic basin and the Yamunā-Chambal catchment area, belong to the years between the second quarter of the tenth and the first half of the eleventh. A study of the political condition of Madhyadeśa during this period, can help us to ascribe possible causes for emigration from this region.

In the second quarter of the tenth century, the Gurjara-Pratihāras of Kanauj had become weaker, and the process of disintegration of their empire had begun. Taking advantage of this, Candella Yaśovarman, c. 925-954 A.D., who was a vassal and contemporary of Gurjara-Pratihāra Devapāla c. 948-949 A.D., tried to enhance his power at the expense of his overlord. He conquered Kālañjara which is situated in the Banda district of U.P. and had been in the possession of the imperial Pratihāras. He followed this up, by pushing the northern frontiers of his kingdom to the banks of the Yamunā.[35] Dhaṅga who succeeded Yaśovarman in c. 954 A.D. and ruled till c. 1002 A.D., is known to have held Gwalior within his dominions. He, however, soon came into conflict with the Kachchhapaghāta Vajradāman. The latter sometime before c. 977 A.D., invaded Gwalior and forced Gurjara-Pratihāra Vijayapāla and Dhaṅga to surrender to him the fortress of Gwalior. The weakness of his Gurjara-Pratihāra overlord, encouraged Dhaṅga to rise against him. He invaded his master's dominions, defeated Vijayapāla and gained control over the eastern portion of his kingdom, to the north of the Yamunā. Benares also fell into his hands. Meanwhile further to the north, the Tomaras who like the Candellas had been feudatories of the imperial Pratihāras, at the beginning of the tenth century, carved out an independent principality around Delhi. But with the rise of the Cāhamānas of Śākambharī, the Tomaras soon came into conflict with them. As the Harṣa Stone Inscription of Cāhamāna Vigraharāja II, dated in *V.S.* 1030/c. 973 A.D. tells us, Čandana who lived in c. 900 A.D. and was the great-grandfather of Vigraharāja, killed in battle, the Tomara Rudrena. Hostilities did not cease with this. The Harṣa Inscription continues, that Cāhamāna Siṁharāja in c. 950 A.D., defeated Sālavana, another Tomara chief. Some other princes, feudatories of the Gurjara-Pratihāras, also suffered at the hands of Siṁharāja. Their overlord, one of the weak successors of Gurjara-Pratihāra Mahendrapāla II, had to come in person, to Siṁharāja, to secure the release of his vassals. This gives further proof of the growing importance of the Cāhamānas and the decline of the imperial Pratihāras. Meanwhile the Cāhamāna-Tomara struggle continued, till about the middle of the twelfth century, and Delhi passed into Cāhamāna hands.[36] So just as in the previous century, the Pālas, Gurjara-Pratihāras and Rāṣṭrakūṭas had been engaged in constant conflicts, to gain control over Kanauj, similarly in the tenth century, the Candellas, Cāhamānas and Tomaras were warring amongst themselves, for supremacy in the Madhyadeśa region.

With the opening of the eleventh century, Madhyadeśa witnessed the invasions of Sultan Mahmūd of Ghazni. Even earlier, in the last quarter of the tenth century, Sabuk-tigīn, father of Mahmūd, shortly after his accession in c. 976 A.D., had led expeditions against the Śāhis ruling over Afghanistan and the Punjab. According to Firishta, Śāhi Jayapāla organized a confederacy of Indian rulers against Sabuk-tigīn. The kings of Delhi, Ajmer, Kālañjara and other neighbouring countries, sent troops to help Jayapāla.[37] The three capital cities mentioned, were under the Tomaras, Cāhamānas and Candellas. But as there is no independent testimony to corroborate the statement of Firishta, it is not possible to say whether the Indian rulers had really combined against Sabuk-tigīn. However, the fact remains, that the Turko-Afghan invasions into India had already begun and Sabuk-tigīn before his death in c. 997 A.D., had annexed the territory between Lamghān and Peshawar.[38] From c. 1000 A.D. onwards, Mahmūd began a series of expeditions, and gradually penetrated into the heart of North India. Thāneśvara under the Tomaras in c. 1011 A.D., Baran, i.e. modern Bulandshahar in U.P., Mathurā, Kanauj, Munj, Asi or Asni near Fatehpur in U.P., Sharwa or Sirsawa near Saharanpur also in U.P., in c. 1018-1019 A.D., Gwalior under the Kachchhapaghātas in c. 1021 A.D., and Kālañjara under the Candellas, once in c. 1019 A.D. and again in c. 1022 A.D., all felt the strength of his arms.[39] So the entire Madhyadeśa region, for a period of ten or eleven years, was threatened by the recurring invasions of the Ghaznavid ruler.

Even during the expeditions of Mahmūd, except probably once, the rulers of North India, had not sunk their differences. The mutual rivalry of the Kachchhapaghātas, Candellas, Kalacuris and Paramāras went on Kachchhapaghāta Arjuna of Dubkund near Gwalior, killed the imperial Pratihāra Rājyapāla in c. 1019 A.D. Vidyādhara, grandson of Candella Dhaṅga, fought successfully against Paramāra Bhoja and also against Kalacuri Kokalla II of Ḍāhala, or the country around Jabalpur. Gāṅgeyadeva, son of Kokalla II conquered Benares and annexed it to his kingdom before c. 1034 A.D. Sometime after c. 1037 A.D., his son Karṇa took Allahabad from Gurjara-Pratihāra Yaśaḥpāla. At the same time, in the years following the period of disorder that resulted from the invasions of Sultan Mahmūd, a branch of the Rāṣṭrakūṭas established themselves in U.P. and came into conflict with Paramāra Bhoja, who was eager to extend his influence in that region.[40] So the struggle for supremacy in Northern India continued unabated, even in the first half of the eleventh century.

Evidently Madhyadeśa during the major part of the tenth and the first half of the eleventh century, was torn by rival ambitions of Indian rulers, and endangered by invasions from outside. It is not strange, that the political instability arising from these factors should have prompted a steady flow of emigration. Like the Brāhmaṇas from Bengal, the majority of those from Madhyadeśa, headed towards Orissa. Among these were Bhaṭṭa Bṛhaspati from Nidhati, known from the Dhenkanal grant of Kulastambha,[41] Bhaṭṭaputra Daṇḍapāṇi of the Keśari Plates, Ājapāla of the Dasapalla grant of the Śatrubhañja from Khaḍuvāvallī, Bhaṭṭaputra Dāmodara, the donee of the Baud grant of the twenty-sixth year of Raṇabhañja, from Khaḍuvāpalī in Madhyadeśa, and the Brāhmaṇa Devahara who was the beneficiary of an undated grant of Raṇabhañja. Others, like the Brāhmaṇa Bhaṭṭa who had lived in Madhura and who was given a village by Mahābhavogupta I's Mahākosala Historical Society's Plates, Tiku from Śāluvigrāma in Madhyadeśa, referred to in the Gaintala Plates of Mahābhavogupta I and Śaṅkhapāṇi, an inhabitant of Śrīvalla-grāma, also in Madhyadeśa, the donee of the Cuttack Plates of Mahāśivagupta I, came to the kingdom of the Somavaṁśis. In Orissa these Brāhmaṇas were granted lands and villages and began a new life in settlements in the Goilla-*viṣaya* of Dhenkanal, in the Khiñjali-*maṇḍala* in Khiching, in Mayūrbhañja and in Dakṣiṇa Kośala.

Two Brāhmaṇas, one from Ayaka and another from an unnamed village, which nevertheless lay within Madhyadeśa, migrated to the Malwa region, where they became co-donees with others, of the Gaonri Plates of Vākpati II. Some moved towards the Deccan. The Brāhmaṇa Navaśiva from Madhyadeśa, received a village within Paṅgarikā near Poona, by a grant of Sinda Ādityavarman. Daddapaiya, whose home like that of Navaśiva had been in Madhyadeśa, along with some other Brāhmaṇas was given the right to enjoy the revenues of villages in the Bassein region, by the Thana Plates of Śīlāhāra Mummuṇirāja. Mummuṇirāja also granted another village, probably lying in the Konkan to the Brāhmaṇa Devadhara Dīkṣita from Muṁjasthāna in Madhyadeśa. Mention may be made here of Dīrghācārya of the Balera Plates of Caulukya Mūlarāja. Emigrating from Kānyakubja, he went towards the kingdom of the Caulukyas of Aṇhilvāḍa and received a village in the modern Jadhpur state. Although he had come from Kanauj and not from Madhyadeśa, it would not be wrong to suggest, that he had been prompted to leave his ancestral home which lay in the same region by the very factors that had driven away other Brāhmaṇas from Madhyadeśa.

So Brāhmaṇas gradually began to move away from Madhyadeśa, travelling in some cases, over considerable distances, to reach areas of greater security. The fact that there is not a single instance of migration of Madhyadeśa during this period, lends added support to the possibility of emigration from that area, due to an extremely disturbed political situation.

Apart from the unidentified places in Madhyadeśa that have been mentioned above, one frequently comes across migrations from Śrāvasti, Ṭakāri, Kolāñca, and Hastigrāma, which in some cases are specifically mentioned as lying within Madhyadeśa. Although sometimes scholars tend to locate these places in Bengal and Assam, generally, they are supposed to lie in the area comprising the Set-Mahet region, on the border of the Gonda and Bahraich districts of U.P. It is rather difficult to ascribe any particular cause, to explain the migrations from this region. However, a possible suggestion may be made. In the latter part of the eighth century, a collateral branch of the Kalacuri family of Tripurī, was ruling on the banks of the Sarayū or modern Gogrā which flows by the Bahraich and Gonda districts.[42] They were probably feudatories of the Gurjara-Pratihāras, who in the time of Mahendrapāla I, are known from his Dighwa Dubauli Plates, to have been holding Śrāvasti-*viṣaya* in U.P.[43] Guṇāmbhodhideva, the fourth in this line, can be referred to in the last quarter of the ninth century. So he was a contemporary of Gurjara-Pratihāra Bhoja, c. 836-885 A.D., whom he perhaps helped in his campaign against the Pālas of Gauḍa.[44] It is possible that as a reward for his services, Guṇāmbhodhideva received some territory from Gurjara-Pratihāra Mihira Bhoja. Later members of this Kalacuri family are found ruling over the Gorakhpur district and extending their territories upto the river Gandaka. So it may be, that Mihira Bhoja handed over the Gorakhpur region to the Kalacuris, after putting an end to the Malayaketu dynasty there.[45] Set-Mahet lay close to Gorakhpur. So it is not unlikely that the Kalacuris extended their hold over that area as well, bringing Śrāvasti and the sites of Ṭakāri, Kalāñca and Hastigrāma which lay in its vicinity, within their control. Guṇāmbhodhideva was succeeded by Ullabha and Bhāmana. The latter as a vassal of the Pratihāras, fought against a king of Dhārā. Nothing is recorded of the five kings, who came after Bhāmana-Śaṁkaragaṇa II, Guṇasāgara II, Śivarāja II, Śaṁkaragaṇa III and Bhīma. On the basis of the Kahla Plates of Soḍhadeva, dated *V.S.* 1135/c. 1077 A.D., H.C. Ray concludes, that in about *V.S.* 1087/c. 1031 A.D., Bhīma was probably dethroned in favour of Vyāsa, a son of Guṇasāgara II. Soḍhadeva the donor of the Kahla Plates, was the son of Vyāsa.[46]

As Guṇāmbhodhideva has been placed in the last quarter of the ninth century, his two successors Ullabha and Bhāmana must have been ruling in the first half of the tenth century. The way in which the rule of Bhīma came to an end, suggests some kind of civil war.[47] Taking this factor into account and the uneventful reigns of the five ancestors of Bhīma, it would not be wrong to suggest that the Kalacuris ruling over the Gorakhpur and Set-Mahet areas in the tenth century and until the time of Ṣoḍhadeva, in the latter half of the eleventh century, were insignificant and torn by internal strife. It is remarkable, that the dates of the records that refer to emigration from the Set-Mahet area, all fall within this period. Already in the days of Hsuan Tsang, the ancient Śrāvasti region had been in a decadent state. It may be mentioned here, that prior to the tenth century, in only one charter, the Prince of Wales Museum Plates of Gurjara Dadda III of *K.S.* 427/c. 676-677 A.D., is a Brāhmaṇa donee found coming from Sāvathi or Śrāvasti. It is possible, that the disturbed condition of North India after the death of Harṣavardhana, and the decline of Śrāvasti into an insignificant town by the middle of the seventh century had prompted the Brāhmaṇa of the above charter to leave his home and go westward to the kingdom of the Gurjaras. Anyway, the condition of ancient centres like Śrāvasti, Ṭakāri, Kolāñca and Hastigrāma, the political ups and downs of the tenth and eleventh centuries and the fear of Muslim arms which at one time, came almost as far as Fyzabad and Benares were undoubtedly responsible for the steady flow of Brāhmaṇas from here to other parts of the country.

Like their couterparts in Bengal and the rest of Madhyadeśa, most Brāhmaṇas emigrating from Śrāvasti, Ṭakāri, Kolāñca and Hastigrāma made Orissa their destination. The Brāhmaṇa Vāvana who had originally lived in Kolāñca, became the donee of a Dhenkanal grant of Śulki Jayastambha.[48] The Bhauma-Kara queens Vakulamahādevī, Daṇḍimahādevī and Dharmamahādevī, gave villages to the Brāhmaṇas Mihadhīchāya of Śāvastha-*deśa*, Bhaṭṭa Mākyadeva of Ṭakāri and Padmanābha and Śrīdharabhaṭṭa of Kolāñca. Harivaṁśa from Hastigrāma and Bhaṭṭa Śubhadāma from Ṭakāri, figure as the donees of two grants from Baud, one of Kanakabhañja, and the other of the fifty-eighth year of Raṇabhañja Kanakabhañja. The beneficiaries of the Somavaṁśi records too—the Brāhmaṇas Śrī Kāko, Mahodadhi, Rāṇaka Rāchcho, Mahattama Sādhāraṇa and Bhaṭṭaputra Yaśakara—came from Śrāvasti, Ṭakāri and Hastigrāma.

Besides Orissa, Brāhmaṇas proceeded in other directions as well. Yaśodhara and Maṅamvanāyaka, whose ancestors had lived in Ṭakāri, migrated, the first to the Candella kingdom, as known from a grant of Dhaṅgadeva and the other to the territory of Yādava Bhillamarāja III, where he received along with others, a village in the Akola-*taluka* of Ahmadnagar. Like Maṅamvanāyaka, another Brāhmaṇa Mādhava Paṇḍita from Hastigrāma in Madhyadeśa, also came to Maharashtra, where he became the donee of the Thane Plates of Śīlāhāra Nāgārjuna. One Brāhmaṇa who had left Kolāñca went to the kingdom of the Paramāras, where he was later to share a village with others, as mentioned in the Gaonri Plates of Vākpati II. In the Bangaon grant of the time of Vigrahapāla III, the names of two other Brāhmaṇas are recorded, whose ancestors had migrated from Kolāñca to Tīrabhukti. Hence owing to the disturbed condition of the Set-Mahet area and its political instability, Brāhmaṇas were compelled throughout the tenth and even during the first half of the eleventh century, to abandon their homes, and they went both far and near to seek residence in safer places.

Migrations from the Gujarat region and some other parts of North India, can be ascribed to the invasion of India by the Arabs and by Sultan Mahmūd of Ghazni. The Arab inroads into Gujarat took place in the first half of the eighth century. The three Brāhmaṇas, Ādityabhaṭṭa, Māula and Govisara, who figure as the donees of the Ellora Plates of Dantidurga of *Śaka* 663/c. 741 A.D., were all emigrants from Navasārikā or Nausari Cāḷukya Avanijanāśraya Pulakeśirāja and Rāṣṭrakūṭa Dantidurga in c. 738 A.D., had been engaged in a fierce battle against the Arabs near Navasari,[49] and had succeeded in repulsing the Arab attack. However, the fear caused by the Arab invasion seems to have compelled the three Brāhmaṇas mentioned above, to leave the Navasari region and migrate to the principality of Dantidurga in Berar. A place within the territory of the Cāḷukyas of Gujarat, could in future be as vulnerable to Arab attacks, as Navasari had proved to be. Hence the Brāhmaṇas preferred to migrate to the Rāṣṭrakūṭa territory, which lay in the heart of the Deccan, and was thus less accessible to the Arabs.

Almost three centuries later, with the opening of the eleventh century, the invasion of Sultan Mahmūd, sent some

Brāhmaṇas moving from North India. According to the Betma grant, dated *V.S.* 1076/c. 1019 A.D., Paramāra Bhoja made a donation of a village in the Kaira district of Gujarat to a Brāhmaṇa coming from Sthānvīśvara. The sack of Thanesar occurred between c. 1011 and 1012 A.D. It was probably after the return of Mahmūd to Ghazni, that Paṇḍita Delha, left Thanesar and went to the kingdom of Bhojadeva. The latter had earlier sent an army to help Śāhi Ānandapāla against Mahmūd in c. 1008-1009 A.D., and was therefore more capable of providing a settled and secure life.

Literary texts give evidence of migration of Kashmir, during the period of Sultan Mahmūd's invasions. Alberuni in his work on India describes how the fear of Mahmūd drove Hindus to Kashmir, Benares and places which had not yet been conquered by him.

From all that has been stated above, it becomes clear, that political upheavals were responsible for quite a large number of migrations. B.N. Sharma,[50] explains that the migration of Brāhmaṇas to the Paramāra kingdom, was due to the great respect of the Paramāras for Brāhmaṇas. This is true to a certain extent. But as has been discussed, the donees of the Gaonri Plates of Paramāra Vākpati II and of the Depalpur and Betma Plates of Bhojadeva had left their original homes possibly due to political factors. The patronage of the Paramāras and other kings might have been an added attraction. But the prime factor behind the movement of so many Brāhmaṇas, was undoubtedly the most natural of human desires for security and safety.

If the political factor compelled Brāhmaṇas to move from their ancestral homes, in some cases the yearning for a better livelihood also prompted their movements. Incidentally it may be pointed out, that in early times, Brāhmaṇas are known to have migrated to south-east Asia. At the end of the fourth and beginning of the fifth century, a Brāhmaṇa named Kauṇḍinya from India, was elected as king by the people of Fu-nan or Cambodia.[51] The Chinese sources mention Brāhmaṇas frequenting the court of Panpan or Bandon. They had come from India, to profit by the munificence of the king who extended his patronage to them.[52] Brāhmaṇas such as these, were prompted by a spirit of adventure to seek their fortune in a distant land. Possibly the less adventurous amongst them travelled from one part of India only to another for better economic prospects.

From about the early years of the seventh century, to the beginning of the eighth, Brāhmaṇas are found emigrating from Ānarttapura or Ānandapura in Gujarat, and moving towards Valabhī. Five records of the Maitrakas bear witness to this fact. It is interesting, that all these migrations were confined within Gujarat itself. As Ānandapura and Valabhī are not situated at a great distance from one another, it is difficult to explain why these Brāhmaṇas left their homes in Ānandapura to go and live in Valabhī. But it is probable, that Ānandapura at this time had been over-populated with Brāhmaṇas of equal learning and calibre. Further Valabhī was growing in importance as the capital of the Maitrakas. Naturally it attracted migrants from outside, who came to Valabhī seeking a better livelihood and took up residence there. It was while they were living in Valabhī, that the Maitraka rulers endowed them with lands and villages in different parts of Surāṣṭra.

The Cambay Plates of Govinda IV, issued in *Śaka* 852/c. 930 A.D., record that a migrant Brāhmaṇa named Nāgamārya who was endowed with the village of Kevañja had originally been living in a holy place called Kāvikā. From there he came to Mānyakheṭa. It is possible that Nāgamārya was a priest, who seeking better prospects migrated to the Rāṣṭrakūṭa capital Mānyakheṭa, where he could get the post of royal *purohita*. While living at Mānyakheṭa, he with some others, performed for the king, sacrifices like *rājasūya, vājapeya* and *agniṣṭoma*, and the village of Kevañja was given to him, in the form of priestly fees for services rendered.

A Yādava charter issued from Devalili, gives the name of a Brāhmaṇa Sillaṇa who had lived in Oyarī-*grāma* in Madhyadeśa. He had come to the kingdom of Paramāra Vairisiṁha of Dhārā, in order to serve under him. Perhaps Sillaṇa too left Madhyadeśa, as during most of the period under survey, this had been a disturbed region. He went towards the Paramāra kingdom which was not very far from Madhyadeśa and there found employment as a *nāyaka* or military officer under Vairisiṁha.

Apart from the epigraphic evidence cited above, another record, the Silimpur Stone Inscription, also seems to allude to the possibility of Brāhmaṇas migrating for economic reasons. The inscription describes, how the ancestors of Prahāsa, originally living in Ṭakāri, within Śrāvasti, migrated to Bālagrāma in Varendrī. It is said that Bālagrāma was the home of many Brāhmaṇa families, all conceited, proud of their learning, lineage and practice of austerities, though none of them acquired individual fame. Some of the *paṇḍita* families who resided in the eastern part of the village, wanted to live apart. So they moved to a neighbouring place called Śīyamva. (ba). From this it becomes clear, that the Brāhmaṇas living in the village of Bālagrāma, did not get along well with one another. It is possible, that those who left the village, were really desirous of better fortune elsewhere, particularly where there might have been a lesser number of academic equals. Hence excessive concentration of Brāhmaṇas in a particular area, might have provided an added impetus to migration.

The same quest for a better livelihood, induced poets and authors like Bhāravi, Bāṇabhaṭṭa, Rājaśekhara and others to leave their homes and take up residence elsewhere.

The fact that they were all learned and came from scholarly families and that some among them moved from the court of one king to another to find a suitable habitat, points to another possibility. The main reason behind their wanderings, must have been the desire to prove their merit in a more congenial atmosphere.

Alberuni's *India* too bears witness to the fact, that Brāhmaṇas on the look-out for a better economic life, often left their homes. He makes detailed references to local festivals and miracles in Kashmir, the knowledge of which he had probably acquired from the *paṇḍitas* who had emigrated from Kashmir.

Stories and popular tales like the *Daśakumāracarita* of Daṇḍin and the *Kathāsaritasāgara* of Somadeva point to the migration of Brāhmaṇas. Although they contain an element of imagination and fantasy, they also reflect the tendency of Brāhmaṇas to move from their original homes for the sake of individual betterment.

Another possible cause of migration can be found in the *Bṛhannāradīya Purāṇa*, written in the ninth century and the *Subhāṣitaratnakoṣa* of Vidyākara of the latter half of the eleventh century, which refer to migrations due to royal oppressions as well as to famines. In these literary texts, however, migrations of Brāhmaṇas are not specifically stated. We are told merely, that people fly from a certain place, when the king is oppressive or when famines occur.[53] There is also reference to a *bhogapati*, whose oppressive measures led to migration.[54] The *Kathāsaritasāgara* too gives several instances of migrations due to famines. Five Brāhmaṇa cow-herds at the time of a famine left Kāśī and came to a word not far from Ujjain. A Brāhmaṇa named Govindasvāmin, living on the bank of the Yamunā had to leave during a famine, and went to Benares. It appears therefore that movement due to famines was not an uncommon occurrence.

Whereas literature and inscriptions provide ample evidence of emigrations from a major part of North India, there were some areas from which no emigrations, other than for religious causes are as yet known. Prominent among these are Sind, the North-West Frontier Provinces and Orissa.

As regards Sind and the Punjab, no instances of migration are available from the eighth to the middle of the eleventh century. Early in the eighth century, Sind was occupied by the Arabs. From that time onwards, it remained under Muslim control. In the ninth century, Multan and Manṣūrah were two of the chief Arab towns. Multan in which was situated the famous Sun-Temple, was a wealthy town. Al-Iṣṭakhrī, who visited India in the tenth century, testifies to the wealth of Multan. The temple stood between the bazar of the ivory-dealers and the shops of the copper-smiths. The eyes of the idol were made of precious gems, and the head was covered with a crown of gold. Manṣūrah too, according to Ibn Hauqal, was situated in a fertile and populous country. Mas-ūdī also points out that it was well cultivated and covered with trees and fields.[55] Moreover, commerce was in a flourishing condition. Caravans moving between Sind and Khurasan used to assemble at Multan. Chinese and Ceylonese products were brought to the sea-ports of Sind and were conveyed by way of Multan, to Turkestan and Khurasan. Meanwhile, the administration of the country was left largely in the hands of Hindu landlords. As regards religion, the Arab conquerors at a later period, wisely adopted a policy of toleration. Existing temples were allowed to stand and sometimes as at Bahamanābād, Brāhmaṇas were permitted to rebuild demolished temples. The iconoclastic outlook of the Arabs underwent such a change, that they did not hesitate to thrive on the income of idols.[56] All these factors taken together, can explain why Brāhmaṇas did not find it imperative to emigrate from Sind. Socially undisturbed and financially well-off due to their hold over the rich temples, the Brāhmaṇas must have considered themselves secure enough in a country that enjoyed a flourishing trade and was reasonably wealthy.

As in the case of Sind, so too in that of the North-West-Frontier Provinces of India, no instances of migration are available. (We exclude here the pilgrims from among migrants). This seems to be rather strange in view of the fact, that ever since the late tenth century, this region which was under the Śāhis, had fallen a prey to Muslim raids. However, some reasons may be suggested to explain this phenomenon. Had people tried to emigrate from there, they would have had to face several obstacles on the way. The states surrounding the Śāhi kingdom, were at this time, not very strong. The Tomaras of Delhi were rather weak. In the heart of Northern India, the Gurjara-Pratihāras, by the tenth century, had become a decadent power. Moreover, Northern India was torn by internal dissensions and rivalries between the ruling houses. Hence migrating Brāhmaṇas would have had to cross several politically disturbed areas, on their way to the comparatively safer regions of Orissa and the south.

Coming to Orissa, it seems to have been the only region, which attracted a large number of Brāhmaṇas, although no emigrations from it are known. Insularity as a trait of the Oriyās till at least the end of the mediaeval period, might have been a basic cause for this. It may also be suggested, that as Orissa had a number of ports, it was perhaps, an important trading centre. This brought wealth to the country, and consequently an increase of national income. This in its turn, might have eliminated the need for emigration of Brāhmaṇas from Orissa.

## References

1. Majumdar, R.C. (ed.) *HBI*, p. 625, Majumdar, R.C., *History of Ancient Bengal*, p. 471
2. Vasu, N., *Vaṅger Jātīya Itihāsa* pp. 92-112, as quoted by R.D. Bandyopadhyaya, *Vāṅglār-Itihāsa*, Vol. I, p. 211.
3. Majumdar, R.C., in *CA*, p. 131.
4. Bandyopadhyaya, R.D., *Vāṅglār-Itihāsa*, Vol. I, p. 210.
5. Chanda, R., *Gauḍa-Rāja-Mālā*, pp. 69-71.
6. Niyogi, P., *BSDSAB*. p. 24.
7. Sharma, B.N., *op. cit.*, p. 16.
8. Sircar, D.C. *SSAAMI*, pp. 12-30.
9. Majumdar, R.C., *HBI*, p. 629.
10. *Ibid.*, p. 580.
11. Sircar, D.C., *Select Inscriptions* I, p. 351, ll. 4-5 (text).
12. Sircar, D.C., *SSAAMI*, pp. 12 and 15-16.
13. Majumdar, R.C., *HB* I, p. 626.
14. Majumdar, R.C., *Bhārat-Koṣa* I, p. 256.
15. Majumdar, R.C., *HB* I, pp. 631-632.
16. *Ibid*, p. 632.
17. *Ibid.*
18. Tripathi, R.S., *History of Kanauj*, pp. 3-6.
19. Majumdar, R.C., *HB* I, p. 633.
20. Niyogi, p., *op. cit.*, p. 47.
21. *Rāmāyaṇa Bālakāṇḍa* p. 24 (ed.), S.S.K. Mudholkara, (1912).
22. Majumdar, R.C., *IK*, pp. 416-417.
23. Mazumdar, B.P., *JAS* X, 1968, p. 16.

24. *JBRS* LXI (1975), p. 131f. This copper plate grant was first noticed by V.N. Srivastava *Bulletin of Museums and Archaeology in U.P.*, (Lucknow, 1970, Nos. 5-6, pp. 67-70) and then by B.N. Mukherjee in the *Asiatic Society, Monthly Bulletin* (Calcutta, Vol. VI, No. 10, Nov. 1971. pp. 4-5).
25. Majumdar, R.C., *HB* I, pp. 128-129.
26. *Ibid.*, p. 129.
27. *Ibid.*, pp. 133-134.
28. Ray, H.C., *DHNI* I, p. 238.
29. Majumdar, R.C., *HB* I, p. 105.
30. Altekar, A.S., *IK*, p. 14.
31. *Ibid.*, p. 15.
32. Ganguly, D.C. *SE*, pp. 166-167.
33. *Ibid.*, p. 165.
34. Altekar, A.S., *IK*, pp. 6-8 and 11-13.
35. Ganguly, D.C., *IK* p. 83.
36. Ray, H.C., *DHNI* II, pp. 1064, 1146 and 1148.
37. Ganguly, D.C., *SE*, pp. 3-4.
38. *Ibid.*, p. 5.
39. Ganguly, D.C., *SE.*, pp. 10-18.
40. *Ibid.*, pp. 50, 57-62 and 66.
41. *JBORS* II, p. 400.
42. Ganguly, D.C., *IK.*, p. 92.
43. Ray, H.C., *op. cit.*, I, p. XXXVII.
44. *Ibid.*, II, p. 746.
45. Ganguly, D.C., *IK*, p. 92.
46. Ray, H.C., *op. cit.*, II, pp. 746-747.
47. Ganguly, D.C., *IK*, p. 94.
48. *JBORS* II, p. 405.
49. Altekar, A.S., *IK*, p. 2.
50. Sharma, B.N., *op. cit.*, p. 16.
51. Majumdar, R.C., *CA*, p. 643.
52. *Ibid.*, p. 649.
53. *Bṛhannāradīya*, pp. 35, 87.
54. *Subhāṣitaratnakoṣa*, verse 1175.
55. Ray, H.C.. *op. cit.*, I, pp. 16-18.
56. *Ibid.*, pp. 21-22.

## Chapter III

# Social Life and Status

Sufficient data are not available for drawing a comprehensive picture of the social life of the migrant Brāhmaṇas. It is not possible to find out the trials and tribulations of these people in their long treks. No one knows what relationship they had amongst themselves after they had settled in a particular area. Similarly no information regarding their food habits, amusements, dress and ornaments or the extent of their contact with the common people of the states to which they had migrated, is as yet available. Hence we have been compelled to study only a few aspects of the social life of the migrant Brāhmaṇas, like the characteristics of their original habitat, their gregarious instinct, their *gotras* and *pravaras*, academic achievements and the position of women. Some attempts have also been made to ascertain the profession of those alone who are mentioned in the relevant epigraphs. How other immigrants about whom we have no record fared in life is a matter of speculation.

**Habitat**

An idea can be formed about the social set-up of villages where the migrating Brāhmaṇas or their ancestors had originally lived. Terms like *bhaṭṭa-agrahāra* or *bhaṭṭa-grāma* indicate predominantly Brahmanical settlements. *Bhaṭṭa-grāmas* were undoubtedly the villages that had once been the homes of Brāhmaṇas. North Bengal had several such settlements. Mūthāutha-*bhaṭṭa-grāma* in Varendrī is known from the second set of Talcher Plates of Gayāḍatuṅga. Besides, unnamed localities in Varendrī referred to merely by the term *bhaṭṭa-grāma* are noticed in the grant of Kulika Vipracandra, and the Hindol Plates Kulika-Vīra Pracaṇḍadeva. South-West Bengal too, could boast of one such settlement. This was Telliṅgabhaṭṭagrāma in Rāḍha-maṇḍala where Paucuka, the donee of a grant of Raṇastambha had lived before coming to Orissa. Three other villages were *Bhaṭṭagrāma* Khaḍuvavāllī which lay in Madhyadeśa, *Bhaṭṭagrāma* Āllavida in Oḍra-*viṣaya* and Kaṇopā-*bhaṭṭagrāma* in Magadha, as known from a grant of Śatrubhañja, the Ādipur Plates of Narendrabhañja and the Gaonri Plates of Paramāra Vākpati II of *V.S.* 1038/c. 981 A.D. and *V.S.* 1043/c. 986 A.D. Sometimes, however, the charters name some *bhaṭṭa* villages that have not yet been identified, like *Kāvaḍa-bhaṭṭagrāma* of the first set of Gaonri Plates of Vākpati II, and Bhaṭaparoli of the Nibinnā grant of Mahāśivagupta, issued in his fifteenth regnal year.

In addition to these villages, which are specifically mentioned as being *bhaṭṭa-grāmas*, there were other settlements from which considerable number of migrations took place. In the sixth and seventh centuries of the Christian era, records discovered in Gujarat show that Ānarttapura or Ānandapura and Girinagara or Girnar, were regions largely populated by Brāhmaṇas. Several of them left their homes and became beneficiaries of the Maitraka, Gurjara and Cālukya rulers. In the later period we do not hear of any emigration of Brāhmaṇas from these places. But other names, Śrāvasti, Ṭakāri, Kolāñca, Hastipada, Hastigrāma in Magadha and Muktāvathi in Śrāvasti in North Bengal, make their appearance as localities inhabited for the greater part by Brāhmaṇas, many of whom had to leave their ancestral homes in these regions.

As was to be expected, having emigrated, the Brāhmaṇas preferred to settle in an area where the population consisted mostly of Brāhmaṇas. Throughout the seventh century, Brāhmaṇa migrants in Gujarat are found coming to Valabhī, as can be seen from the records of the Maitrakas. It is remarkable, that with a few exceptions, almost all the Brāhmaṇas from Ānandapura, at first took up residence in

Valabhī. The exceptions were Viṣṇumitra, of a grant of Dharasena II, issued in the year 270/c. 589-590 A.D., and Nārāyaṇa known from the plates of *Gupta saṁvat* 337/c. 656-657 A.D., issued by Kharagrāha II. They like Mātrakāla of the grant of Dhruvasena II of the *Gupta* year 312/c. 632 A.D., and Aditiśarman of a grant of Dharasena IV, migrated to Kheṭaka or Kaira which like Valabhī seems to have been a Brāhmaṇa stronghold. Later, all these Brāhmaṇas received lands in different parts of Gujarat. The Brāhmaṇas Agnisvāmin, Dattasvāmin and Saṅgaravi, donees of the two sets of Nogawa Plates of Dhruvasena II, having left their ancestral homes, were residing in Agastikāgrahāra and Ayānakāgrahāra, at the time when they received grants from the king. Another Brāhmaṇa Devasvāmin known from the Navasari Plates of Jayabhaṭa III of *K.S.* 456/c. 705-706 A.D., was living in the village of Śrāddhikāgrahāra before Jayabhaṭa III donated a village to him. Oḍra-*viṣaya* or coastal Orissa, seems to have contained within its limits, a number of such Brahmanical settlements. We hear of Sāvira-*bhaṭṭa-grāma* and Kuruva-*bhaṭṭa-grāmà* from the second set of Talcher Plates, and Asiatic Society's Plates of Gayāḍatuṅga, of Bhaṭṭa Tadalā in the Baud grant of Raṇabhañja, issued in his fifty-eighth year, and of *Bhaṭṭgrāma* Āllavida from a set of Ādipur Plates of Narendrabhañja, all situated in Oḍra-*viṣaya*. While residing in these villages, the Brāhmaṇas were granted lands in different parts of Orissa. The choice of villages like these, inhabited by Brāhmaṇas, may have been prompted by the feeling, that it might be easier to settle in a place where the majority of the people were those, with whom cultural, social and intellectual affinity was possible. It speaks much for the gregarious nature of the migrant Brāhmaṇas, that just as several of them coming from Ānandapura, preferred to live in Valabhī, most of the emigrants from Ṭakāri, Śrāvasti, Kolāñca, Hastipada, Hastigrāma and Muktāvathi, headed towards Orissa, and in some cases to Bengal, where other Brāhmaṇas had already made their homes.

But the final stage in the settlement of migrant Brāhmaṇas was reached when they became donees of the land grants of ruling kings. Although the term *bhaṭṭa* or *agrahāra*, as a prefix or suffix, is not found in connection with the donated villages in any of the records, sometimes the donated fields, or a village were bounded by plots belonging to other Brāhmaṇas. Some of the charters, like a Copper Plate of Dharasena I, the Lunsadi Plates of Śīlāditya II (Śīlāditya III?) of the *Gupta* year 350/c. 669-670 A.D. the two sets of Jesar Plates of Śīlāditya III, and the Gurjara grants, e.g. the Sankheda Plates of Dadda II, issued in *K.S.* 392/c. 642 A.D., and the Navasari Plates of Jayabhaṭa III of the *Kalacuri* year 456/c. 705-706 A.D., show that Brāhmaṇas were already living in the vicinity of the donated lands and villages. Hence in these cases, grants were being made to the immigrant donee Brāhmaṇas, in the regions where Brāhmaṇas were already settled.

The fact, that lands were not always granted in *bhaṭṭa-grāmas* may be due to the reason, that the choice of the locality of the donated plots lay with the king. Considerations of political expediency, and social and economic factors probably guided the rulers. The charters of the Pālas, Gopāla II, Mahīpāla I and Vigrahapāla III, show how several areas like Kuddalakhāta-*viṣaya*, Gokalikā-*maṇḍala* Phāṇitavīthī-*viṣaya* and Brāhmaṇī-*grāma*, all lying within Puṇḍravardhana-*bhukti*, were handed over to migrant Brāhmaṇa donees. Puṇḍravardhana-*bhukti* comprises North Bengal, where Brāhmaṇas had been living,, as is proved by a number of migrations from this region. Hence efforts were made to resettle the areas with immigrant Brāhmaṇas, by means of grant of lands.

But in Gujarat and Orissa, where considerable Brahmanical settlements gradually grew up, the case was not the same. Various settlements in Surāṣṭra including Kālāpaka, Kālāsamaka-*grāma*, Bahumūla-*grāma* in Vaṭapallikā-*sthalī*, Dhūṣā village, Desenaka-*grāma*, villages in Hastavaprāhāra, and several others, all of which lay within Surāṣṭra, gradually came to be peopled by Brāhmaṇas, as a result of grants made in this region by the Maitrakas. In the same way, the lands around Kheṭaka or Kaira were occupied by Brāhmaṇa donees who received grants from Dharasena II, Dhruvasena II and Dharasena IV.

Meanwhile, the contemporary dynasty of the Gurjaras under Dadda II, Jayabhaṭa III and Jayabhaṭa IV, helped to colonize the villages near Baroda and in the Broach region. In later years, the Rāṣṭrakūṭa feudatories made grants of lands in and around Baroda, while Caulukya Bhīmadeva I did the same in Cutch. So by and large, the whole of Gujarat, gradually came under Brahmanical influence.

Coming to Orissa, villages like Santīra-*grāma* and Komyosaṅga in Dakṣiṇa Tosala, Chhoḍātavutsā in Uregoḍḍā-*khaṇḍa* in Uttara Tosala, and Tarataloi or Taltalai, near Angul in the Cuttack district, were made subjects of grants by the Bhauma-Kara queens. The Goilla-*viṣaya* including within itself villages like Candrapura and Jhaḍabādā, lay in the former Dhenkanal state, where the Śulkis Jayastambha and Kulastambha bestowed lands on some Brāhmaṇas. The Tuṅgas ruling over the Yamagarta-*maṇḍala*, settled their donees in villages like Toro-*grāma* in the Veṇḍuṁga-*viṣaya* and Vāmāitāllo-*grāma* in Tuṁkerā-*viṣayà*. Under the Bhañjas, Brāhmaṇas received villages like Syallāmāyi in Urtti-*viṣaya*, Amvasari in Sivara-*khaṇḍa* both in the Mayurbhañja region, and others like Singharā, Vāllāśṛṅga in the Khātiā-*viṣaya*, and Jamarāpura and Sihipura in Vāhulāveṇḍaka, located in the Baud-Sonpur region. The Somavaṁśis Mahābhavagupta I, Mahāśivagupta I, Yayāti and Mahābhava-gupta II, held sway over a large part of Dakṣiṇa Kośala. They bestowed on their donees, villages like Jambūgrāma in Potā-*viṣaya*, Liñjira near Prithaurā-*bhukti*, Mārañja and Murā, situated in the Santovardā-*khaṇḍa*, Cāndagrāma in Marada-*viṣaya*, Gauḍasimiṇilligrāma in the Kośala-Sākhaṅgadyanhā-*viṣaya*, Loisarā in the Giḍāṇḍā-*maṇḍala* and many other villages, all lying within Dakṣiṇa Kośala. Thus throughout Orissa. Brahmanical settlements were gradually coming into existence. The fact that all the dynasties mentioned above, ruled either as contemporaries, or followed shortly one after the other, perhaps helped to maintain the continuous process of settling immigrant Brāhmaṇas.

A pertinent question arises, regarding the reason for so many Brāhmaṇas from outside being settled in and around

Surāṣṭra, Baroda, Kaira and Cutch and in Orissa. A positive answer cannot be given. But some assumptions may be made. The local Brāhmaṇas of these areas, perhaps constituted a strong element, which the rulers wanted to curb. This could be achieved by creating a section of people, who would be attached to their patrons, by donations of lands and villages, and who enjoying accompanying privileges, would develop into a fairly powerful group, independent of the local Brāhmaṇas. On the other hand, there may have been a real paucity of local Brāhmaṇas in these regions. Dr. J.G. de Casparis and Dr. Bivar were kind enough to suggest, that in the early phase of the period under review, Orissa had been a Buddhist stronghold. At the same time, there were tribal elements present in its society. As a result, the rulers were prompted by the necessity of Hinduising their principalities. By making landgrants, they encouraged Brāhmaṇas who had been driven away or who had voluntarily moved from various centres of Northern India, to settle in Orissa. Hence it was a two-way phenomenon, each supplying the need of the other. The Brāhmaṇas were looking for a more secure life, while the kings were eager to introduce Brāhmaṇas into their kingdom,. which would help to create a society in keeping with the accepted tradition. Consequently, the selection of sites for grants of land to immigrant Brāhmaṇas depended on the desire of the kings, to extend and strengthen Brahmanical influence in these areas and thereby to ensure their own hold over them. Whatever the reasons may have been, the fact remains, that immigrant Brāhmaṇas helped to build up Brahmanical settlements, wherein they could begin a new life.

**Gotras**

The records of the period make it possible to count a fair number of *gotras* among the migrant Brāhmaṇa population, as almost all of them mention the *gotras* of the donee Brāhmaṇas. The word *gotra*, which originally meant a herd of cattle, or a pen for cattle, gradually came to indicate a kin-unit with a common ancestor. In course of time, according to Brough, *gotra* denoted "an exogamous patrilineal sibship," whose members traced their descent back to a common ancestor.[1] The *Baudhāyana Śrauta Sūtra* (c. 6th century B.C.), describes that the descendants of the seven *ṛṣis*, Viśvāmitra, Jamadagni, Bharadvāja, Gautama, Atri, Vaśiṣṭha, Kaśyapa and of Agastya, constitute the original *gotras*. Puruṣottama, who flourished before the twelfth century A.D., states in his *Pravaramañjarī* that there were three *koṭis* of *gotras*. But Kane counted the number of *gotras* in this text, as only five thousand.[2]

The Brāhmaṇas faithfully recorded their *gotras* alongside their names. The importance of *gotra* was varied in character. A Brāhmaṇa who kept the sacrificial fire, had to know to which *gotra* he belonged.[3] Social life too laid stress on the importance of the *gotra*, inasmuch as customs differed on the basis of an individual's *gotra*, with regard to inheritance, *śrāddha* or funeral oblations and tonsure.[4] Moreover religious and legal texts forbade marriage within the same *gotra*.

Closely connected with the *gotra*, was the *pravara* of the migrant Brāhmaṇa. Literally meaning choice or invocation, the word *pravara* came to denote, one or more illustrious *ṛṣi* ancestors of a sacrificer, whose names had been used in early times, to invoke Agni to carry offerings to the gods.[5] According to Ghurye, *pravaras* in theory at least, since Baudhāyana's time, are those further ascendants of the sage, after whom a *gotra* is called, who are looked upon by the members of the *gotra* as its eponyms. Brough describes *pravaras* as a stereo-typed list of names of ancient *ṛṣis* or seers, believed to be the remote founders of the family. This list had to be regularly recited at specific points in the sacrificial ritual. As with *gotra*, so with *pravara* too, a man was to avoid marriage with a woman having the same *pravara* as himself. Brough further explains the significance of the *pravara* system. He points out, that in the course of linguistic development, the meaning of the word *gotra* gradually came to be applied to individual families as well as to the sub-divisions of family units. Hence, to preserve the exogamous nature of society, the *pravaras* which were classified according to the main exogamous *gotras*, were brought into use, as they clearly offered a precise method of determining a man's position in the exogamous structure. The *pravara* rule in marriage, came to be applied, as an "infallible test of the exogamous group to which a man belonged."[6] It further confirmed the prohibitions as to *gotra* in marriage, Ghurye, however, lays greater stress on the Śrauta ritual of group-based sacrificial rites, in connection with which, according to him, the use of *pravaras* was most required.[7]

Scholars hold divergent views, as regards the period of the origin and development of the system of *gotras* and *pravaras*. Brough traces the beginning of the *gotras* to the earliest stage of the formation of the *Ṛgveda*, and explains, that by the *Brāhmaṇa* period, the use of the word *gotra* in the sense of clan had become quite frequent.[8] As for the *pravaras*, he holds, that it was during the formative period of the *Yajurveda*, that the use of *pravaras* proper, i.e. names directly connected with the sacrificer's own clan, as distinct from the freer usage of the *Ṛgveda*, was gradually coming into use. However, the form in which the system is preserved in the *Brāhmaṇa* and *Sūtra* texts, developed over a period of years, by the time of the early *Brāhmaṇas*.[9] Kane agrees with Brough in this matter and takes back the conception underlying the idea of *gotra*, to the age of the *Ṛgveda*,[10] and holds that by the time of the *Brāhmaṇas* and ancient *Upaniṣadas*, the system of *gotras*, with several subsections was well established.[11] Despite the fact, that the word *pravara* is not found in the *Ṛgveda*, Kane mentions, that the word *ārsheya* occurs therein, and on this basis concludes, that the system of *pravara* goes back almost to the *Ṛgveda*.[12]

Ghurye, however, does not accept either of these views. According to him, the origin of the scheme of eight *gotras* or the unit source of all Brāhmaṇa families, was definitely post-Atharvavedic, and not Ṛgvedic, as Kane and Brough would have us believe.[13] The system developed fully not much before the eighth century B.C., and it is to this date, that he assigns the beginning of the *gotra* system. Coming to *pravara*, Ghurye thinks that its antecedents lay in ancient Ṛgvedic practice and gradually developed in the intervening period, between the *Brāhmaṇas* and the *Śrauta-Sūtras*. He believes, that the process of *pravara* systematization, must have begun after the *gotras* came to be considered as kin-units, named after the eight *ṛṣi* families about 800 B.C., and was almost complete by 500 B.C.[14]

Inscriptional evidence of the standard *gotra* specification of an individual, dates back to the first century of the Christian era. During the period under review, c. 475-1030 A.D., as far as migrant Brāhmaṇas are concerned, the records yield the names of thirty-six *gotras*,[15] spread over different regions. It is to be noted, that only the *gotras* of Brāhmaṇas as known from epigraphs, and just two from literature, have been taken into consideration.

The *gotra* that could claim the largest number of adherents, thirty-four in all, was the Kauśika, a *gaṇa* under the Viśvāmitra group of *gotras*. Of these, as many as twenty-seven are found to have migrated to Orissa. The Asiatic Society's Plates of Gayāḍatuṅga record, that a Brāhmaṇa of the Kauśika *gotra* had migrated to Orissa, and with twenty-one other Brāhmaṇas, he became the recipient of a village. Although the *gotras* of the other donees are not mentioned, D.C. Sircar holds that all the donees may have belonged to the same family and the same *gotra*. So a single charter accounts for twenty-two migrant Kauśikas in Orissa. The remaining five figure as the donees of the Patna Museum Plates of Somavaṁśi Mahābhavagupta I issued in his sixth year, the Orissa State Museum Plates of his son Mahāśivagupta I, issued in his fourth year, two sets of Patna Plates of the same king, dated in his twenty-fourth and twenty-eighth years, and the Cuttack Plates of the third year of Mahābhavagupta II.

It may be mentioned here, that the Keśari Plates of Śatrubhañja, refer to a single donee, although two *gotras* namely Kauśika and Vaśiṣṭha are given.[16] According to R.C. Majumdar who edited the plates, the Kauśika *gotra* was inscribed by mistake. The correct *gotra* was Vaśiṣṭha, followed by Vaśiṣṭha *pravara*[17] On the other hand, B. Misra who has also edited the same plates, believes, that there were two donees, one of each *gotra*[18] although Bhaṭṭaputra Daṇḍapāṇi, son of Bhaṭṭaputra Cakrapāṇi and grandson of Bhaṭṭaputra Nārāyaṇa, is the only donee mentioned. If. B. Misra's view is accepted, there might have been twenty-eight instead of twenty-seven Kauśika donees in Orissa. His argument, however, seems to be unacceptable. The name of only one donee occurs in the charter. Besides, the fact that the *pravara* of the donee is given as Vaśiṣṭha, lends greater support to R.C. Majumdar's view, that the donee belonged to the Vaśiṣṭha *gotra*.

There were lesser numbers of Kauśika Brāhmaṇas in Gujarat, Madhya Pradesh, Maharashtra and U.P. Four Kauśikas migrated to settle in Gujarat. One is known from a grant of Dhruvasena III of *saṁvat* 334 c. 653-654 A.D., two from the two sets of Jesar Plates of Śīlāditya III, dated in the *Gupta* year 347/c. 666-667 A.D. and the *Valabhī* year 357/c. 676-677 A.D., and one from the Betma grant of Bhojadeva of *V.S.* 1076/c. 1019 A.D. Three other Kauśikas find mention, one in the Nogawa Plates of Dhruvasena II, issued in the *Gupta* year 320/c. 639-640 A.D., one in the Sāngli grant of Rāṣṭrakūṭa Govinda IV, dated in *Śaka* 855/c. 933 A.D., and one in the Benares Inscription of Kalacuri Karṇa of the *Cedi* year 793/c. 1042 A.D. They settled respectively in the modern states of Madhya Pradesh, Maharashtra and U.P. Migrant Brāhmaṇas of the Kauśika *gotra*, are so far not known to have settled in Bihar, Bengal and Rajasthan.

Two *gotras* common to migrant Brāhmaṇas in all territorial divisions except Bihar and Rajasthan, were the Bharadvāja and Vatsa. Of these two, the twenty-five Bharadvājas, were numerically more ponderant than the Vatsas. Orissa had the largest number of these. Daṇḍimahādevī by her Santiragama grant, Raṇabhañja by his Tasapaikera charter, and his Baud grant issued in his fifty-eighth year, Mahābhavagupta I in his thirty-first year and Mahāśivagupta I in his ninth year, by two sets of Cuttack plates, and the latter Mahāśivagupta I by his Nibinnā grant, dated in his fifteenth regnal year, made grants of lands and villages to six migrant Brāhmaṇas of the Bharadvāja *gotras*. By three other charters,[19] three other Brāhmaṇas with the same *gotra* affiliation, were settled in Orissa.

Next to Orissa, Gujarat had the maximum number of Bharadvājas. Seven records from Gujarat,[20] refer to eight migrant Bhāradvājas, who received lands from the Maitrakas, and Gurjaras. It may be pointed out, that compared to Brāhmaṇas of other *gotras*, there were more migrant Bharadvājas in the kingdom of the Maitrakas, as merely three Kauśikas, three each of Parāśaras and Śārkarākṣis and one or two of other *gotras* are referred to in their charters.

In Maharashtra, Madhya Pradesh and Bengal, there were a lesser number of Bharadvājas. By the Ellora Plates of Dantidurga of *Śaka* 663/c. 741 A.D., and the Kalas Budrukh Plates of Bhillamarāja III of *Śaka* 948/c. 1025 A.D., four migrant Brāhmaṇas of this *gotra* were settled near Ellora in the Aurangabad region and in the Akola-*taluka* of Ahmadnagar district of the Bombay Presidency. Madhya Pradesh had three Bharadvājas known from the Deoli Plates of Kṛṣṇa III of *Śaka* 862/c. 940 A.D., and the first set of Gaonri Plates of Vākpati II of *V.S.* 1038/c. 981 A.D. In contrast, a grant of Vigrahapāla III from Belwa, refers to just one Bharadvāja Brāhmaṇa who had come to live in North Bengal.

Fifteen instances of migrating Brāhmaṇas belonging to the Vatsa *gotra*, a member of the Bhṛgu section of *gotras*, are known from inscriptions of Northern India. Like the Bhāradvājas, most of the Vatsas came to Orissa, where the Bhauṃa-Karas, Tuṅgas, Bhañjas and Somavaṁśis patronized as many as seven Vatsa Brāhmaṇas.[21] Gujarat and Madhya Pradesh together could claim six Vatsas.[22] Maharashtra and Bengal, each became the home of one migrant Vatsa Brāhmaṇa. They were the donees of the Navasari Plates of Pulakeśirāja of *K.S.* 490/c. 739-740 A.D. and of the Irda Plates of Nayapāla.

Literature provides the name of another Vatsa Brāhmaṇa Bāṇabhaṭṭa, the author of the *Kādambarī* and *Harṣacarita* who had come to settle in Kanauj in U.P. In the introductory verses to his *Kādambarī*, Bāṇa while describing his family lineage, mentions, that his ancestor Kubera, belonged to the Vātsyāyana *gotra*[33] Kane too, in his notes on the *Harṣacarita* says, that Bāṇa was a member of the Vātsyāyana or Vatsa *gotra*.

Within the larger group of the Vaśiṣṭhas, were included the members of the Parāśara *gotra*. Fourteen adherents of this *gotra* are heard of, half of whom had migrated to Orissa. Kanakabhañja by his Baud grant, Mahābhavagupta I by the Kalibhanā Plates of his sixth year, and Mahāśivagupta I by his Mārañja-Murā grant of his third year, gave lands to one Parāśara Brāhmaṇa each. Another Brāhmaṇa Viṣṇusomācārya of this *gotra* came from Kāmarūpa to settle in the Ganjam district, as known from a grant of the Eastern Gaṅga king Anantavarman, of the *Gaṅga* year 204/c. 700 A.D. On the other hand, Devānandadeva by a single charter bestowed a village in Airāvaṭṭamaṇḍala, to three migrant Parāśaras. Four Brāhmaṇas of this *gotra* went to Madhya Pradesh,[24] one to Gujarat,[25] one to Maharashtra[26] and one to Bengal.[27]

Attention may be drawn to a Dhenkanal grant of Jayastambha, where the donee belonged to the Yajñāḍha Parāśara *gotra*[28] This *gotra* does not find a place in Brough's list of *gotras.* Neither has it been mentioned by Ghurye. This seems to cast some doubt, both on the validity of the *gotra*, and the reading of the plates.

The Kaśyapas were thirteen in number. Nearly half of them are known from Orissa, which became the home of six[29] such Brāhmaṇas. Compared to Orissa, they were fewer elsewhere. That two settled in Bengal, can be seen from the Jājilpārā grant of Gopāla II and a grant of Śulki Raṇastambha. Two others became co-donees of the Gaonri Plates of Vākpati II and went to live in Madhya Pradesh. Bhaṭṭa Mātṛgaṇa, was a Kaśyapa Brāhmaṇa, benefited by the Hilol Plates of the year 470 in Gujarat. Another Brāhmaṇa of the same *gotra*, Bhaṭaputra Ugranandī emigrated from Bengal, and came to live in Karnataka where he received a village from Kulika Vipracandra.

Literature, as in the case of Bāṇa, gives information of another Kaśyapa Brāhmaṇa. He was Bhavabhūti, composer of the *Mahāvīracarita* *Mālatī-Mādhava* and *Uttararāmacarita.* In the prologue of the *Mahāvīracarita* the poet while giving details of his birth and heritage, described his forefathers as Udumbaras and says, that they belonged to the Kaśyapa *gotra*[30] So U.P., where Bhavabhūti had migrated received a Kaśyapa Brāhmaṇa, together with a Bharadvāja and a Vatsa.

Included in the larger *gotra* family of the Kāśyapas, were

the Brāhmaṇas of the Śāṇḍilya *gotra*. Six Śāṇḍilya Brāhmaṇa donees are known to have settled in the ratio of two in Orissa, two in Madhya Pradesh, one in Bengal and one in Bihar.[31] The seventh Brāhmaṇa of this *gotra* was the poet Gadādhara, eulogized in the Kolagallu Inscription of Khoṭṭigadeva, dated in *Śaka* 889/c. 967 A.D. As the record itself states, he left his home in North Bengal, and came to South India, to the court of the Rāṣṭrakūṭas.

Only five Brāhmaṇa immigrants of the Gārgya *gotra*, included in the Bharadvāja group of *gotras*, are mentioned in the charters of the period. Maitraka Śīlāditya III by two grants dated in *G.S.* 346/c. 666 A.D., and in the *Valabhī* year 352/c. 671-672 A.D., settled two Brāhmaṇas of this *gotra* in Gujarat. A third Brāhmaṇa of the Gārgya *gotra*, who also came to live in Gujarat, was the donee of a grant of Śīlāditya, issued in the year 403/c. 722-723 A.D. Another migrant Gārgya is included in the long list of donees of the Gaonri Plates of Vākpati II of *V.S.* 1038/c. 981 A.D. Besides this, Śīlāhāra Mummuṇirāja by his Thana Plates issued in the *Śaka* year 970/c. 1048-1049 A.D., made a grant of land to a Gārgya Brāhmaṇa, who having left Madhyadeśa, was settled in the Bassein area of North Maharashtra.

Inscriptions refer to four Brāhmaṇas. They were immigrants of the Kuṇḍina *gotra*, a *gaṇa* of the Vaśiṣṭha group. The Vakratentalī grant of Mahābhavagupta I of his third year, the Kudopali charter of Mahābhavagupta II, issued in his thirteenth year, the Prince of Wales Museum Plates of Jayabhaṭa IV of *KS* 486/c. 735-736 A.D., and grant of Sinda Ādityavarman of *Śaka* 887/c. 965-966 A.D., show that two Brāhmaṇas of the Kuṇḍina *gotra* received lands in Orissa, one in Gujarat and one in Maharashtra. The Mudgala *gaṇa* is included by Baudhāyana both within the Atri *gotra* and the Kevala Angirasa group.[32] However, Āpastamba, Kātyāyana and Laugākṣī Āśvalāyana and the *Matsya Purāṇa*,[33] mention it only with the other *gaṇas* of the Kevala Agnirasa group, but not within the Atri *gotra*. Three Maudgalyas are known to have settled, in Orissa[34] and one in Madhya Pradesh.[35]

Four Brāhmaṇas of the Gautama *gotra* are known to have

emigrated in this period. Three of them who went to Orissa, figure as donees in the Patna Plates of Mahābhavagupta I of his sixth regnal year, and in his Nagpur Museum Plates, issued two years later, and in the Talcher Plates of Vinītatuṅga II. The fourth Gautama who came to Madhya Pradesh is included among the beneficiaries of the Gaonri Plates.

Instances of three Brāhmaṇas of the Agasti and three of the Atri *gotra* are available. Among the former two migrated to live in Madhya Pradesh and one in Orissa. In Madhya Pradesh they became the donees of the Gaonri Plates of Vākpati II and the Ujjain grant of Paramāra Bhoja. In Orissa, Mahābhavagupta I, by his Patna Plates of his sixth regnal year, donated a village to four Brāhmaṇas, among whom one belonged to the Agasti *gotra*. None of the Atris, however, is known from Orissa. The Prince of Wales Museum Plates of Govindarāja of the viceregal Rāṣṭrakūṭa family of Gujarat, dated in the *Śaka* year 732/c. 810 A.D., the Kolhapur Copper Plate of Akālavarṣadeva of *Śaka* 882/c. 960 A.D., and the Depalpur Plates of Paramāra Bhoja, dated in *V.S.* 1079/c. 1022 A.D., show, that three Brāhmaṇas of the Atri *gotra*, came to live in Gujarat, in South Maharashtra and in Madhya Pradesh.

Brāhmaṇas of the Vaśiṣṭha *gotra* who left their ancestral homes during the period under survey, are three in number. They went to live in Madhya Pradesh, Gujarat and Orissa respectively as proved by the Gaonri Plates, the Banswara grant of Bhojadeva and the Keśari Plates of Śatrubhañja.

A member of the larger Vaśiṣṭha complex was the Kapiṣṭhala *gotra*. Two migrant Brāhmaṇas with this *gotra* affiliation, are found in Gujarat, and one in Orissa.[36] The Sāvarṇa or Sāvarṇi *gotra*, of the Baṛgu family, could claim just two members. One of them was the Brāhmaṇa Dāmadīkṣita, an emigrant from Girnar, who received a village in the Nasik district of Maharashtra by means of the Lohaner Plates of Pulakeśin II, dated in the *Śaka* year 552/c. 630 A.D. The other Brāhmaṇa migrated to Bihar, and there received a village, as recorded in the grant of Saurāditya of *V.S.* 1077/c. 1020 A.D.

Unlike these *gotras*, the members of which had settled in two or more different regions, there were others confined to particular areas. Seven such *gotras* are known, adherents of which all came to Gujarat. Three Maitraka charters[37] refer to three Brāhmaṇas of the Śārkarākṣī *gotra*, which finds a place in Brough's list as a *gaṇa* of the Bhṛgu group. Two Brāhmaṇa brothers of the Dauṇḍavya *gotra* which is not mentioned by Brough, were the donees of the Lunsadi Plates of Śīlāditya II (Śīlāditya III ?) of the *Gupta saṁvat* 350/c. 669-670 A.D. The other five *gotras* to be discussed below, had a single member each. The Cauli *gotra* of the Śyāma-Parāśara group of the Vaśiṣṭha family can be traced in the Kaira Plates of Dadda II of *KS* 380/c. 629-630 A.D. Two *gotras* Dokṣṇa and Prāgāyaṇa which do not occur in Brough's list, are available from the Amreli Museum Plates of Dhruvasena II, of *saṁvat* 323/c. 642-643 A.D., and the Navasari Plates of Jayabhaṭa III, issued in the *Kalacuri* year 456/c. 705-706 A.D. The remaining two *gotras*, Lakṣmaṇa and Māṭhara, are found at slightly later dates. In a grant of Rāṣṭrakūṭa Indra III, of *Śaka* 836/c. 914-915 A.D., the donee belonged to the Lakṣmaṇa *gotra*. This is regarded as a *gaṇa* under the Kaśyapas, by Kātyāyana and Laugākṣī, the *white Yajurveda-pariśiṣṭa* and the *Mānava-pravarādhyāya*, and as a *gaṇa* of the Upamanyu *gotra*, under the Vaśiṣṭhas by Baudhāyana.[38] The other *gotra*, Māṭhara occurs in the Cambay Plates of Govinda IV of *Śaka* 852/c. 930 A.D. According to the *Mānava-pravarādhyāya*, it was a component of the Śāṭhara-Māṭhara *gaṇa* of the Viśvāmitra *gotra*.[39] On the other hand, Baudhāyana and Kātyāyana and Laugākṣī, include the Māṭharas within the Kaśyapa group.[40] It may be pointed out, that Ghurye makes no reference to the above mentioned *gotras*.

It is interesting to note, that among all these Brāhmaṇas with uncommon *gotras*, Śārkarākṣi, Dauṇḍavya, Cauli, Dokṣṇa, Prāgāyaṇa, Māṭhara and Lakṣmaṇa, those of the first six, had emigrated from places within Gujarat. The three Śārkarākṣis and the donee of the Dokṣṇa *gotra* came from Ānarttapura near Valabhī. The donee of the Cauli *gotra* hailed from Bharukachchha or Broach. The original home of the two Dauṇḍavya brothers was in Dvīpa or Diu, on the coast of Gujarat. The Brāhmaṇa who belonged to the Prāgāyaṇa *gotra* had been living in Girnar in Kathiawar, while Kāvikā near Kaira, was the place from where the donee of the Māṭhara *gotra* had moved.

The charters of the period also point to six *gotras*, the migrant members of which had all come to Orissa. One such *gotra* was the Viśvāmitra, to which three Brāhmaṇas[41] belonged. The Kṛṣṇātreya *gotra* of the Atri group, is referred to as the *gotra* of a donee in the Patna Plates of the sixth year of Mahābhavagupta I, and in the Baripada Museum Plates of Devānanda. Another charter of Devānanda, the Jurerpur grant, gives the name of a Brāhmaṇa of the Ulūka *gotra*, included in the Viśvāmitra group. The Khargaprasad Plates of Vinītatuṅga II and the undated Baud grant of Raṇabhañja, both benefited Brāhmaṇas of the Kāṇva *gotra*, a *gaṇa* of the larger body of the Kevala Angirases. The reference to the Rohita *gotra* in a Baud grant of Raṇabhañja of his fifty-fourth year, is rather puzzling. This *gotra* is not recorded by Brough or Ghurye. But Baudhāyana includes the *gaṇa* Lohita in the Viśvāmitra group, giving it the *pravara* formula of "Vaiśvāmitra, Āṣṭaka, Lauhita".[42] As the donee of this grant had the same three *pravaras*, it may be suggested, that he belonged to the Lohita and not the Rohita *gotra*, which may have been an error on the part of the engraver. Mahābhavagupta I by his Patna Plates of the sixth year, granted a village to a Brāhmaṇa of the Kauchchatsa *gotra*, probably the same as the Kautsāḥ of Baudhāyana, mentioned with the Kevala Angirases.[43]

Four Brāhmaṇas of four other different *gotras* migrated to Madhya Pradesh, where they became co-donees of the Gaonri Plates of Vākpati II. They belonged to the Sāṁkritya, Maitreya, Bhārgava and Mauni *gotras*. Of these Kātyāyana and Laugākṣī, the *Mānava-pravarādhyāya*[44] and the *Matsya Purāṇu*,[45] include the first, Sāṁkritya, both in the Viśvāmitra and Bhṛgu sections. The Maitreya *gotra* was a *gaṇa* of the Bhṛgu family. As for the Bhārgava *gotra*, as Ghurye points out, Brough's list does not include a Bhārgava *gotra* as such, but describes the Bhṝgus as a whole complex.[46] The last of the four *gotras*, the Mauni, was probably the same as Mauno, placed by Baudhāyana within the Yaşka *gaṇa* of the Bhṛgus.[47]

Another *gotra* is heard of, only in Rajasthan. A grant of Guhila Bhāvihita of the Harṣa year 48, proves the existence of a Brāhmaṇa of the Dauṇḍāyana *gotra* who had migrated to Rajasthan. It must be mentioned, that this *gotra* does not occur in Brough's list of *gotras.*

It is difficult to pin-point any *gotra* that was special to any particular kingdom, as Brāhmaṇas of different *gotras* settled down under the various ruling houses. However, on the basis of the above account, some conclusion regarding the *gotras* and their state-wise distribution can be arrived at.

It is clear, that none of the *gotras* known for migrant Brāhmaṇas during the period under study, was common to all territorial divisions, as far as their new places of habitation are concerned. However, Orissa, Gujarat and Madhya Pradesh were regions where most of the *gotras* could be found. The table furnished herewith shows that the Kauśikas formed the largest group, almost 20.6% of the total migrant population. Twenty-seven of the thirty-four Kauśikas were settled in Orissa, where the Brāhmaṇas of this *gotra*, made up about one-third of the total number of migrant Brāhmaṇas living there. So although the immigrant Brāhmaṇas in Orissa belonged to a fairly large variety of *gotras*, the members of the Kauśika *gotra*, constituted by far, the largest single majority. Of course, there were Kauśikas in Gujarat, Maharashtra, Madhya Pradesh and U.P., but their total number was just about one-fourth the number of Kauśikas found in Orissa.

The Bharadvājas forming approximately 15.1% of the migrant population, lived mostly in Orissa, where more than one-third of them had become recipients of lands and villages. However, it was only in Gujarat and Maharashtra, that compared to members of other *gotras*, they were the largest single majority. This was not the case with Orissa, Madhya Pradesh and Bengal. As regards Orissa, it had more Kauśikas than Bharadvājas. In Madhya Pradesh, there were four Parāśaras and three Bharadvājas, while Bengal became the home of two Kaśyapas, but just one Bharadvāja Brāhmaṇa.

The migrant Vatsas who were numerically lesser than the

Table showing the number and location of adherents of the more common ***gotras*** of immigrant Brāhmaṇas, c. 475-1030 A.D.

| Gotra | Total No. | Orissa | Gujarat | M.P. | Maha-rashtra | Bengal | Bihar | U.P. | Rajasthan | South India |
|---|---|---|---|---|---|---|---|---|---|---|
| 1 Kauśika | ā34 | 27 | 4 | 1 | 1 | — | — | 1 | — | — |
| 2 Bharadvāja | ā25 | 9 | 8 | 3 | 4 | 1 | — | — | — | — |
| 3 Vatsa | ā16 | 7 | 3 | 3 | 1 | 1 | — | 1 | — | — |
| 4 Parāśara | ā14 | 7 | 1 | 4 | 1 | 1 | — | — | — | — |
| 5 Kaśyapa | ā13 | 6 | 1 | 2 | — | 2 | — | 1 | — | 1 |
| 6 Śāṇḍilya | ā 7 | 2 | — | 2 | — | 1 | 1 | — | — | 1 |
| 7 Gārgya | ā 5 | — | 3 | 1 | 1 | — | — | — | — | — |
| 8 Kuṇḍina | ā 4 | 2 | 1 | — | 1 | — | — | — | — | — |
| 9 Mudgala | ā 4 | 3 | — | 1 | — | — | — | — | — | — |
| 10 Gautama | ā 4 | 3 | — | 1 | — | — | — | — | — | — |
| 11 Agasti | ā 3 | 1 | — | 2 | — | — | — | — | — | — |
| 12 Atri | ā 3 | — | 1 | 1 | 1 | — | — | — | — | — |
| 13 Vaśiṣṭha | ā 3 | 1 | 1 | 1 | — | — | — | — | — | — |
| 14 Kapiṣṭhala | ā 3 | 1 | 2 | — | — | — | — | — | — | — |
| 15 Sāvarṇa | ā 2 | — | 1 | — | — | — | 1 | — | — | — |
| 16 Śārkarākṣi | ā 3 | — | 3 | — | — | — | — | — | — | — |
| 17 Viśvāmitra | ā 3 | 3 | — | — | — | — | — | — | — | — |
| 18 Kṛṣṇātreya | ā 2 | 2 | — | — | — | — | — | — | — | — |
| 19 Kāṇva | ā 2 | 2 | — | — | — | — | — | — | — | — |
| 20 Kauchchatsa | 1 | 1 | — | — | — | — | — | — | — | — |
| 21 Ulūka | 1 | 1 | — | — | — | — | — | — | — | — |
| 22 Rohita | 1 | 1 | — | — | — | — | — | — | — | — |
| 23 Sāṁkritya | 1 | — | — | 1 | — | — | — | — | — | — |
| 24 Maitreya | 1 | — | — | 1 | — | — | — | — | — | — |
| 25 Bhārgava | 1 | — | — | 1 | — | — | — | — | — | — |

Table showing the number and location of adherents of rare and unusual *gotras** of immigrant Brāhmaṇas, c. 475-1030 A.D.

| Gotras | Total No. | Gujarat | Madhya Pradesh | Rajasthan |
|---|---|---|---|---|
| 26 Dauṇḍavya | 2 | 2 | — | — |
| 27 Cauli | 1 | 1 | — | — |
| 28 Dokṣṇa | 1 | 1 | — | — |
| 29 Prāgāyaṇa | 1 | 1 | — | — |
| 30 Lakṣmaṇa | 1 | 1 | — | — |
| 31 Māṭhara | 1 | 1 | — | — |
| 32 Mauni | 1 | — | 1 | — |
| 33 Dauṇḍāyana | 1 | — | — | 1 |

*These *gotras* have till now, not been found in inscriptions of Orissa, Maharashtra, Bengal, Bihar and U.P. as *gotras* of immigrant Brāhmaṇas in the period under survey.

Bharadvājas, made up 9.6% of the Brāhmaṇa immigrants. About half of them were living in Orissa, although in Orissa and Gujarat, there were more Bharadvājas than Vatsas. Maharashtra knew of one Vatsa, but four Bharadvājas. On the other hand, Madhya Pradesh and Bengal had an identical number of Bharadvājas and Vatsas. One Vatsa is also seen in U.P., which, however, could claim no Bharadvājas at all.

The Parāśaras and the Kaśyapas could claim 8.4% and 7.8% respectively of the migrant population. Orissa, Gujarat, Madhya Pradesh and Bengal, were regions common to both. It is remarkable, that although there were fewer Brāhmaṇas of the Kaśyapa *gotra* than there were Kauśikas and Bharadvājas, the Kaśyapas were more widely spread over six regions, instead of the five to which the others and the Parāśaras were confined. The largest section of the Parāśaras and Kaśyapas were living in Orissa, with little difference in their numbers. In other regions, a slight variation is visible. While there were four Parāśaras in Madhya Pradesh, there were only two Kaśyapas. On the other hand, only one migrant Parāśara Brāhmaṇa, but two Kaśyapas are recorded in Bengal. Maharashtra and U.P., each had one Parāśara and one Kaśyapa respectively, while South India had become the home of another Kaśyapa Brāhmaṇa. It may be noted, that this donee is one of the only two Brāhmaṇas among many others who may have migrated to the south, during the period under review, and whose *gotra* and *pravara* are known.

As regards the other *gotras*, their percentage ranged between 4.2% to just 0.6% in some cases. The majority of the Śāṇḍilyas, Kuṇḍinas, Gautamas and Mudgalas had migrated to Orissa. On the other hand, there were two Brāhmaṇas of the Agasti *gotra* in Madhya Pradesh, and two of the Kapiṣṭhala in Gujarat, but just one of each in Orissa. There were no Gārgyas in Orissa, nor any Atris. The greater number of the former settled in Gujarat. The three Atris were evenly distributed between Gujarat, Madhya Pradesh and Maharashtra.

On the basis of the available evidence it can be said, that the largest variety of *gotras* can be found in Orissa, Gujarat and Madhya Pradesh. Gujarat, however, could claim more of the rare and unusual *gotras*, than either Orissa or Madhya Pradesh. There were no Kaśyapas, Gautamas, Agastyas, Maudgalyas, Vaśiṣṭhas or Kapiṣṭhalas in Maharashtra. Bengal could claim only five of the thirty-three *gotras* Bharadvāja, Vatsa, Parāśara, Kaśyapa and Śāṇḍilya. The Kauśika, Vatsa and Kaśyapa *gotras* are the only three known from U.P., and the Śāṇḍilya and Sāvarṇa, are the two from Bihar. In Rajasthan there was just one migrant Brāhmaṇa of the Dauṇḍāyana *gotra*.

It may be pointed out that some of the *gotras* which are known from earlier charters, are no longer heard of in the later phase of the period under survey. Among these are the Śārkarākṣi, Dokṣṇa, Dauṇḍavya, Cauli, Prāgāyaṇa and Dauṇḍāyana *gotras*. These are not mentioned in charters after the seventh century. Of course, the maximum number of adherents of these *gotras* was three, so that it would not be wrong to suggest, that they were rare, even in the earlier days. The families of the donees of these *gotras*, may have gradually become extinct.

Just as there was a large concentration of Kauśikas in Orissa, earlier there had been several other pockets of Brāhmaṇas of particular *gotras* in Northern India. The difference was, that while Orissa was a place to which migrating Brāhmaṇas came, the other areas, discussed below, had once been the original homes of several Brāhmaṇas. As the Brāhmaṇas in the years between c. 475-1030 A.D., are known to have emigrated from various places all over the country, it is impossible to assign particular *gotras* to particular centres of emigration. Hence only a few outstanding and special cases have been taken into account. It should also be mentioned, that henceforth, even those charters will be taken into consideration, wherein the places to which the donees migrated, are not identified with certainty. Names like Hastipada, Hastigrāma in Magadha, Kolāñca, Ṭakāri, Muktāvathi in Śrāvasti and Ahichchhatra in U.P., occur time and time again in the records of the period. It is remarkable, that with a single exception, Brāhmaṇas who emigrated from each of these regions, were members of a particular *gotra*.

The exception is Hastipada. Only one Brāhmaṇa emigrant from Hastipada, belonged to the Kuṇḍina *gotra*, as can be seen from the Kudopali grant of Mahābhavagupta II. The other five Brāhmaṇas who had left Hastipada to live in Orissa and Bengal,[48] all belonged to the Parāśara *gotra*. Like these Brāhmaṇas, the three emigrants from Hastigrāma,[49] were also Parāśaras.

Takkārikā or Ṭakāri, seems to have been at one time, the home of Bharadvāja Brāhmaṇas. Six charters[50] bear witness to the fact, that only Bharadvāja Brāhmaṇas left Ṭakāri, to take up residence in other parts of the country. Another locality, Kolāñca, seems to have included only Brāhmaṇas of the Śāṇḍilya *gotra* within its population. Six sets of plates,[51] show how six Śāṇḍilya Brāhmaṇas from Kolāñca, went to live in Orissa, Madhya Pradesh, North Bihar and Bengal.

The second set of Talcher Plates of Gayāḍatuṅga, the Kalibhanā Plates of the thirty-fourth year of Mahābhavagupta I and the Jājilpārā grant of Gopāla II, give the names of three Brāhmaṇa donees who had emigrated from Mūthāutha-*bhaṭṭa-grāma*, Muktāvathi and Muktāvastu all probably identical with one another. These three Brāhmaṇas belonged to the Kaśyapa *gotra*. The name of Ahichchhatra near Bareilly occurs in only two grants, as a place of emigration. One from Madhya Pradesh, says nothing about the *gotra* of the donee. The other, the Asiatic Society's Plates of Gayāḍatuṅga, records the grant of a village to twenty-two Brāhmaṇas, all members of the same family, of the Kauśika *gotra*, and all emigrants from Ahichchhatra.

On the basis of this evidence, it may be suggested that in the days before these migrations took place, each of these regions—Hastipada, Hastigrāma, Ṭakāri, Kolāñca, Muktāvathi and Ahichchhatra, had been the home of adherents of a particular *gotra*. The desire of Brāhmaṇas of a particular *gotra*, to live together in a particular region, may possibly have had something to do with this.

Apart from the thirty-three *gotras* that have already been discussed, there were three more known during the period under discussion. One of these, the Upamanyu, was a member of the larger group of Vaśiṣṭhas. Only two charters, the Mudgapadra grant of Śryāśraya Śīlāditya, of *KS* 420/c. 668-669 A.D., and a copper plate of Śīlāhāra Mummuṇirāja, dated in the *Śaka* year 971/c. 1049 A.D., record grants to two Aupamanyavas, of villages whose actual location is uncertain.

The two other *gotras* were Autathya and Jātukarṇa. By a set of Talcher Plates, Kulastambha granted a village to a Brāhmaṇa of the Autathya *gotra*, which was a *gaṇa* of the Gautama group. The Jātukarṇa *gotra* of the Vaśiṣṭha family, is known from the first set of Talcher Plates of Gayāḍatuṅga. The two donees of these two charters, received villages, which have not yet been identified.

**Pravaras**

As has been said earlier, the *gotra* system is closely linked with that of *pravara*. Not only a *gotra*, but each *gaṇa* or group into which it was sub-divided, has been given a specific *pravara*. All the *gaṇas* within one *gotra*, normally have at least one *pravara* name in common, that of the eponymous *ṛṣi* of the major *gotra*[52] The case of the *gaṇas* of the Vaśiṣṭha *gotra* helps to prove this point. The Parāśara, Kuṇḍina and Jātukarṇa *gaṇas* of the Vaśiṣṭha *gotra* all include the name of Vaśiṣṭha in their *pravara* formulae that of Parāśara being Vāśiṣṭha, Śāktya, Pārāśarya, that of Kuṇḍina being Vāśiṣṭha, Maitrāvaruṇa. Kauṇḍinya, and that of Jātukarṇa being merely Vāśiṣṭha.[53] Besides, the law givers prescribe for the *gotras* and the *gaṇas*, usually a one *ṛṣi*, or a three *ṛṣi*, or a five *ṛṣi pravara* and sometimes a two *ṛṣi* one.

It may be pointed out that no mention of *pravaras* of migrant Brāhmaṇas, is made in the copper plates of the Rāṣṭrakūṭas and their feudatories. It was under the various ruling houses of Orissa, that the *pravaras* of the *gotras* of the donees, came to be named and enumerated. They were also recounted by the Pālas, Paramāras, Candellas, Kalacuris and Caulukyas. Although the *pravara* systematization had been completed in theory by about 500 B.C., generally speaking, it was not until the middle of the eighth century of the Christian era, that it first began to be mentioned in the inscriptions of the time. Ghurye has pointed out, that even Bhāsa, Bāṇabhaṭṭa and Bhavabhūti did not mention their *pravaras*. He, therefore, concluded, that '*pravara*' was not regularly employed to qualify one's '*gotra*' by a Brāhmaṇa, even perhaps till the tenth century A.D.[64] Hence the wide gap between the dates of systematization of *pravaras* and their introduction in the land-grants, was possibly due to the fact, that the *pravara* formulae was necessary only during the marriage ceremony, and not in other socio-economic matters, in the period between c. 500 B.C. and c. 700 A.D.[55]

The sacred texts not only refer to the *pravaras*, but also lay down the order in which they are to be recited. But copper plates do not observe the rules faithfully. The Bharadvājas have been given a three *ṛṣi pravara*, which runs Āṅgirasa, Bārhaspatya, Bhāradvāja. In two grants, one of Candella Dhaṅgadeva of *VS* 1055/c. 998 A.D. and another of Vigrahapāla III, from Belwa, the *gotra* of the donees have been further qualified as Bharadvāja, Āngirasa, Vā(hā)rhaspatya[56] and Bhāradvāja, Āngirasa, Vā(Bā)rhaspatya,[57] respectively.

In the same way, the correct form for the Kauśika *gaṇa* of the Viśvāmitra group is, Vaiśvāmitra, Daivarāta, Audala. But in the Benares Inscription of Kalacuri Karṇa of the *Cedi* year

793/c. 1042 A.D., the *pravaras* appear as Audālaka, Devarāta, Viśvāmitra,[58] and in the two sets of Patna Plates of the twenty-fourth and twenty-eighth years of Mahāśivagupta I, as Devarāta, Audala, Viśvāmitra.[59] A special mention may be made here of the Patna Museum Plates of the sixth year of Mahābhavagupta I. The donees of this charter are two Kauśika Brāhmaṇas, whose *pravara* formula reads, Daladeva-rājaviśvāmitra.[60] Even if we assume, that the scribe should have written Audala, Devarāta, Viśvāmitra, the proper order for the recitation of the names of the *pravara ṛṣis* of the Kauśikas, has not been observed.

The Rohita or Lohita *gotra* of the Viśvāmitra family should correctly have the *pravaras* Vaiśvāmitra, Āṣṭaka, Lauhita. But in the Ganjam grant of Vidyādharabhañja, the order has been changed to Rohita, Āṣṭaka, Viśvāmitra.[61]

The Vatsa *gotra* of the Bhṛgu complex is known to have the *pravaras* Bhārgava, Cyavana, Āpnavana, Aurva, Jāmadagnya. But two donees, one of the Irda Plates of Nayapāla, and the other of the Aidā Plates of Raṇabhañja, do not conform to this rule. They have the *pravaras* Bhārgava, Chyavana, Aurvvya, Jāmadagnya, Āpnuvana,[62] and Bhārgava, Au(au)rvya, Chyavana, A(ā)tma(pna)vana, Jāmadagni,[63] respectively. The same is the case with the Parāśara Brāhmaṇa donee of the Bangarh grant of Mahīpāla. Instead of the correct formula Vāśiṣṭha, Śāktya, Pārāśarya, he is introduced with the *pravaras* Śakti, Vasiṣṭha, Parāśara.[64]

According to the Nagpur Museum Plates of Mahābhavagupta I, the donee belonged to the Gautama *gotra* and Gautama, Āngirasa, Autathya *pravaras*.[65] Such a *pravara* formula does not appear either in Baudhāyana's list, or in the one in the *Matsya Purāṇa*.[66] However, Āpastamba, Kātyāyana, Laugākṣī and Āśvalāyana,[67] have for the Aucathya or Ucathya Gautamas, the three *ṛṣi pravara* of Āngirasa, Aucathya, Gautama. Taking Autathya to be the corrupt form of Aucathya, the donee's *pravaras* should have been Āngirasa, Autathya, Gautama.

Sometimes all the *pravaras* of a particular *gotra* were not written down in full in the charters. Several records bear witness to this fact. The Bharadvājas are entitled to a three *ṛṣi pravara* or Āngirasa, Bārhaspatya, Bhāradvāja. But a set of plates of Neṭṭabhañja,[68] gives only the Āngirasa *pravara*, while the Tasapaikera charter of Raṇabhañja,[69] the Ganjam grant of Śatrubhañja,[70] and the Cuttack Plates of Mahābhavagupta I of his thirty-first year,[71] give only Vārhaspatya or Bārhaspatya and Angirasa *pravaras*. Their exclusion of Bhāradvāja from the list, makes one feel, that the composer of the charter thought it enough to mention Bhāradvāja only as a *gotra* and saw no need to repeat it again as one of the *pravara* names.

Likewise, the Kuṇḍinas are supposed to have a three *ṛṣi pravara*, Vāśiṣṭha, Maitrāvaruṇa, Kauṇḍinya. But all three names are not found in the *pravaras* of two Brāhmaṇa donees. In the Vakratentalī charter of Mahābhavagupta I, the *pravara* ascription is Vāsiṣṭha and Maitrāvaruṇa,[72] and in the Kudopali grant of Mahābhavagupta II, it is merely Mitrāvaruṇa.[73] Kauṇḍinya, which is their *gotra*, does not figure in the *pravara* lists.

All law givers agree, that the Kaśyapa *gotra* has the three *ṛṣi pravara*, Kāśyapa, Āvatsāra, Naidhruva. But only one of these, Naidhruva is the *pravara* of the donee of a grant of Jayastambha [74] The Talcher Plates of Vinītatuṅga II and those of Gayāḍatuṅga, give their donees, Vachchhāra, Naidhruva[75] and Vachhāyana-Naidhruva[76] *pravaras* respectively. The beneficiaries of the Hindol Plates of Kulika Vīra Pracaṇḍadeva, have been given the *pravaras* Vachchāra or Vatsāra and Naidhruva.[77] Vachhāyana and Vachchhāra, may be alternatives for Āvatsāra, which still omits Kāśyapa from the formulae.

A *gaṇa* of the Kaśyapa *gotra*, Śāṇḍilya, has a three *ṛṣi pravara* of Śāṇḍila, Āsita, Daivala. Yet the donee of a Dhenkanal grant of Jayastambha has been given only two, Āsita and Devala.[78] Vaiśvāmitra, Daivarāta and Audala is the prescribed *pravara* of the Brāhmaṇas of the Viśvāmitra *gotra*. But only one of these, Devarāta is the *pravara* of the Brāhmaṇa who received a village from Daṇḍimahādevī.[79]

The Patna Plates of Mahābhavagupta I issued in his sixth year, record the grant of a village conjointly to four Brāhmaṇas of four different *gotras*. Three of them with the *gotras*, Kṛṣṇātreya, Agasti and Gautama, have not been described with their full *pravara* specifications. While Kṛṣṇātreya should be given the three *ṛṣi pravara* of Ātreya, Ārchanānasa, Śyāvāśva, the Brāhmaṇa of this plate has only Ārchanānasa *pravara* and Śyāvāśva *anupravara*[80] Similarly, whereas the Agastyas are entitled to Āgastya, Dārḍhyacyuta, Aidhmavāha, only the last Idhmavāha occurs as the *pravara* and Chyavana as the *anupravara* of another donee.[81] The third donee belonged to the Gautama *gotra*, Āngirasa *pravara* and the Bārhaspatya *anupravara*[82] As Ghurye puts it, *anupravara* consists in reciting or recording the *pravara ṛṣis* in the reverse order of the statement of the *pravara* formula.[83] In that case Śyāvāśva, Chyavana and Bārhaspatya should have formed part of the *pravara* lists of the three Brāhmaṇas of the Kṛṣṇātreya. Agasti and Gautama *gotras* respectively.

Brough[84] recounts the following *pravaras* for the Śāṇḍilas. Three *ṛṣi pravaras* recommended by Baudhāyana are Kāśyapa, Āvatsāra, Śāṇḍila; Kāśyapa, Āvatsāra, Daivala; Śāṇḍila, Āsita, Daivala; and Kāśyapa, Āvatsāra, Āsita. Āpastamba prescribes for them Daivala, Āsita, and Kāśyapa, Daivala, Āsita. Kātyāyana and Laugākṣī lay down Kāśyapa, Āsita, Daivala and Śāṇḍila, Āsita, Daivala. Āśvalāyana gives two forms Śāṇḍila, Āsita, Daivala and Kāśyapa, Āsita, Daivala. The *Matsya Purāṇa*, however, puts forward only one formula of Āṣita, Devala and Kāśyapa. But none of them give Vārihaspatya, Yamadagnī, Daivallya as the *pravara* of this *gotra*, which can be seen in the Angul Copper Plate of Dharmamahādevī.[85] The editor of this plate, P. Banerji, does not give any explanation for the entry of Vārihaspatya and Yamadagnī. It may be, that there were two other donees of the charter, one of the Bharadvāja and another of the Vatsa *gotra*, whose names may have been left out by mistake, but whose *pravara ṛṣis* have been recorded, albeit one in each case. However, in the absence of any solid proof, this is a mere conjecture.

Coming to the Parāśara *gotra*, its three *ṛṣi pravara* prescribed by the law-givers is Vāśiṣṭha, Śāktya, Pārāśarya. But with complete disregard for this, the donee of the Mārañja-Murā charter of Mahāśivagupta I, issued in his third year, is described as belonging to the Parāśara *gotra* and Ātreya *pravara*.[86] Ātreya is conspicuous by its absence from the Parāśara *pravara* list. This leads one to doubt whether the donee really belonged to the Parāśara *gotra* or to one of the Atri group. In the same way, in a Dhenkanal grant, the donee of the Yajñāḍha-Parāśara *gotra*, has been ascribed the tri-Gārgya *pravara*.[87] It is true, that Brough in his list makes no mention of this particular *gotra*. But even if its inclusion in the Parāśara group is accepted, the *pravara* Gārgya is most inappropriate.

One of the donees of the Patna grant of the sixth year of Mahābhavagupta I, belonged to the Gautama *gotra*, Āngirasa *pravara*, and Bārhaspatya *anupravara*[88] Bārhaspatya being mentioned as the *anupravara*, indicates that it must have been one of the *pravara ṛṣis* of the *gotra*. On the other hand, with the exception of Āśvalāyana, none of the texts include Bārhaspatya or Vārhaspatya within the *pravara* formulae of any of the *gaṇas* comprising the Gautama group. Āśvalāyana gives the *pravara* Āngirasa, Bārhaspatya, Bhāradvāja, Vāndana, Mātavacasa, for the Ṛkṣas, one of the *gaṇas* of the Gautama group.[89] It is remarkable, that the name Gautama is not present in this prescription. So while on the one hand, it leads one to doubt whether the Ṛkṣas should have been included among the Gautama *gaṇas*, the *pravara* and *anupravara* designations, Āngirasa and Bārhaspatya, of the Brāhmaṇa donee lose credibility. As a matter of fact, with all these Brāhmaṇas whose *pravara* names are not what they should be, one begins to wonder if they are all errors to be attributed to the scribes, or whether the Brāhmaṇas were not very sure of their *pravaras*. If the latter is true, the custom of remembering the *pravara ṛṣis* was gradually being given up.

Incorrect *pravaras* appear sometimes in the charters. Daladevarājaviśvāmitra of the Patna Museum Plates of Mahābhavagupta I of his sixth year, should have been Audala Devarāta, Viśvāmitra. Vāchchāyana of a grant of Raṇastambha and Vachchāra of the Talcher Plates of Vinītatuṅga, may have been corrupt forms of Āvatsāra. However, as D.C. Sircar points out, Āvatsāra was sometimes written in records in

Orissa as Āvāchhyāyana.[90] A grant of Raṇabhañja, dated in his twenty-fourth year, instead of Śyāvāśva as one of the *pravaras* of the Kṛṣṇātreya *gotra*, gives Śāvāśmasya,[91] along with Ātreya and Ārchanānasa for the donee. Likewise in the Patna Plates of Mahābhavagupta I of the sixth year, the *pravara ṛṣis* of a donee of the Kauchchatsa *gotra* are Āngirasa-Varsha-Yo(yau)vanāśva.[92] Varsha, the name of the second *ṛṣi* should have been Amvarīṣa

Mention may be made here of a Dhenkanal grant of Jayastambha, which gives an example of an unusual *pravara*. The donee's *gotra* is not given, although he is said to belong to the Śuṅga *pravara*.[93] According to Brough, while Baudhāyana and Āpastamba prescribe a Śuṅga *gaṇa* under the Bharadvāja *gotra*, Kātyāyana and Laugākṣī and the *Matsya Purāṇa*, have in their place, Śauṅgi.[94] The *pravara* for this *gaṇa* has been laid down as Āngirasa Bārhaspatya, Bhāradvāja by Baudhāyana, Kātyāyana and Laugākṣī, and the *Matsya Purāṇa*.[95] Āpastamba, however, gives a five *ṛṣi pravara* namely Āngirasa, Bārhaspatya, Bhāradvāja, Kātya, Ātkila.[96] But it is remarkable, that none of them include the name Śuṅga in the *pravara* list. So it is difficult to decide with any certainty on the correct *gotra* and *pravara* affiliation of this particular Brāhmaṇa.

While some copper plates, like the Nagpur Museum Plates of the eighth year of Mahābhavagupta I, give both the number and names of the *pravaras*, there are quite a few in which only the number but not the names of *pravaras* of a particular *gotra* is stated. Several such grants are available for the period under discussion. The two sets of Gaonri Plates of Paramāra Vākpati II, as well as the Mahudi Plates, the Banswara grant and the Ujjain grant of his nephew Bhojadeva, do not record the names of *pravara ṛṣis*, but just the number in each case. It is remarkable, that the Paramāra charters should make no mention of the names of the sages constituting the *pravara* formula. Likewise, in the Bhadresar Plates of Caulukya Bhīmadeva I and the Jodhpur grant of Siṁharāja, the *pravaras* are merely enumerated. In the latter, even the *gotra* of the donee is conspicuous by its absence. In several charters from Orissa[97] as well, the *pravara ṛṣis* have not been named.

Of all these records, four give wrong numbers of *pravaras*. In the Gaonri Plates of Vākpati II of *V.S.* 1038/c. 981 A.D., a Brāhmaṇa of the Parāśara *gotra* is said to have five *pravaras*, whereas all the relevant texts maintain, that this *gotra* has a three *ṛṣi pravara* namely Vāśiṣṭha, Śāktya, Pārāśarya. Similarly in the Angul C.P. of Śāntikara, a donee of the Maudgalya *gotra*, is ascribed five instead of the three *pravaras* meant for the Mudgalas, Āngirasa Bhārmyaśva, Maudgalya. In the Juraḍa grant of Neṭṭabhañja too, one comes across a Brāhmaṇa of the Viśvāmitra *gotra* again with five *pravaras* instead of the prescribed three, Vaiśvāmitra, Daivarāta, Audala. Finally in the Jurerpur Plates of Devānanda, the donee belonged to the Ulūka *gotra* and had five *pravaras*. D.C. Sircar, the editor of these plates points out, that the donee should have been given only three *pravaras*, Udala, Devarāta and Viśvāmitra, as recognized by the *Gotra-pravara-nibandhakadamba*[98]. Āpastamba, Kātyāyana and Laugākṣī and the *Matsya Purāṇa*[99], all ascribe a three *ṛṣi pravara* to the Ulūka *gotra*.

**Anupravaras**

In some of the charters from Orissa, one finds the inclusion of *anupravaras*, as a further specification of *gotras* of Brāhmaṇa donees. As Brough points out, this term is unknown to the *Sūtras.*[100] He, however, fails to explain it. Ghurye on the other hand, describes it as the recitation of the *pravara ṛṣis* in the reverse order of the statement of the *pravara* formula.[101] However, he also says, that on the basis of Pāṇini's explanation of the term *anubrahmaṇam* as supplementary Brāhmaṇas, the term *anupravara* can only mean secondary *pravara*[102].

Two grants of Mahābhavagupta I, the Gaintala Plates and the Patna Plates of the sixth year, show the correctness of Ghurye's view, that the *anupravaras* should be in reverse order of the *pravaras*. In the former, the donee of the Vatsa *gotra* has the *pravaras*, Bhārgava, Cyavana, Āpnuvana, Aurva, Yamadagni and the *anupravaras*, Yamadagni, Aurva,

Āpnuvana, Cyavana, Bhārgava.[103] Likewise, one of the donees of the Patna Plates, who belonged to the Kauchchatsa *gotra*, enjoyed the *pravaras* Āngirasa, Varsha, Yauvanāśva and the *anupravaras* Yuvanāśva, Amvarīṣa, Āngirasa.[104]

In the Baud grant of Raṇabhañja of his fifty-fourth year, the donee has the *pravaras* Rohita-ashṭakāya-Viśvāmitra,[105] while in the Ganjam grant of Vidyādharabhañja, the donee is given the *pravaras* Rohita, Āṣṭaka, Viśvāmitra, and the *anupravaras* Viśvāmitravat, Aṣṭakavat, Rohitavat,[106] thereby indicating Viśvāmitra, Āṣṭaka and Rohita as the *anupravaras* of the donee. It should be pointed out, that the order of the *pravaras* in these two charters and of the *anupravaras* in the Ganjam grant have been reversed, but not in the correct way. As a matter of fact, what has been formulated for the *anupravara*, should have taken the place of the *pravara* and *vice versa*. As prescribed by the law-givers, the Rohita or Lohita *gotra* of the Viśvāmitra family, should rightly have the *pravaras* Vaiśvāmitra, Āṣṭaka, Lauhita, in which case its *anupravaras* should have been Lauhitavat, Aṣṭakavat, Viśvāmitravat.

As regards the three other donees of the Patna Plates of the sixth year of Mahābhavagupta I, two of the Kṛṣṇātreya and Agasti *gotras* have been given one *anupravara* each, Śyāvāśva and Cyavana respectively.[107] The third donee belonging to the Gautama *gotra* has been ascribed Bārhaspatya *anupravara*,[108] which is one of the *pravara ṛṣis* of the Ṛkṣas, as has been discussed earlier. In the same way, in a grant of Daṇḍimahādevī, for a donee of the Viśvāmitra *gotra*, only one *anupravara* Audala,[109] and in a grant of Neṭṭabhañja, for a Brāhmaṇa of the Bharadvāja *gotra* only the Bārhaspatya *anupravana*[110] have been mentioned.

In one other charter, the enumeration of *anupravaras* is not correct. In the Phulsara Copper Plate of Kīrttirājadeva, a Brāhmaṇa of the Viśvāmitra *gotra* is the donee. Although he is rightly given a three *ṛṣi* unnamed *pravara*, the charter describes him as having five *anupravaras*.[111] This would go against Ghurye's theory in that, there are more *ṛṣi* names in the *anupravara* list, than in the *pravara*. The view that the *anupravara ṛṣis* should be in reverse order of the *pravara* ones, presupposes an identical number of both.

From the above discussion regarding *pravaras*, it seems, that they were at all times, open to various kinds of errors. The incorrect order in the recitation of the *pravara ṛṣis*, the omission of one or more *ṛṣi* names from the *pravara* lists, the inclusion of inappropriate *pravaras* in the formulae, the mere enumeration of numbers of *pravaras* in quite a few cases, and the mistakes sometimes made in their numbering, all point to the fact, that not much care and attention was given to their recording. To account for this careless and casual attitude, it may be suggested, that the Brāhmaṇa society of the time, did not attach much importance to the *pravara* system. Besides, the provision by Baudhāyana, Āpastamba and Āśvalāyana, that in the case of doubt or ignorance regarding one's own *pravara*, the word *Manuvat*, indicating Manu as the *pravara*, can be recited,[112] perhaps implies, that the recital of one's *pravara* was not always essential. It may also help one to understand the absence of *pravaras* as further qualifications of *gotras* in some of the charters. It is improper to explain all the errors and omissions as being due to the scribes. At the same time, one should not always doubt the authenticity of the caste of the donees, when such mistakes are found. It is true, that we frequently come across the proper *pravara* formulae in the charters. But on the whole, the *pravara* specification of the *gotra* of a donee, was either far from being stadardized, or was not being strictly adhered to, in the period under discussion.

**Austerities and Asceticism**

Just as the migrant Brāhmaṇas in all possibility, observed the *gotra* rule in their daily lives, so too in other spheres they tried to conform to the code laid down for them by the *Dharmaśāstras*. The ideal life for a Brāhmaṇa is explained by Yājñavalkya. According to this lawgiver, a Brāhmaṇa who although entitled to accept a gift on account of his Vedic learning and *tapas*, did not do so, attained to the highest world.[113] To this may be added the study of the *Vedas* and the performance of religious duties. As the inscriptions show, most of the migrant Brāhmaṇas studied at least one *Śākhā* of the *Veda* and were engaged in the maintenance of *bali* and *caru*, in the worship of gods, honouring of guests and *Vaiśvadeva*.

Practice of Austerities and piety too, were prescribed for Brāhmaṇas. As a matter of fact, some migrant Brāhmaṇas tried to live up to this ideal. One was Dīrghācārya, the donee of the Balera Plates of Caulukya Mūlarāja I of *V.S.* 1051/c. 994-995 A.D. The charter itself describes him as *aśeṣa vidyāpāraga taponidhi*. Another Brāhmaṇa was Gadādhara of the Kolagallu Inscription of Khoṭṭiga, dated in the *Śaka* year 889/c. 967 A.D. He was renowned for his learning, asceticism and austerities. He had to his credit, the consecration of an image of the god Kārttikeya, with divine hymns, as well as the installation of images of deities like Viṣṇu, Brahmā, Maheśvara and Pārvatī. A third Brāhmaṇa was Prahāsa of the Silimpur Stone Inscription of the eleventh century. A scion of a learned and respectable migrant family, he too was responsible for the installation of an image of Amaranātha, the dedication of an image of Trivikrama and the excavation of a tank. Moreover the inscription describes how in spite of being pressed by king Jayapāla of Kāmarūpa, who was making a *tulāpuruṣa* gift, Prahāsa refused to accept nine-hundred gold coins and a grant of land, yielding an income of a thousand measures of rice.

**Profession and Avocation**

Brāhmaṇa Prahāsa mentioned, above, however, was an exception rather than a rule. Migrant Brāhmaṇas, who for the greater part had left their homes in search of a better financial status, were at times forced to abandon this high principle by the necessity of earning a livelihood. They followed the advice of Gautama and Laghu Vyāsa,[114] to approach a king for their *yogakṣema*, or for their livelihood and support. Consequently, they received lands, villages, gifts and donations, and drew from these, their means of sustenance. Whether the income thus derived, was according to Manu's injunction, just sufficient to enable Brāhmaṇas to maintain themselves and their families, and to perform their religious duties,[115] or whether there was something left over which was accumulated by the Brāhmaṇa donees, is not known. But some of them, specially those who were recipients of two or more plots of lands and villages with accompanying tax-privileges, e.g. Brāhmaṇas like Sūrya of the Sankheda Plates of Dadda II of *K.S.* 392/c. 642 A.D. Nārāyaṇamitra, of a grant of Dharasena IV of the *Gupta saṁvat* 330/c. 649-650 A.D., Sarvānanda of the two sets of Gaonri Plates of Paramāra Vākpati II, Bhaṭṭa Mahattama Sādhāraṇa of the Cuttack Plates of the thirty-first year of Mahābhavagupta I and Mahodadhi, of the Patna Plates of the twenty-fourth and twenty-eighth years of Mahāśivagupta I, were undoubtedly quite rich and well-to-do individuals. So the ideal of poverty and plain living which was insisted upon by the *Dharmaśāstras*, was not always strictly followed by the migrant Brāhmaṇas. Besides, Parāśara lays down a gradation, on the basis of which a gift could be classified. The best gift was made when the donor himself went to the place of a worthy donee. Slightly inferior was the one given when the donor called the donee to his place, before making the grant. But the worst and most inferior, was the gift made as a result of supplication by the donee.[116] The inscriptions and texts of the period are silent as regards these three ways of making a gift. They say nothing, either about the king inviting the immigrant donee or the Brāhmaṇa himself begging for a grant. It may, however, be assumed, that having migrated to a new area, the Brāhmaṇa applied to the king for a grant of land. Satisfied with his worthiness and his qualities, the king accordingly acceded to the request.

A Brāhmaṇa is expected to teach the *Vedas* and allied subjects, and a few of the migrant Brāhmaṇas lived up to this expectation. An *adhyāpaka* is known from the Kaira Plates of Dadda II of *K.S.* 380/c. 629-630 A.D., where he figures as one of the donees of a collective grant. There were others with the epithets *upādhyāya* and *ācārya* added to their names. According to the Bonda Plates of Mahāśiva Tīvara, the Brāhmaṇa Vikrama was an *upādhyāya*, who had come from Avanti. Another *upādhyāya* was Nannaka, the donee of the

Jodhpur grant of Siṁharāja dated in the *Vikrama* year 1054 c. 997 A.D. In a charter from Bengal, the Amgachi grant of Vigrahapāla III, the father of the donee Khoduladevaśarman, was a *mahopādhyāya* named Arkkadeva. The names of *ācāryas* too are recorded. One was Viṣṇusomācārya of a grant of Anantavarman of the Eastern Gaṅga family, of the *Gaṅga* year 204/c. 700 A.D. Another was Vasantācārya who had come from Ahichchhatra and was the donee of the Dharmapuri grant of Vākpati II, issued in *V.S.* 1031/c. 974 A.D. By his Balera Plates of *V.S.* 1051/c. 994-995 A.D., Caulukya Mūlarāja I, donated a village to Dīrghācārya, son of Durlabhācārya, both of whom must have also followed the same profession of a teacher. It may, however, be pointed out that during the period under discussion, immigrant Brāhmaṇas are not known to have been connected with any temple, where education might have been imparted to students.

Literature introduces us to two immigrant Brāhmaṇas who rose to high positions as royal *gurus* and chief *paṇḍitas*. One was Rājaśekhara, the *guru* or preceptor of Pratīhāra Mahendrapāla. The other Bilhaṇa came to the kingdom of the Cāḷukyas of Kalyāṇī where king Paramāḍi or Vikramāditya VI Tribhuvanamalla honoured him with the office of Chief Paṇḍita or *Vidyāpati*.

Some of the immigrant Brāhmaṇas officiated as priests in sacrifices, which was allowed by the *Dharmaśāstras*. The charters tell us about a number of *adhvaryu* priests,[117] whose function was, to execute all the sacrificial acts, muttering simultaneously the prose prayers and sacrificial formulae of the *Yajus Saṁhitā*. Other than these, there were some Brāhmaṇas, who also served as priests. In the Bonda Plates of Mahāśiva Tīvara, a donee named Phalihasvāmin had come from Lāṭa. Both he and Vikramopādhyāya, who has been mentioned earlier, have been described as priests of the *Caraka* section of the *Yajurveda* and *Sāmaveda*.[118] In the Cambay Plates of Govinda IV of *Śaka* 852/ c. 930 A.D., the immigrant Brāhmaṇa Nāgamārya who was perhaps a priest, received a village as priestly fees for the performance of *śrāddha* and sacrifices like *rājasūya, vājapeya, agniṣṭoma* and for *soma* sacrifices.[119] So he along with other local Brāhmaṇas, was performing religious rituals for the king. Mention may be made here of Bhaṭṭaputra Śrīdharaśarman the donee of the Jājilpārā grant of Gopāla II. He has been referred to as a *Yājñika*[120] Brāhmaṇa, probably engaged in sacrifices. At times Brāhmaṇas from outside, were attached to temples in their new areas of residence. Priests from Lāṭa, are found attending to the god Nunna-Nārāyaṇa, in the Khalimpur Plates of Dharmapāla of Bengal.[121]

But immigrant Brāhmaṇas did not always confine themselves to the above-mentioned permitted professions. Several among them, entered the service of the king, a course allowed to them by law-givers, only in times of distress. Yet it was not very desirable. Aparārka who lived in the thirteenth century, quoting Śātātapa who belongs to an earlier date, speaks of six groups of Brāhmaṇas, who although born Brāhmaṇas, were really not so, one among the six consisting of those who had taken service with the king.[122]

Nevertheless, some immigrant Brāhmaṇas with the requisite qualifications, came to be employed as *mantrins* and held other posts as well. Bhaṭṭa Mahattama Sādhāraṇa of the Cuttack Plates of Mahābhavagupta I, served as the *mantrin* or minister of the king.[123] Another Brāhmaṇa, Ghaṇṭīśa, whose maternal ancestors had emigrated from Kolāñca, and who was the actual donor of the Bangaon Plates of the times of Vigrahapāla III, was a *vidheya*, meaning literally a servant of the king.[124]

Two inscriptions also refer to immigrant Brāhmaṇas in military service. This profession too, was permitted by writers of the early *Dharmaśāstras*, only in particular circumstances, i.e. in times of distress, to prevent the inter-mingling of the castes, to maintain *dharma* and protect the twice-born classes.[125] The Brāhmaṇa Sillaṇa referred to in a Yādava charter from Devalili, has been described as a *nāyaka*.[126] So he was probably employed in a military capacity by Paramāra Vairisiṁha of Dhārā. From the Siyadoni Inscription of Devapāla,[127] we learn about the Brāhmaṇa Vaśiṣṭha, who had come from Rāyakka near Kanauj to Siyadoni near Jhansi. He was killed in battle, as the last line of the inscription seems to suggest. It is also known from the same source, that his son Dāmodara became a *senāpati.*

Some migrant Brāhmaṇas, perhaps followed the profession of astrologers. Two charters from Orissa, the Kalibhanā Plates of the thirty-fourth year of Mahābhavagupta I and the Antirigam grant of Yaśabhañja, give the names of some such astrologers.[128] The first refers to the *Kāladeśī* Devu, who belonged to the Kaśyapa *gotra* and was a student of the *Ṛgveda.* The donee of the grant of Yaśabhañja, was Dhīradīkṣita Jagadharaśarman, who came from a family of astrologers, as his father Vidyādhara and grandfather Śrīdhara had been astrologers before him. Jagadharaśarman was a Bharadvāja Brāhmaṇa, who had studied the Mādhyaṁdina *śākhā* of the *Yajurveda.* However, despite their lineage and learning, these Brāhmaṇas were probably looked down upon by their fellowmen, who were only engaged in sacrifices and the teaching profession. The *Bṛhaddharma Purāṇa* regards the astrologer class of Brāhmaṇas who worshipped the planets, as a degraded set of people.[129] Hence astrology too as a profession, according to the law-books, was not to be adopted by high and noble-minded Brāhmaṇas.

Other Brāhmaṇas sometimes held humble posts. Dhavala, the donee of a grant of Daṇḍimahādevī, served as a doorkeeper, as the charter states, that he was a *pratihāra*[130] Few served as composers and writers of *praśastis* and land-grants. There is reference to two composers, Iśāna of the Mahua Inscription of Vatsarāja and Vimalamati of the Mandakila Tal Inscription of *V.S.* 1043/c.986 A.D. Two other Brāhmaṇas were employed as writers of charters. One was Bhaṭṭa Kakka of the Hansot Plates of Bhartṛvaḍḍha II of *V.S.* 813/c. 756 A.D. and the other was *Vandya* Devabhadra writer of the Russellkonda Plates of Neṭṭabhañja.

So as far as the study of the *Vedas* and performance of daily religious rites were concerned, migrant Brāhmaṇas might have maintained the ancient tradition, sometimes imparting knowledge as teachers and sometimes officiating as priests.

**Study of the Vedic Literature (Śākhā)**

In theory at least, most of the migrant Brāhmaṇas who could qualify as teachers, were students of some branch of the *Vedas*. The Vedic affiliation of Brāhmaṇas was usually indicated in the records, by two terms, *caraṇa* and *śākhā*. According to Ghurye, they pertained more or less to one and the same phenomenon and institutional or organizational aspect.[131] Both could be used to denote a school or branch of the *Veda*. Monier Williams further explains, in the context of the word *śākhā*, that each school adhered to its own traditional text and interpretation in the *Caraṇavyūha*, a work by Śaunaka, about the various schools.[132] Five *śākhās* of the *Ṛgveda*, have been enumerated those of the Śākalas, Bāshkalas, Āśvalāyanas, Śāṅkhāyanas, and Māṅḍukāyanas. Forty-two or forty-four out of eighty-six have been mentioned of the *Yajurveda*, of which fifteen belonged to the Vājasaneyins, including those of the Kāṇas and Mādhyaṁdinas. Twelve out of a thousand, are said to have existed of the *Sāmaveda* and nine of the *Atharvaveda*. M. Winternitz describes *śākhās* as *Saṁhitās*, or collections of hymns, prayers, incantations, benedictions, sacrificial formulae and litanies. There must have once existed a fairly large number of *Saṁhitās*, which originated in different schools of priests and singers and which continued to be handed down in the same. However, many of these collections were nothing but slightly diverging recensions — *śākhās* or branches of one and the same *Saṁhita*[133]. Although the words *caraṇa* and *śākhā* are sometimes used simultaneously, yet *caraṇa* properly applies to the sect or collection of persons united in one school, and *śākhā* to the traditional text followed, as can be seen from the phrase *śākhām adhīte*, where the Brāhmaṇa recites a particular version of the *Veda*.[134]

This is further borne out by the Santiragama grant of Daṇḍimahādevī and the Dasapalla grant of Śatrubhañja, where the Brāhmaṇa donees were students of the Vājasaneya *caraṇa* and Mādhyaṁdina *śākhā*. Likewise in the Aidā Plates of Raṇabhañja, and the Irda Plates of nayapāla, the donees belonged to the Chhāndoga *caraṇa* and Kauthuma *śākhā*. The

Mādhyaṁdina and Kauthuma *śākhās* were particular texts of the Vājasaneya and Chhāndoga schools.

But such formulation was not always the rule. In five Maitraka charters,[135] We come across beneficiaries of the Chhāndoga *śākhā* and Vājasaneya *śākhā*. In the Ganjam grant of Śatrubhañja, the Brāhmaṇa Bappi, is said to have belonged to the Taittirīya *śākhā*. These are all unusual descriptions of Vedic qualifications as Chhāndogya, Vājasaneya and Taittirīya, are in fact common names for students of the *Sāmaveda* and for the theologians of the *White Yajus* and *Black Yajus* schools respectively,[136] rather than being particular recensions of the same. Perhaps the most discordant note is struck by the Cuttack Plates of Mahābhavagupta II, issued in his third regnal year. There the donee Rāchcho belonged to the Kauthuma *caraṇa* and Chhāndogya *śākhā*. Both the Kauthuma *śākhā* and *Chhāndogya Upaniṣad* belong to the *Sāmaveda*. Yet it has been surmised by some scholars, that the *Chhāndogya* forms a part of the Tāṇḍya-Mahā-Brāhmaṇa, which is distinct from the Kauthuma *śākha*. This may explain why the abovementioned Brāhmaṇa of the Cuttack Plates, was a student of the Kauthuma *caraṇa* and Chhāndogya *śākhā*. However, whatever may have been the form of expression, the term *caraṇa* occurs less frequently than *śākhā*, which appears time and time again to indicate the Vedic affiliation of Brāhmaṇa donees.

Of the four *Vedas*, the one that could claim the largest number of students, at least as far as the migrant Brāhmaṇas were concerned, was the *Yajurveda*. B.K. Ghosh observes on the *Ṛgveda*, that "the hymns constituting the Ṛik-Saṁhitā, though certainly not always composed or manufactured directly for the sacrificial ritual, yet owe their inclusion in the Saṁhitā, which guaranteed their preservation, wholly to the fact that at some time or other the ritual offered a place to each of them.[137] But V.M. Apte writes, that even in the age of the *Ṛgveda*, "the cult of the Grand Sacrifices, especially the Soma sacrifices, was gradually developing by the side of the cult of the domestic rites .... They were, however, so elaborately developed and systematized during the period under review that the *Sāmaveda* and *Yajurveda Saṁhitās* have been compiled solely for use at these Grand Sacrifices."[138] Perhaps it was this purpose of the *Yajurveda*, that made it the most widely read of the *Vedas*.

Immigrant donees in the charters are sometimes described merely as belonging to a particular *Veda*. Henceforth the *śākhās* of only such immigrant Brāhmaṇas will be discussed, the identification of whose new places of residence or granted villages is certain. Seven students of the *Yajurveda* are known from the Bangarh grant of Mahīpāla I, from Bengal, the Thana Plates of Śīlāhāra Nāgārjuna of *śaka* 961/c. 1039 A.D. from Maharashtra, the Singharā Plates of Raṇabhañja from Orissa, a grant of Kulika Vipracandra and the Hindol Plates of Kulika Vīra Pracaṇḍadeva, from the Kanara district of Karnataka. At other times, the term *adhvaryu* was used. The *adhvaryu* priest was proficient only in the *Yajus Saṁhitā*, because he muttered the prose formulae collected in it for his use, and he executed all the sacrificial acts. Three charters, two from Gujarat, one of Śīlāditya II (Śīlāditya III?) of the year 352/c. 671-672 A.D., and the Jesar Plates of Śīlāditya III of *G.S.* 347/c. 666-667 A.D., and one from Maharashtra, the Ellora Plates of Dantidurga of *śaka* 663/c. 741 A.D., speak of five *adhvaryu* Brāhmaṇas who were priests proficient in the *Yajurveda*.

Usually, however, the records mention the specific branch of a particular *Veda* to which a Brāhmaṇa belonged. In records from Gujarat, Madhya Pradesh, U.P. and Orissa, immigrant Brāhmaṇa donees are described as Vājasaneya Brāhmaṇas. The *Vājasaneya Saṁhitā* or the *Saṁhitā* of the *White Yajurveda*, takes its name from Yājñavalkya Vājasaneya the chief teacher of this *Veda*.[139] During the period under survey, eight such adherents of the Vājasaneya school are found in Gujarat.[140] Two Vājasaneyas in Madhya Pradesh are found in the Nogawa Plates of Dhruvasena II, dated in the *Gupta* year 320/ c. 639-640 A.D. A charter from U.P., the Benares Plates of Kalacuri Karṇa of the *Cedi* year 793/c. 1042 A.D., gives the name of another Vājasaneya Brāhmaṇa. Orissa, like U.P. had jast one immigrant Brāhmaṇa of this Vedic school, referred to in the Cuttack Plates of Mahābhavagupta I of his thirty-first regnal year.

Generally, however, the charters record the specific recensions of the Vājasaneya school. Two recensions of the *Śukla Yajurveda* are known, the Kāṇva and Mādhyaṁdina. Weber is of the opinion, that they resemble one another very closely, and that the Kāṇva recension was older than the Mādhyaṁdina. Twenty migrant Brāhmaṇas of the Kāṇva *śākhā* are known from the land grants of the period, sixteen of them being from Orissa.[141] Three Rāṣṭrakūṭa charters[142] refer to three other Brāhmaṇas of this Vedic school, who settled in Gujarat, Maharashtra and Madhya Pradesh respectively. One Kāṇva Brāhmaṇa is known from Bengal, the donee of a grant of Śulki Raṇastambha. It is remarkable, that not a single specific mention of the Kāṇva *śākhā* is found in the period prior to the eighth century, at least as far as migrant Brāhmaṇas of North India are concerned.

The Mādhyaṁdina Vājasaneya Brāhmaṇas far exceeded the adherents of the Kāṇva śākhā. Thirty-one Mādhyaṁdinas are referred to in the records. Madhya Pradesh had the largest share. Only one Maitraka grant, the Nogawa Plates of Dhruvasena II of the year 321/c. 640-641 A.D., refers to a Brāhmaṇa of the Mādhyaṁdina branch who settled in Madhya Pradesh. The Gaonri Plates of Vākpati II of *V.S.* 1038/c. 981 A.D., alone account for nine such Brāhmaṇas. A Yādava charter from Devalili, mentions a Brāhmaṇa whose ancestor served under the king of Dhārā. He had specialized in the Mādhyaṁdina school and was an emigrant from Madhyadeśa.

Eight Mādhyaṁdina Brāhmaṇas became donees of land-grants in Gujarat. Three of them are known from two sets of Sankheda Plates of Gurjara Dadda II, both dated in *K.S.* 392/c. 642 A.D., the Navasari Plates of Jayabhaṭa III, *K.S.* 456/c. 705-706 A.D., and the Prince of Wales Museum Plates of Jayabhaṭa IV, issued in *K.S.* 486/c. 735-736 A.D. Rāṣṭrakūṭa Indra III in the *Śaka* year 836/c. 914-915 A.D., settled a single Brāhmaṇa of the Mādhyaṁdina school in Gujarat. In the same may, the Hilol Plates of the year 470 and the Baroda grant of Karkka Suvarṇavarṣa, issued in *Śaka* 734/c. 812 A.D., each mentions one Brāhmaṇa versed in the Mādhyaṁdina *śākhā* of the Vājasaneya school, Paramāra Bhojadeva by the Betma and Banswara grants, both of *V.S.* 1076/c. 1019 A.D., donated lands to two Mādhyaṁdina Brāhmaṇas, also in Gujarat.

Orissa knew of nine migrant Brāhmaṇas of the Mādhyaṁdina school.[143] Besides these Guhila Brāvihita by a charter issued in the *Harṣa* year 48, Gopāla II by the Jājilpārā grant of his sixth year and Bhillamarāja III by his kalas Budrukh Plates of *Śaka* 948/c. 1025 A.D., settled three Mādhyaṁdinas in Rajasthan, Bengal and Maharashtra respectively.

Compared to the students of the Mādhyaṁdina *śākhā* of the *White Yajus*, more migrant Brāhmaṇas of the Kāṇva *śākhā* figure in charters from Orissa. Maharashtra and Bengal had an identical number of each. But in Madhya Pradesh and Gujarat, their numerical difference was quite striking. Just one Brāhmaṇa of the Kāṇva school had come to live in each of these regions, in contrast with the eleven immigrants of the Mādhyaṁdina branch in Madhya Pradesh, and eight of the same school in Gujarat. Rajasthan had no Kāṇva Brāhmaṇas and merely one Mādhyaṁdina, while the adherents of both these schools were absent from Bihar. The case of Orissa is remarkable. There were more Kāṇvas in Orissa, than Madhyaṁdinas, despite the fact, that the Mādhyaṁdinas on the whole, far exceeded the Kāṇvas in other parts of North India. Perhaps Brāhmaṇas of the Kāṇva *śākhā* of the *Śukla Yajus* found greater favour in Orissa, than those of the other school.

The *Kṛṣṇa Yajurveda* had a lesser number of students than the *Śukla Yajus*. Just as the term *Vājasaneya* was sometimes used as a name for the *White Yajus*, so was Taittirīya for the *Black Yajus*. The charters refer to only two Brāhmaṇas of this school. Avanijanāśraya Pulakeśirāja issued his Navasari Plates in *K.S.* 490/c. 739-740 A.D. bestowing a village in Maharashtra on a Brāhmaṇa versed in the Taittirīya *Śākhā*. The other immigrant learned in the Taittirīya school is known from Orissa, as the donee of the Ganjam grant of Śatrubhañja.

Literature gives the name of the poet Bhavabhūti, whose ancestors had been educated in the Taittirīya branch. In the prologue of his *Mahāvīracarita*, while describing his lineage, he refers to his forefathers, as being Taittirīyas.[144] It can be inferred, that he too belonged to the same Vedic school.

A school of the *Black Yajus*, is the Maitrāyaṇī *śākhā*. The charters of the period, give evidence of six migrant Brāhmaṇas of this section who benefited from the patronage of kings in Madhya Pradesh, Maharashtra, Gujarat and Orissa. The Bonda Plates of Mahāśiva Tīvara from Madhya Pradesh record a collective grant made to Brāhmaṇas, among whom the three immigrants were of the Maitrāyaṇī *śākhā* of the *Black Yajus*. Cālukya Pulakeśin II in the *Śaka* year 552/c. 630 A.D., issued the Lohaner Plates, in which the donee was a Brāhmaṇa of the Maitrāyaṇī *śākhā* and Vārāhaka *sūtra*, which like the Maitrāyaṇī, belongs to the school of the *Black Yajurveda*.[745] In Gujarat, Śīlāditya III by a charter of *Gupta saṁvat* 342/c. 661-662 A.D., and much later in Orissa, Mahābhavagupta I by his Mahākosala Historical Society's Plates, donated villages to two Brāhmaṇas of the Maitrāyaṇī school.

It may be mentioned here, that sometimes Brāhmaṇa donees who had specialized in any of the branches of the *Yajurveda* are also described as being learned in other unnamed Vedas. Bhūtakumāra of a grant of Śīlāditya III of *Gupta saṁvat* 342/c. 661-662 A.D., a student of the Maitrāyaṇī

*Geographical Distribution of the Śākhās of the Yajurveda to which Migrant Brāhmaṇas Belonged (c. 475-1030 A.D.)*

| Name as given in epigraphs | No. | Orissa | Gujarat | M.P. | Maharashtra | Bengal | Bihar | U.P. | Rajasthan | South India |
|---|---|---|---|---|---|---|---|---|---|---|
| Yajurveda | 7 | 1 | | | 1 | 1 | | | | 4 |
| Adhvaryu | 5 | | 2 | | 3 | | | | | |
| Sukla: | | | | | | | | | | |
| Vājasaneya | 12 | 1 | 8 | 2 | | | | 1 | | |
| Mādhyamdina | 31 | 9 | 8 | 11 | 1 | 1 | | | 1 | |
| Kāṇva | 20 | 16 | 1 | 1 | 1 | 1 | | | | |
| Kṛṣṇa: | | | | | | | | | | |
| Taittiriya | 3 | 1 | | | 1 | | | 1 | | |
| Maitrāyaṇī | 6 | 1 | 1 | 3 | 1 | | | | | |

school was well versed in the *Vedas*, just as the *adhvaryu* Brāhmaṇa Magopadatta of the plates of Śīlāditya II, (Śīlāditya III?) dated in the year 352/c. 671-672 A.D., was learned in the *three Vedas*. A third Brāhmaṇa, Kāñcala, the beneficiary of the Navasari Plates of Cālukya Pulakeśirāja of *K.S.* 490/c. 739-740 A.D., although belonging to the Taittirīya *śākhā*, was learned in two *Vedas*.

It becomes quite clear from the above chart, that the *Śukla Yajus*, was by far the more popular of the two *Yajus* schools, there being seven times as many White Yajurvedic Brāhmaṇas, as Black Yajurvedic ones. While the former came to settle in Orissa, Gujarat, Madhya Pradesh, Maharashtra, Bengal, U.P. and Rajasthan, the latter cannot be found as immigrant donees either in Bengal or in Rajasthan. Even in the regions, where the Brāhmaṇa population incorporated members of both groups, there was a remarkable numerical difference. In Orissa, Gujarat and Madhya Pradesh, there were twenty-six, seventeen and fourteen adherents of the *White Yajus*. On the other hand, there were just three members of the *Black Yajus* in Madhya Pradesh, two in Orissa and one in Gujarat. This enormous gap can perhaps be explained by suggesting, that the systematic and orderly character of the *Śukla Yajus* was responsible for its attracting more students. This led to their being patronised in greater numbers by the ruling dynasties, than the Brāhmaṇas of the *Kṛṣṇa Yajus*.

While the Yajurvedic Brāhmaṇas numbered eighty-four in all, the charters yield the names of only twenty-eight migrant Brāhmaṇa students of the *Sāmaveda*. The *Sāmaveda* is mostly an anthology of hymns taken from the *Ṛgveda*, made up of those verses, which had to be chanted during the *soma* sacrifice.[146] The common name of the theologians of this *Veda* was Chhāndogya, and Kauthuma was one of its recensions.

Nine Brāhmaṇa adherents of the *Sāmaveda* are known to have migrated to Gujarat. Six Maitraka charters[147] record the names of eight such Brāhmaṇas, who studied the Chhāndoga *Śākhā*. The Prince of Wales Museum Plates of Govindarāja, of *Śaka* 732/c. 810 A.D., mentions a Sāmavedic Brāhmaṇa, who was given a village in Gujarat. In Orissa,[148] Jayastambha by a Dhenkanal grant, Raṇabhañja by his Aidā Plates of the fiftieth year and his Baud grant of his fifty-fourth year, Śatrubhañja by his Sonpur Plates, Mahābhavagupta I by the Vakratentalī charter of his third year, and three years later by his Patna grant, his son Mahāśivagupta I by his Cuttack Plates of his ninth year and Mahābhavagupta II by his Cuttack Plates of his third regnal year, settled eight Brāhmaṇas in different villages. They are described sometimes as merely students of the *Sāmaveda* or of the Chhāndoga-Kauthuma school, or sometimes as Chhāndogyas or as followers of the Kauthuma *śākhā*. Mention may be made here of the donee of the two sets of Patna Plates issued in the twenty-fourth and twenty-eighth years of Mahāśivagupta I. He was a student of the Gautama *śākhā*. According to Monier Williams, Gautama is the name of a Sāman.[149] So it may be assumed, that he too belonged to the Sāmavedic school, thereby bringing the number of Sāmavedins in Orissa, up to nine. In Madhya Pradesh, seven immigrants of the Kauthuma school, are found as donees of the Gaonri Plates of Vākpati II of *V.S.* 1030/c. 981 A.D. Three other charters, the Irda Plates of Nayapāla, the Amgachi grant of Vigrahapāla III of his twelfth year and the Bangaon Plates of his seventeenth year, benefited three Sāmavedic Brāhmaṇa migrants in Bengal and Bihar.

Fourteen migrant Bahvṛchas are recorded in the charters of the period. Four Maitraka plates and a Gurjara grant, contain the names of five of these Brāhmaṇas.[150] Four others figure as donees in land grants of Orissa.[151] Of these the affiliation of the donee of the Kalibhanā Plates of the thirty-fourth year of Mahābhavagupta I, was to the *Ṛgveda caraṇa*, which is rather strange. The Gaonri Plates of Vākpati II of *V.S.* 1038/c. 981 A.D., and the Depalpur grant of his nephew Bhoja, dated in *V.S.* 1079/c. 1022 A.D., prove the existence of three Bahvṛchas in Madhya Pradesh, who had come to settle in the Paramāra kingdom. Two Ṛgvedic Brāhmaṇas migrated to settle in Maharashtra. A grant of Sinda Ādityavarman of *Śaka* 887/c. 965-966 A.D., and the Thana Plates of Śīlāhāra Mummuṇirāja, dated *Śaka* 970/c. 1048-1049 A.D., refer to these two Bahvṛchas who received lands in Maharashtra.

Sometimes, the Ṛgvedic affiliation of the donee was further specified by stating, that he belonged to the Āśvalāyana *śākhā* of the *Ṛgveda*, or to the Bahvṝcha *caraṇa*. Āśvalāyana according to Weber, is one of the *Sūtra* texts of the *Ṛgveda*, both in the *Śrauta Sūtra* and *Gṛhya Sūtra* sections.[152] Six such Brāhmaṇas can be found in the records. The donees of a grant of Vakulamahādevī, the undated Baud grant of Raṇabhañja, and the Ādipur Plates of Narendrabhañja, all belonged to the Āśvalāvana *śākhā* of the *Ṛgveda* and settled in Orissa. Two others are known to have moved to Madhya Pradesh, where they appear as donees of the Gaonri Plates of Vākpati II of *V.S.* 1038/c. 981 A.D. and *V.S.* 1043/c. 986 A.D., and the Ujjain grant of Bhojadeva of *V.S.* 1078/c. 1021 A.D. The sixth Brāhmaṇa of the Āśvalāyana school, was one of the many donees of the Kaira Plates of Gurjara Dadda II, dated in *K.S.* 380/c. 629-630 A.D. from Gujarat.

Perhaps the least popular of all was the *Atharvaveda*. In spite of verses relating to magical formulae for protection against the baneful influences of divine powers, against diseases, animals and enemies, and invocations of healing herbs, and for luck in gaming, the *Atharvaveda* failed to find any considerable following among the Brāhmaṇas of the time. The Paippalāda *śākhā* referred to in two land grants, was one of its recensions.[153] One of the two charters in which reference is found to the *Atharvaveda*, comes from Gujarat. The Brāhmaṇa affiliated to this branch was one of the donees of the Kaira Plates of Dadda II of *K.S.* 380/c. 629-630 A.D. The other charter, though later than our period, comes from North Bengal. The Brāhmaṇa mentioned therein, was the donee of the Belwa Plates of the eleventh year of Vigrahapāla III.

*Geographical Distribution of Migrant Brāhmaṇas on the basis of four Vedas (c. 475-1030 A.D.)*

| | No. | Crissa | Gujarat | Madhya Pradesh | Maharashtra | Bengal | Bihar | U.P. | Rajasthan | South India |
|---|---|---|---|---|---|---|---|---|---|---|
| Yajurveda | 84 | 29 | 20 | 17 | 8 | 3 | - | 2 | 1 | 4 |
| Sāmaveda | 28 | 9 | 9 | 7 | — | 2 | 1 | | - | - |
| Ṛagvedá | 20 | 7 | 6 | 5 | 2 | – | | | | |
| Atharvaveda | 2 | | 1 | | — | 1 | | | – | |

Certain factors emerge from a study of the above chart. Undoubtedly, the *Yajurveda* had the largest number of adherents among the immigrant Brāhmaṇas. With the exception of Bihar, students of the *Yajurveda* can be found among Brāhmaṇa migrants in all other regions, Orissa, Gujarat, Madhya Pradesh, Maharashtra, Bengal, U.P., Rajasthan and in the Kanara district of Karnataka. Of these, the first three had the majority of Yajurvedic Brāhmaṇas, while elsewhere they were present in smaller numbers. In the case of Rajasthan, their number went down to just one.

Compared to these Yajurvedic Brāhmaṇas, members of the Sāmavedic school, were a little less than one-third the number of Yajurvedins in Orissa, and less than half in Gujarat and Madhya Pradesh. No Brāhmaṇas versed in the *Sāmaveda* during the period under review, came to live in Maharashtra, although eight of the *Yajurveda* belonging to its different schools, are known to have migrated there. In Bengal, the difference was slight, there being three Yajurvedic and two Sāmavedic Brāhmaṇas. In U.P. and Rajasthan there were no Sāmavedins, who had come from other regions. On the other hand, the only Brāhmaṇa donee who went to Bihar, whose Vedic affiliation is known, and who became a recipient of a grant, belonged to the Sāmavedic school. So the *Sāmaveda* was both confined to a smaller group of Brāhmaṇas than the *Yajurveda*, and was at the same time, chanted less. It should, however, be pointed out that in some instances Brāhmaṇas pertaining to particular *śākhās* of the *Yajurveda*, were nevertheless versed in the *Sāmaveda* as well. In the Bonda Plates of Mahāśiva Tīvara, the three Brāhmaṇas of the Maitrāyaṇī *śākhā* are further described as being priests of the *Caraka* section of the *Yajurveda* and *Sāmaveda*[154]. Likewise, the donee of the Jājilpārā grant of Gopāla II, was a student of the Mādhyaṁdina *śākhā* of the *White Yajus* and also a reciter in three varieties of the *Sāmaveda*[155]. In the Taltalai Plates of Dharmamahādevī, the Brāhmaṇa Śrī Padmanābha, having studied the Chhāndoga *śākhā* was at the time of the grant, a student of the Mādhyaṁdina *śākhā* of the *Yajurveda*[156].

Coming to the Ṛgvedic Brāhmaṇas, they were almost one-fourth the number of Yajurvedins in Orissa, a little less than one-third of their number in Gujarat and Madhya Pradesh, and one-fourth in Maharashtra. As far as the *Sāmaveda* was concerned, however, the difference was not so striking. In Orissa and Madhya Pradesh, there were nine and seven students of the *Sāmaveda* and seven and five members studying the *Ṛgveda*, respectively. In Gujarat, the six Ṛgvedic Brāhmaṇas were two-thirds of the number of the Sāmavedins, of whom there were nine. Two Brāhmaṇasof the *Ṛgveda* are known to have settled in Maharashtra but none of the *Sāmaveda*. In Bengal, Bihar, U.P. and Rajasthan, however, no immigrant Brāhmaṇas are known to have belonged to the Bahvṛcha section.

As for the *Atharvaveda*, its study was confined to just two geographical regions, Gujarat and Bengal. After its mention in the Kaira Plates of Dadda II of *K.S.* 380/c. 629-630 A.D., there is no reference to it in North India until much later. It is found again in the second half of the eleventh century, in the Belwa Plates of the eleventh year of Vigrahapāla III. This may mean that affiliation to this particular *Veda* was dying out. It may also be suggested, that the ruling houses viewed Brāhmaṇas of this school with disfavour, as a result of which they fail to appear in the land grant charters of the period.

A study of the chart further shows, that Brāhmaṇas affiliated to different Vedic *śākhās*, except those of the *Atharvaveda*, enjoyed the patronage of almost all the existing ruling families viz. the Maitrakas, Gurjaras, Pālas, Paramāras and those in Orissa. One exception is, however, noticeable in the case of the Rāṣṭrakūṭas. Of the charters available for this dynasty, wherein migrant Brāhmaṇas figure as donees, only five mention their Vedic qualifications. These records together refer to grants of villages to seven Brāhmaṇa adherents of the *Yajurveda*, specially the *Śukla Yajus*. Four of them, of the plates of Indra III, Govinda IV and Kṛṣṇa III, definitely belonged to the Vājasaneya school, while the other three, mentioned in the charter of Dantidurga, acted as *adhvaryus*. Although the point cannot be stressed too far, in the absence of the mention of Vedic *śākhās* of donees of all available records, it may be suggested, that the Rāṣṭrakūṭas extended their patronage, as regards immigrant Brāhmaṇas, almost exclusively to Yajurvedins.

As Brāhmaṇas emigrated from various places all over the country, it is difficult to assign particular Vedic *śākhās* to each of these regions. Hence only a few outstanding cases have been selected for discussion. It is also to be noted, that henceforth even those instances will be utilized, where the identity of the places where the migrants settled, is not established with certainty. Inscriptions show, that some of the original homes of emigrating Brāhmaṇas, were the seats of learning of particular *Vedas*. One such area was Ṭakāri. Six charters, a grant of Candella Dhaṅgadeva of *V.S.* 1055/c. 998 A.D., the Kalas Budrukh Plates of Bhillamarāja III of Śaka 948/c. 1025 A.D. the Santīragama grant of Daṇḍimahādevī, the Antirigam grant of Jayabhañja, the Baud charter of the fifty-eighth year of Raṇabhañja, and the Cuttack Plates of Mahābhavagupta I, dated in his thirty-first year, record grants of land to Brāhmaṇas from Ṭakāri. What is remarkable about them is, that all these donees belonged to the Bharadvāja *gotra* and at the same time to the *Śukla Yajurveda* school. They were either adherents of the Mādhyaṁdina or Kāṇva *śākhā* of the *Vājasaneya Saṁhitā* or merely Vājasaneya Brāhmaṇas of the *Yajurveda*. Another centre of emigration was Hastigrāma in Magadha. Of the three records which mention Brāhmaṇas from this region, only two, the Mārañja-Murā grant of Mahāśivagupta I and the Thana Plates of Śilāhāra Nāgārjuna, dated in *Śaka* 961/c. 1039 A.D., give the Vedic affiliation of their donees. Both belonged to the Parāśara *gotra* and the *Yajurveda*. So perhaps those belonging to one *gotra* in a particular place, used to read one recension or branch of a single *Veda*.

Of the thirty-six *gotras* available for migrating Brāhmaṇas, during the period under discussion, only two can with some degree of certainty, be linked to two Vedic schools. One was the Gautama *gotra*. Five Brāhmaṇa immigrants of this *gotra* are known. The *śākhās* of four of them have been mentioned in the Abhona Plates of Kalacuri, Śaṁkaragaṇa of *K.S.* 347/c. 596-597 A.D., the Gaonri Plates of Vākpati II of *V.S.* 1038/c. 981

A.D., the Patna Plates of the sixth year of Mahābhavagupta I, and his Nagpur Museum Plates issued in his eighth year. All these were students of the *Yajurveda*, the first of the Taittirīya *śākhā* of the *Kṛṣṇa Yajus*, and the others of the Mādhyaṁdina or Kāṇva *śākhā* of the *Śukla*. The second *gotra* was the Śārkarākṣi. Three adherents of this appear in a grant of Dharasena II of *saṁvat* 270/c. 589-590 A.D., one of Dharasena IV of the *Gupta saṁvat* 330/c. 649-650 A.D., and another of Kharagrāha II, dated in *G.S.* 337/c. 656-657 A.D. All these three Brāhmaṇas were well versed in the *Ṛgveda*. It is possible, that Brāhmaṇas of the Gautama and Śārkarākṣi *gotras* had a preference for and tended to attach themselves to the *Yajurveda* and *Ṛgveda*. The case of the only donee of the Cauli *gotra* may also be mentioned. He was one of the beneficiaries of the Kaira Plates of Dadda II of *K.S.* 380/c. 629-630 A.D., and was a student of the Paippalāda *śākhā* of the *Atharvaveda*.

In conclusion then, it can be said, that the *Yajurveda* was by far, the most widely read by the migrant Brāhmaṇas of the period, its members far exceeding those of the three other *Vedas* put together. Of its two divisions, it was the *Śukla Yajus* which due to its clarity and organized nature, attracted the largest group of Brāhmaṇas. The *Sāma* and *Ṛg* being for the greater part, collections of hymns, did not afford as wide a scope, as did the *Yajus*. As for the *Atharvaveda*, magical formulae for protection and prosperity, were not enough to win for its adherents, the patronage of the ruling houses.

**Knowledge of Other Subjects**

Mention should be made here of some Brāhmaṇas who are specifically described as having studied the *Vedāṅgas* and the *Śrutis*. Among these were Govindabhaṭṭa known from the Kolhapur Copper Plates of Akālavarṣadeva of *Śaka* 882/c. 960 A.D., Bhaṭṭa Mātṛgaṇa of the Hilol Plates of the year 470, and Ādityabhaṭṭa, Yajñubhaṭṭa and Khaṇḍidevabhaṭṭa of the Cheedivalasa Plates of Eastern Gaṅga Devendravarman of *Gaṅga* 397/c. 893-894 A.D.

Subjects like *Mīmāṁsā Vyākaraṇa* or grammar and *Tarka* or logic too, formed part of the education of some migrant Brāhmaṇas. Kṛṣṇādityaśarman, a donee of the Bangarh grant of Mahīpāla I had knowledge of these, in addition to the branch of the *Veda* in which he was an expert. Likewise, another Brāhmaṇa, mentioned in the Irda Plates of Nayapāla, claimed the same academic attainments.

Perhaps science too, was included in the course of study. Vasantācārya, the donee of the Dharmapuri grant of Vākpati II, dated *V.S.* 1031/c. 974 A.D., is said to have been well versed in *jñāna* and *vijñāna*. Of course the term may conjointly mean merely, that he was a learned and knowledgeable person, although the possibility of his having learnt some science, cannot be totally ruled out. Besides this, the reference to the *Kāladeśī* Devu in the Kalibhanā Plates of the thirty-fourth year of Mahābhavagupta I, to the family of astrologers in the Antirigam Plates of Yaśabhañja, and to the *nāyaka* and *senāpati* in the Yādava charter from Devalili, and the Siyadoni Inscription of Devapāla show, that astrology and military science, must have formed a part of the curriculum of the times.

Inscriptions do not directly mention the study of subjects like literature or poetics, by migrant Brāhmaṇas. But the literature of the period introduces us to migrant poets and dramatists like Bhāravi, Bhavabhūti, Indurāja, Rājaśekhara and Bilhaṇa. It would not be wrong to say, that all these Brāhmaṇas definitely had good knowledge of poetics, as well as literary training, without which their compositions could hardly have achieved high standards. It may be mentioned here that the Mahua Inscription of Vatsarāja, and the Mandakila Tal Inscription of *V.S.* 1043/c. 986 A.D., are silent about the academic qualifications of their composers Iśāna and Vimalamati, although Durlabharāja the father of the latter, is said to have been well versed in literature. However, it cannot be denied, that they too must have had a good knowledge of both grammar and literature, without which they could hardly have been appointed as composers of *praśastis*.

**Participation in Religious Observances**

The close affinity of immigrant Brāhmaṇas with religious and auspicious occasions, becomes evident from the days on which grants were made to them. Rāṣṭrakūṭa Indra III and Govinda IV bestowed lands on their donees during *paṭṭabandha* i.e. the crowning ceremony, or on the occasion of the installation of images of gods. The eclipses of the sun or the moon, and the full-moon day were popular for this purpose. The grant of Sinda Ādityavarman of *Śaka* 887/c. 965-966 A.D., the Thana Plates of Sīlāhāra Nāgārjuna, dated in the *Śaka* year 961/c. 1039 A.D., and some charters from Orissa, like the Santiragama grant of Daṇḍimahādevī, the Baud grant of the fifty-eighth year of Raṇabhañja, the Cuttack Plates of Mahābhavagupta II of his third year, and the Cheedivalasa Plates of Eastern Gaṅga Devendravarman of the *Gaṅga* year 397/c. 893-894 A.D., all refer to the *Ravi-saṁkrānti* (The Sun's entry into any sign of the Zodiac) as the fitting day for grants to be made to Brāhmaṇas. The donees of the Navasari Plates of Jayabhaṭa III of *K.S.* 456/c.705-706 A.D., the Gaonri Plates of Vākpati II of V.S. 1038/c. 981 A.D., the Mahudi Plates of Bhoja of *V.S.* 1074/c. 1017 A.D., the Angul Copper Plate of Śāntikara, and of the two sets of plates of Śīlāhāra Mummuṇirāja, of the years *Śaka* 970/c. 1048-1049 A.D., and *Śaka* 971/c. 1049 A.D., received their gifts when the moon was in eclipse. The full-moon day or *pūrṇimā* too, in the months of *Vaiśākha*, as in the Prince of Wales Museum Plates of Govindarāja of *Śaka* 732/c. 810 A.D., or *Śrāvaṇa*, as in the Sāngli grant of Govinda IV, dated in the *Śaka* year 855/c. 933 A.D., or *Kārtika*, as in the charter of Dhaṅga of *V.S.* 1055/c. 998 A.D., was another suitable day for grants to immigrant Brāhmaṇas. Likewise, at the time of *tithis* like the *udgayana* or winter solstice, as in the Gaonri Plates of Vākpati II of *V.S.* 1043/c. 986 A.D. and *uttarāyaṇa* or summer solstice, as mentioned in the Jājilpārā grant of Gopāla II, the Taltalai Plates of Dharmamahādevī, and the Phulsara Plates of Kīrttirājadeva, Brāhmaṇas became beneficiaries. While the Jodhpur grant of Siṁharāja of *V.S.* 1054/c. 997 A.D., refers to *Makara-saṁkrānti*, the Bangarh grant of Mahīpāla names the *Viṣuva-saṁkrānti*, as the time for making donations. Sometimes, on socio-religious occasions, for example, the performance of funerary rites, a grant could be made to a Brāhmaṇa. The Benares Plates of Kalacuri Karṇa of the *Cedi* year 793/c. 1042 A.D., record, that while performing the *śrāddha* ceremony of his father Gāṅgeyadeva, Karṇa made over a village to a migrant Brāhmaṇa. This, however, may have been in the nature of fees to the officiating Brāhmaṇa.

**Family-life and Position of Women**

As regards the family-life of the immigrant Brāhmaṇas, few ideas can be formed from the little evidence provided both by inscriptions and literature. The head of the immigrant Brāhmaṇa family, might have been the father, as was usual in ancient India. What lends support to this view is the fact, that hardly ever in the land-grant charters referring to immigrant Brāhmaṇas, do we come across the name of the mother, or the mother's family of the donee. It is always, the father, grandfather and great-grandfather who are mentioned. The one exception where the mother's name is mentioned, is in the Guakuci Plates of Indrapāla. Apart from this, it was only when a Brāhmaṇa was being eulogized as in the Silimpur Inscription, or if he figured as the donor, as in the later Bangaon Plates of the time of Vigrahapāla III, did his mother merit a mention in his family-tree.

A family seems to have been fairly large. A man might have had as many as six sons, the largest number known from the available charters. In the Asiatic Society's Plates of Gayāḍatuṅga, which record a collective grant, small units are ascribed to groups of brothers, the largest being six. This, however, does not preclude the possibility of there having been more than six uterine brothers. Besides, there might have been daughters as well, although the charters are usually silent about them.

The joint family system seems to have been the order of the day. A plate of Dharasena I from Kathiawar, refers to the brothers Ajuna and Mankasvāmin, who were to share a field and a well among themselves.[157] By the Lunsadi Plates of Śīlāditya II (Śīlāditya III?) of *G.S.* 350/c. 669-670 A.D., a pond and some pieces of land were given conjointly to the uterine brothers Īśvara and Bhaṭṭi. As has been said earlier, the Asiatic Society's Plates of Gayāḍatuṅga, refer to small shares of a village being enjoyed by groups of brothers. Another charter shows, that three brothers Duvanandī, Thiranandī and

Bhaganandī were made co-owners of a village in the Kanara district of Karnataka by the Hindol Plates of Vīra Pracaṇḍadeva. Granting of common plots of lands to brothers means, that they were to share the income accruing from the village, and it is possible that they may have lived together.

Except for a single instance, it is not known whether a migrant Brāhmaṇa had wives belonging to different *varṇas*. The term *pāraśava* has been used in the *Harṣacarita* of Bāṇabhaṭṭa, to describe Candrasena, a brother of the author.[958] *Pāraśava* means a person, whose father is a Brāhmaṇa and whose mother belongs to the Śūdra caste. The fact that Candrasena is said to have brought Bāṇa some news while the latter was resting at home, perhaps shows, that sons of one father, by wives of different castes, lived together as a single family unit. This speaks well for the close affinity that existed even between half-brothers.

Family ties between different branches seem to have been fairly strong. Members were bound together by feelings of affection. The Mudgapadra grant of Śryāśraya Śīlāditya, of *K.S.* 420/c. 668-669 A.D., refers to the grant of a village to two cousins, Revāditya and Varasyaka, whose mothers were sisters. Revāditya's father Bambhasvāmin, had brought up Varasyaka, who is described as a *putraka* to him, and whose father is not mentioned. It seems therefore, that Varasyaka's father was possibly not alive at least some time before the grant, and Bambhasvāmin had taken him into his own family and had brought him up like a son.

Various branches of the same family, at times are known to have settled in the same region. A Maitraka charter, the Goras C.P. of Dhruvasena II of *G.S.* 313/c. 634 A.D., bears witness to this fact. In it the two donees Devakula and Bhāda, were cousins, as Bhāda has been described as being the nephew of Brāhmaṇa Śarmma, the father of Devakula. As both the donees were emigrants from Valāpadra, and residents of Gorakeśa, it may be assumed, that these two families lived close to one another. Another charter, the Asiatic Society's Plates of Gayāḍatuṅga, records a collective grant. Eleven major shares were made, each going either to a single

Brāhmaṇa, or to a group of Brāhmaṇa brothers, e.g. the two brothers—Trivikrama and Puruṣottama, or Rāmadeva and his five brothers, and Manorathadevaśarman and his two brothers. In the last two units, the names of the brothers are absent. The plates mention the *gotra* of only the first donee, Bhaṭṭaputra Dādo. D.C. Sircar the editor of the charter, is of the opinion, that the rest of the donees may have belonged to the same *gotra* and the same family. If this view is accepted, it may also be assumed, that they had all emigrated from Ahichchhatra, the original home of Dādo. They came to Oḍra-*viṣaya*, and while living there, received a village from Gayāḍatuṅga. Of course, each unit was to enjoy the village according to the share stipulated in the charter. However, they were probably on good terms with one another. From their original habitat Ahichchhatra, all of them moved to the same region and ultimately settled down as donees in the same village.

Inscriptions and literature of the period, provide very little information about the women in the household of the immigrant Brāhmaṇas. Anurādhā, the mother of the donee Devādeva of the Guakuci Plates of Indrapāla, was born in a *Kulīna* or high class Brāhmaṇa family. She herself was of a noble character, in which respect she has been compared to Arundhatī, wife of Vaśiṣṭha.[159] Kaliparvā was the mother of Prahāsa of the Silimpur Inscription. She was the great-grand-daughter of a *Kavi-prava(ba)rhāgrya* or foremost among poets.[160]

So on the whole, the family life of the migrant Brāhmaṇas was marked by bonds of affection between different members. It is likely, that the womenfolk were largely dependent on their male relatives. Inscriptions give us no idea as to whether they received any education. Even if they did enjoy a respectable place in their homes, they played no part in public life.

Literature shows, that immigrant Brāhmaṇas sometimes had matrimonial relationship with non-Brahmanical royal families. Rājaśekhara in his *Karpūramañjarī*, describes his wife Avantisundarī as the crest-garland of the Chauhan family[161], she was therefore, a Rajput princess.

It is rather difficult to infer from inscriptions, whether migrant Brāhmaṇas were polygamous or monogamous. When recording the names of Brāhmaṇa brothers as donees, the charters with one exception, are silent as to whether they were sons of the same mother, or whether they were half-brothers. The exception is the case of the Lunsadi Plates of Śīlāditya II (Śīlāditya III?) of *G.S.* 350/c. 669-670 A.D. Therein the two brothers Īśvara and Bhaṭṭi have been qualified thus-*sodarabhrātṝbhyām*[162], or uterine brothers. This or any similar term indicating the relationship on the mother's side, of two or more Brāhmaṇa brothers, is absent from all other charters. So on the basis of its specific mention in this grant, it may be suggested that Īśvara and Bhaṭṭi, had other brothers as well, who were sons of their father, by a wife, other than their own mother. Apart from this, there is nothing in the inscriptions, pointing to polygamy among the immigrant Brāhmaṇas.

**Nomenclature**

A study of the nomenclature of immigrant Brāhmaṇas reveals some interesting facts. As regards their proper names, sometimes the names of gods were given to the Brāhmaṇas. Although the *Mānavagṛhyasūtra* lays down, that the name of a deity was not to be given directly to an individual (vide Kane, *IHQ*, XIV, p. 233), but was to be followed by another word, this rule was not always strictly observed. Brāhmaṇas called Sūrya, Īśvara, Gadādhara, Kṛṣṇa, Viṣṇu, Nārāyaṇa, Vāsudeva, Keśava and Dāmodara, are found in the records of the period. Sometimes Brāhmaṇas were given names consisting of two parts. This was in keeping with Brahmanical tradition. Kane explains, that some *Gṛhya Sūtras* like the *Āpastamba* say, that a name should have two parts, the first being a noun and the second, a derivative from a verb, generally a past passive participate ending in "ta",[163] e.g. datta. Names like Yajñadatta and Śrīdharadatta in a grant of Śīlāditya III of *G.S.* 346/c. 666 A.D., conformed to this rule. It is noteworthy, that Yajñadatta had the second name Prakāśa. Likewise, another Brāhmaṇa in the Jesar Plates of Śīlāditya III, dated in the *Gupta* year 347/c. 666-667 A.D., was called Saggala, whose second name was also Prakāśa. According to the *Taittirīya Saṁhitā*, a Brāhmaṇa who has two names, prospers,[164] or is successful. The word Prakāśa meaning light, when used in the context of a man, possibly indicates, that he is famous or celebrated in some field or the other. G.C. Acharya who edited the plates of *G.S.* 346/c. 666 A.D. translates *Yajñadatta Prakāśa-dvināma-yajñaya*, as Yajñadatta, popularly known as Yajña.[165] However, it may be suggested that the two Brāhmaṇas Yajñadatta and Saggala might have acquired fame due to some reason, and in keeping with Brahmanical tradition, might have assumed the name Prakāśa.

The names of two Brāhmaṇas in a grant of Candella Dhaṅga of *V.S.* 1055/c. 998 A.D., show a deviation. The donee of the plates was Rudra Śrī Yaśodhara, son of Rudra Jayakumāra. The fact that Rudra occurs in the names of both father and son, may mean either, that it was a family name or that it was indicative of something which is not revealed by the charter. In later years, Rudra was to become a lineage name, like so many others in Bangal.

Sometimes a Brāhmaṇa was named after a place. It is not improbable that those names also indicate their original homes, as we find in some parts of modern South India. The Navalakhi Plates of Śīlāditya I of *G.S.* 286/c. 545-546 (?) (c. 605-606 A.D.), record a collective grant made to a large number of Brāhmaṇa immigrants from Samgapurī or Shahapur, near Junagadh. According to H.M. Bhadkamkar who edited the plates, some of these names may be indicative of the villages to which Brāhmaṇas originally belonged. One of them Guhilabhaṭṭi, has been traced by him to Gohilwadpranta of Kathiawar. In another charter, the Bonda Plates of Mahāśiva Tīvara, the two migrant donees, were Avanti-Vikramopādhyāya and Lāṭa-Phalihasvāmin.

At times, however, these place-names were not directly attached to the proper name of a Brāhmaṇa. In a grant of Eastern Gaṅga Devendravarman, the Cheedivalasa Plates of *Gaṅga* 397/c. 893-894 A.D., the three donees have been described as *Vaṅgajebhya*, which shows that their ancestral homes were in Bengal. Another charter, the Muṁdaka grant of Caulukya Bhīmadeva I of *V.S.* 1086/c. 1030 A.D., speaks of an

*Udīcya* Brāhmaṇa who settled in the Varddhi-*viṣaya* of Gujarat. *Udīcya* was probably used to denote a Northerner. Even when Brāhmaṇas migrated from Rajasthan and Mālwa to the Gujarat area between c. 1000 and 1300 A.D., some of them have been described as *Udīcyas* or Northerners.[166] Literature provides us with a third name of this kind. Indurāja who wrote a commentary on the *kāvyālaṁkāra* of Udbhaṭa, and who had migrated to Kashmir, added the suffix Konkana[167] to his name, indicating that he was an original inhabitant of the Ratnagiri District of Maharashtra. Mention must be made here of two more names from the Navalakhi Plates of Śīlāditya I of *G.S.* 286/c. 545-546 (?) c. 605-606 A.D. According to H.M. Bhadkamkar, the names Bappaṭaka and Bhānu of two migrant donees of the charter, are in modern times, names of two Kokanastha families viz. Bapat and Bhanu.[168] He also explains that although the two Brāhmaṇas like their co-donees, had emigrated from Shahapur near Junagadh, at present, the names Bapat and Bhanu are found only among the Dakṣiṇī Brāhmaṇas, and no longer in Gujarat and Kathiawar.

Frequently in the records, one comes across the word *bhaṭṭa* used both as a prefix e.g. Bhaṭṭa Āchchaḍa, Bhaṭṭa Brahmadhara, Bhaṭṭa Mahattama Sādhāraṇa, and also as a suffix e.g. Siddhapabhaṭṭa, Ādityabhaṭṭa, Yajñubhaṭṭa and Khaṇḍidevabhaṭṭa. *Bhaṭṭa* was attached to the name of an individual, so as to make it obvious, that he was a Brāhmaṇa, just as *bhaṭṭaputra* or *bhaṭaputra* has been added to names like Bhaṭṭaputra Velluka, Bhaṭṭaputra Daṇḍapāṇi Bhaṭṭaputra Sānthakara and Bhaṭaputra Ugranandī. In other words, *bhaṭṭa* was a term to be used exclusively for Brāhmaṇas.

Brāhmaṇas used the titles *śarman* and *svāmin*. Unlike *bhaṭṭa*, they were never used as prefix, but only as suffix or titles. The *Pāraskaragṛhyasūtra* and the *Manusmṛti*, both prescribe the addition of the *upapada śarman* to the name of a Brāhmaṇa. As Manu puts it, *śarman* indicates happiness.[169] A large number of migrant Brāhmaṇas with names ending in *śarman* can be found in the charters.

In the early days of the period under survey, however, *śarman* was not frequently attached to Brahmanical names.

None of the immigrant donees of the Gurjara grants, or those of the viceregal Cāḻukya family seem to have adopted it. Only those of the Maitraka charters, the Navalakhi Plates of Śīlāditya I of *G.S.* 286/c. 545-546 (?) (c. 605-606 A.D.), the Amreli Museum Plates of Dhruvasena II of the year 323/c. 642-643 A.D., and a grant of Dharasena IV, mention Brāhmaṇas like Kumāraśarman, Khaṇḍaśarman, Govaśarman, Agniśarman, Somaśarman and Aditiśarman. One Guhila charter from Rajasthan, speaks of the Brāhmaṇa Āsaṅgaśarman, who was benefited by a grant of Guhila Bhāvihita of the *Harṣa* year 48. In later years, however, *śarman* came to be more widely used, as can be seen from some grants from Orissa,[170] and a grant of Paramāra Bhoja.[171] In Bengal, however, it became the most popular name-ending. Three records available from Bengal,[172] two of the Pālas and one of a Kamboja chief, give the names of immigrant Brāhmaṇas ending in *śarman*. Strangely enough, this is not the case with any of the donees of the Rāṣṭrakūṭas or the Śīlāhāras.

At times, however, the title was absent in one generation, although present in others. Devaśarman, one of the donees of the second set of Talcher Plates of Gayāḍatuṅga, was the son of Pauma and grandson of Dhanaśarman. Likewise in the Irda Plates of Nayapāla, a family of Brāhmaṇas is mentioned. Their names in descending order are as follows, Divākaraśarman, Prabhākaraśarman, Anukulamiśra, and Aśvatthaśarman, the donee of the charter. Probably *śarman* was the title of both these families. Pauma of the Talcher Plates and Anukula of the Irda Plates did not adopt it for some reason. Anukula preferred to call himself *miśra*, which usually in the present day, is like *śarman* or *śarmā* a Brahmanical surname.

Unlike the two examples noted above, in some other cases, it is perhaps possible to trace when *śarman* actually began to be used as a family name. In the Indian Museum Plates of Devendravarman of the *Gaṅga* year 308/c. 804-806 A.D., the donee Govindaśarman, was the son of Bhaṭṭa Nārāyaṇa, just as Vāmanasvāmiśarman of the Angul Plates of Śāntikara, was the son of Padmanābha. Gopāla II by his Jājilpārā grant, donated a village to Bhaṭṭaputra Yājñika Śrīdharaśarman, son of Bhaṭṭaputra Śrīgarbha and grandson of Bhaṭṭaputra Nāga.

Pramāra Bhoja by his Mahudi Plates issued in *V.S.* 1074/c. 1017 A.D., bestowed a village on Mārkaṇḍaśarman, son of Bhaṭṭa Śrīpati and grandson of Bhaṭṭa Gokarṇṇa. It may be suggested, that Govindaśarman, Vāmanasvāmiśarman, Śrīdharaśarman, and Mārkaṇḍaśarman, were perhaps introducing the name-ending *śarman* for the first time in their respective families.

Less popular than *śarman* was *svāmin*, known from four Maitraka grants, a Gurjara, record and the Bonda Plates of Mahāśiva Tīvara. *Svāmin* as a part of the Brāhmaṇa's name seems to have become rare in the later period. Proceeding on the line, that the addition of *Svāmin* to the names of both father and son would indicate that it was a family name, the two sets of Nogawa Plates of Dhruvasena II of *G.S.* 320/c. 639-640 A.D., and *saṁvat* 321/c. 640-641 A.D., seem to be the only ones to conform to this rule. But Mankasvāmin of the plate of Dharasena I, was the son of Brāhmaṇa Guhadḥya, and Devasvāmin of the Navasari Plates of Jayabhaṭa III of *K.S.* 456/c. 705-706 A.D., was the son of the Brāhmaṇa Datta. The names of the fathers of Boppasvāmin of the Navalakhi charter of Śīlāditya I, and of Lāṭa-Phalihasvāmin of the Bonda Plates, are not mentioned.

It should, however, be pointed out, that the word *Svāmin* which indicates a spiritual preceptor, or learned Brāhmaṇa, may well have been used as an epithet for some of the immigrants. This can be true of Lāṭa-Phalihasvāmin of the Bonda Plates. He was well versed in the Maitrāyaṇī *śākhā* of the *Yajurveda* and at the same time has been described as a priest of the *Caraka* section of the *Yajurveda* and *Sāmaveda*. Moreover, one of his co-donees. Vikrama was a migrant *upādhyāya* from Avanti. It would not therefore be wrong to suggest, that Lāṭa-Phalihasvāmin, had added the appellation *svāmin* to his name, as a proof of his vocation and learning.

Two other professional epithets for Brāhmaṇa teachers were *upādhyāya* and *ācārya*. Vikrama of the Bonda Plates of Mahāśiva Tīvara. Nannaka of the Jodhpur grant of Siṁharāja of *V.S.* 1054 c. 997 A.D., Viṣṇusomācārya of a grant of Anantavarman of the *Gaṅga* year 204/c. 700 A.D.,

Vasantācārya of the Dharmapuri grant of Vākpati II, issued in *V.S.* 1031/c. 974 A.D., and Dīrghācārya and his father Durlabhācārya of the Balera Plates of Mūlarāja I of *V.S.* 1051/c. 994-995 A.D., were Brāhmaṇa teachers who had adopted *upādhyāya* and *ācārya* to indicate their occupation.

Another epithet *dīkṣita* could be used in a wider context than *upādhyāya* or *ācārya*. Literally meaning consecrated or initiated, the term could be applied to a priest engaged in *dīkṣā*, may be for a religious ceremony, to one who had taken a vow, or to a teacher, and to a pupil.[173] Several *dīkṣitas* are known from the records. The Lohaner Plates of Pulakeśin II of *Śaka* 552/c. 630 A.D., refer to the Brāhmaṇa student Dāmadīkṣita, while the Jesar Plates of Śīlāditya III of *G.S.* 347/c. 666-667 A.D., mention Saggala, who has been qualified as a *dīkṣita*. One *dīkṣita* known from Orissa, was Puṇḍarīkaśarman of the Nibinnā grant of Mahāśivagupta I. Two others Mahindrahūti Dīkṣita and Vāsuhūti Dīkṣita were donees of a plate of Devānandadeva. Maharashtra became the home of three Brāhmaṇa immigrants also called *Dīkṣita*—Keśava Dīkṣita of the Sāngli grant of Govinda IV of *Śaka* 855/c. 933 A.D., and Yajña Dīkṣita and Sūdana Dīkṣita of a grant of Mummuṇirāja issued in *Śaka* 971/c. 1049 A.D. It is difficult to say whether all these Brāhmaṇas were teachers or pupils or even priests. But *dīkṣita* in the instances cited above, was probably more a qualifying epithet, than a family title.

The Betma grant of Bhoja of *V.S.* 1076/c. 1019 A.D., the Aidā Plates of Raṇabhañja and the Thana Plates of Śīlāhāra Nāgārjuna of *Śaka* 961/c. 1039 A.D., refer to Brāhmaṇas who had *Paṇḍita* added to their names. *Paṇḍita* is a term generally used to indicate a learned man, although in the present day it also applies to a priest. Hence in either case, *Paṇḍita* too seems to have been an educational or religious epithet. It is notable, however, that no immigrant Brāhmaṇa in the charters prior to the tenth and eleventh centuries, has been described as a *Paṇḍita*.

Another epithet, which is definitely a religious one is known from the Jājilpārā grant of Gopāla II. The donee Śrīdharaśarman has been given the full name of Bhaṭṭaputra

*Yājñika* Śrīdharaśarman. Perhaps Śrīdhara was a priest engaged in the performance of sacrifices, hence the epithet *Yājñika*.

Brāhmaṇa name-endings were, however, not confined to merely *śarman* and *svāmin*. Maitraka charters give suffixes like *vasu, mitra* and *datta* added to the names of the immigrant Brāhmaṇas mentioned in them. In the Navalakhi Plates of Śīlāditya I of *G.S.* 286/c. 545-546 (?) (c. 605-606 A.D.), two of the donees are named Ādityavasu and Indravasu. As Āditya and Indra are the names of two Vedic gods, *vasu* may have been used as a title by these Brāhmaṇas. The other suffix *mitra* is known from a grant of Dharasena II of *saṁvat* 270/c. 589-590 A.D., and one of Dharasena IV of the *Gupta saṁvat* 330/c. 649-650 A.D., where Brāhmaṇas called Viṣṇumitra, Nārāyaṇamitra and Keśavamitra are found. The suffix *mitra* attached to these names, can just as well be part of the proper names of the Brāhmaṇas, or merely their hereditary title. Viṣṇu, Nārāyaṇa and Keśava, taken individually, are all names of a god of the Vaiṣṇavite pantheon, in which case it would be wrong to say, that *mitra* was the title of the three Brāhmaṇas. But by adding the word *mitra* to the names, they become, friend of Viṣṇu, friend of Nārāyaṇa and friend of Keśava, which again are complete units in themselves. So it is rather difficult to come to a definite conclusion, regarding the use of the suffix *mitra* in these charters. Coming to the third suffix *datta* a grant of Śīlāditya II (Śīlāditya III?) of *saṁvat* 352/c. 671-672 A.D., records the name of a donee Magopadatta, son of Kikkaka. It is not possible to explain the meaning of his name, which seems to have been a complete whole and *datta* attached to it was a part of that unit, and not a title. It may be pointed out, that *datta* according to Yama, was a name-ending prescribed for the Vaiśyas and not for Brāhmaṇas.[174] Apparently this rule too, like so many others, was not always observed faithfully by the Brāhmaṇas of the time.

In the tenth and eleventh centuries, other suffixes occur, like *kara, ghoṣa, dhara, pāla* and *nandī*, some of which are usually titles of Kāyasthas in modern times. The Mārañja-Murā grant of the third year of Mahāśivagupta I, gives the name of the Brāhmaṇa Yaśakara, son of Śāntikara. Its grammatical errors are not taken into consideration. Yaśa and Śānti, mean fame and peace. Though *kara* may have been the lineage name of this family, yet it is very likely that here it was not so.

Two other suffixes, *ghoṣa* found in the Asiatic Society's Plates of Gayāḍatuṅga, in connection with Śrīghoṣa, and *pāla* which occurs in the Dasapalla grant of Śatrubhañja, as Ājapāla, were probably parts of the Brāhmaṇas' proper names. The name Kuladevapālabhaṭṭa, son of Devapāla and grandson of Samarapāla, found in the Jurerpur Plates of Devānanda, does not clearly prove that the *pāla* title was borne by a Brāhmaṇa. Of course Samara means a fight or a battle, Deva means god and Kuladeva the guardian deity of a family. However, the suffix *bhaṭṭa* added to the name of the donee perhaps indicates, that *pāla* was not their family title.

Coming to the suffix *dhara*, in two grants, one of Candella Dhaṅga of *V.S.* 1055/c. 998 A.D., and another, the Tasapaikera charter of Raṇabhañja, two Brāhmaṇas are found, Yaśodhara and Śrīdhara, respectively, whose fathers Jayakumāra and Vāpula did not have *dhara* attached to their names. Yaśa, and not Yaśo means fame. Śrī meaning fortune or the goddess Lakṣmī, is not by itself, a very appropriate name for a man. Taken with the word *dhara*, however, they would mean one who holds fame and one who harbours fortune. Hence *dhara* here, cannot be taken as the title of these Brāhmaṇas.

In another charter of the Kanara region, we come across the suffix *nandī*. Here, Kulika Vipracandra, handed a village to the Brāhmaṇa Ugranandī, whose father was Vīranandī and grandfather was Suvananandī. Vīra means brave, while Ugra gives the feeling of harshness. Adding the suffix *nandī* gives them no extra meaning. Hence *nandī* may have been their family name. Although in the present day, Brāhmaṇas having the title *nandī* are known, it was an unusual lineage name for Brāhmaṇas in early times. The Nidhanpur Copper Plates of Bhāskaravarman, include among the long list of Brāhmaṇas, just one, named Gopāla Nandī Svāmin.

It may be pointed out, that the titles discussed above, *vasu, mitra, datta, kara* and *ghoṣa*, are in modern times no longer used by Brāhmaṇa families. In modern Bengal these are titles of non-Brāhmaṇas. *Pāla* is at present usually adopted by sculptors, while *dhara* belongs to the non-Kāyasthas. So what at one time may have been the lineage names of immigrant Brāhmaṇas in Gujarat, Bengal and Orissa, underwent a change, and in later years, became confined to Bengal, as mostly the titles of the Kāyasthas.

In conclusion it can be said, that immigrant Brāhmaṇas can be accredited with some contributions. Bringing with them their ancient traditions, they helped to colonize new areas. A social set-up sanctioned by the law-books grew up, and helped to bring a picture of uniformity to regions like Gujarat, Bengal and Orissa. As the Brāhmaṇas carried with them, their knowledge of the *Vedas* and of literature, poetics, grammar and philosophy, they helped in the spread of education and culture. Some among them left behind works which have become immortal. Advocates of closely knit family life, they encouraged people to live together in harmony. At the same time, some of them made a new beginning, by adopting various designations which in later years were to become family names of both Brāhmaṇas and non-Brāhmaṇas. Besides, the trend of naming groups of people on the basis of their original homes also began with them. On the whole, therefore, their advent in their new areas of settlement, proved to a certain extent, to be beneficial for society.

## References

1. Brough, J., *ERSGP*, p.2.
2. Kane, P.V., *HDS*, II, p. 489.
3. Ghurye, G.S., *TBIGC*, p. 7.
4. Kane, P.V., *JBBRAS*, XI, p. 2.
5. *Ibid*, XI, p. 11.
6. Brough, J., *op. cit.*, pp. 3-7.
7. Ghurye, G.S., *op. cit.*, p. 158.
8. Brough, J., *op. cit.*, p. 25.
9. *Ibid.*, p. 23.
10. Kane, P.V., *JBBRAS*, XI, p. 5.
11. Kane, P.V., *HDS*, II, pp. 479-481.

12. *Ibid.*, p. 486.
13. Ghurye, G.S., *op. cit.*, p. 125.
14. *Ibid.*, p. 152.
15. It must be mentioned here, that in the following pages, at first the *gotras* of only such migrant Brāhmaṇas will be discussed, the identification of whose new homes is certain. Consequently, only thirty-three *gotras* have been examined. The other three, Upamanyu, Autathya and Jātukarṇa, will be considered later, as the places to which their adherents came to settle, have not yet been definitely located.
16. *EI*, XXV, p. 161.
17. *Ibid.*, (1939-1940), p. 163, cf. fn. 19.
18. *IHQ*, XIII, (1937), p. 431.
19. *OHRJ*, IV, p. 67, Ganjam grant of Śatrubhañja; *EI*,. XVIII, p. 298, Antirigam grant of Yaśabhañja, *Ibid.*, XIX, p. 41, Antirigam grant of Jayabhañja.
20. *IA*, I. p. 14, Copper Plate of Dharasena I; *JBBRAS*, N.S.I, p. 28, grant of Śīlāditya I, *GS*. 287/c. 608 A.D., *Ibid*, p. 69, grant of Dhruvasena II, *GE* 312/c. 631-632 A.D., *CII*, IV, pp. 75 and 78, Sankheda Plates of Dadda II, *KS*. 392/c. 642 A.D., *JBBRAS*, N.S.I., p. 73, grant of Śīlāditya III, *GS*. 346/c. 666 A.D., *EI*, XXVII, p. 197, PWM, Plates of Dadda III, *KS*. 427/c. 676-677 A.D.
21. *EI*, XXXVI, p. 307, grant of Vakulamahādevī; *Ibid*, XXXIV, p. 96, second set of Talcher Plates of Gayāḍatuṅga, *OHRJ*, XI, p. 155; *EI*, XXXVII, p. 257; Aidā Plates of Raṇabhañja; *EI*, XXV, pp. 147 and 157, Ādipur Plates of Narendrabhañja; *OHRJ*, XI, p. 192, *IO*, IV, p. 124. Gaintala Plates of Mahābhavagupta I.
22. *CII*, IV, p. 57, Kaira Plates of Dadda II, *KS*. 380/c. 629-630 A.D., *IA*, XII, p. 156; *JASB*, N.S. VIII, p. 292, Baroda Plates of Karkka Suvarṇavarṣa *Śaka* 734/c. 812 A.D., *EI*, XXXVII, p. 37, Bhadresar Plates of Bhīmadeva I, *V.S.* 1117/c. 1060 A.D., *Ibid.*, XXIII, p. 108, Gaonri Plates of Vākpati II, *V.S.* 1038/c. 981 A.D., *Ibid*, XXXVII, p. 74, Yādava charter from Devalili.
23. *Kādambarī* (ed.) M.R. Kale (1924), p. 2, verse 10.

24. *EI*, VIII, p. 188, Nogawa Plates of Dharasena II, *GS* 320/c. 639-640 A.D.; *Ibid*, p. 194, Nogawa Plates of Dharasena II, *saṁvat* 321/c. 640-641 A.D., *Ibid*, XXIII, p. 108, Gaonri Plates.
25. *IA*, XV, p. 335, grant of Dharasena IV.
26. *EI*, XXXVII, p. 247, Thana Plates of Śīlāhāra Nāgārjuna.
27. *Ibid*, XIV, p. 324, Bangarh grant of Mahīpāla I.
28. *JBORS*, II, p. 412.
29. *Ibid*, p. 400, Dhenkanal grant of Kulastambha; *EI*, XXXIV, p. 96, second set of Talcher Plates of Gayaḍatuṅga, *JBORS*, VI, p. 481, Singharā Plates of Raṇabhañja; *EI*, XI p. 98, Sonpur Plates of Śatrubhañja; *IHQ*, XX, p. 243, *IO*, IV, p. 151, Kalibhanā Plates of thirty-fourth year of Mahābhavagupta I, *JASB*, NS. I, p. 14, *IO*, IV, p. 167, Patna Museum Plates of Mahāśivagupta I, eighth year.
30. Quoted in V.V. Mirashi: *Bhavabhūti*, p. 32; cf. also Kane and Joshi (ed.), *Uttararāmacarita*, p. 1f.
31. *IHQ*, XXI, p. 213, Taltalai Plates of Dharmamahādevī, *JBORS*, II, p. 405; Dhenkanal grant of Jayastambha; *EI*, XXIII, p. 108, Gaonri Plates of Vākpati II; *Ibid*, XV, p. 293, Amgachi grant of Vigrahapāla III; *Ibid*, XXIX, p. 48, Bangaon Plates of the time of Vigrahapāla III.
32. Quoted by Brough, J., *op. cit.*, pp. 123 and 140.
33. *Ibid*, pp. 125, 129, 131, 134.
34. *OHRJ*, XIII, p. 1, Angul Copper Plates of Śāntikara; *EI*, XII, p. 325; Baud grant of twenty-sixth year of Raṇabhañja; *OHRJ*, I p. 208, *EI*, XXIX, p. 189, Dasapalla grant of Śatrubhañja.
35. *EI*, XXIII, p. 108, Gaonri Plates of Vākpati II.
36. *JBBRAS*, N.S. I, p. 50, Goras C.P. of Dhruvasena II; *EI*, XXII, p. 135; *IO*, IV, p. 212, Mahākosala Historical Society's Plates of Mahābhavagupta I.
37. *IA*, VII, p. 70, grant of Dharasena II; *Ibid*, p. 73, grant of Dharasena IV; *Ibid*, p. 76, grant of Kharagrāha II.
38. Quoted by Brough, J., *op. cit.*, pp. 163 & 174.
39. *Ibid*., p. 35.
40. *Ibid*., pp. 158, 163.

41. *EI*, VI, p. 133, grant of Daṇḍimahādevī; *Ibid*, XXIV, p. 15, Juraḍa grant of Neṭṭabhañja; *JAHRS*, III, p. 30, Phulsara Copper Plate of Kīrttirāja.
42. Quoted by Brough, J., *op. cit.*, p. 147.
43. *Ibid.*, p. 121.
44. *Ibid.*, pp. 87 & 150.
45. *Ibid.*, pp. 95 & 156.
46. Ghurye, G.S., *op. cit.*, p. 188.
47. Quoted by Brough J., *op. cit.*, pp. 82-83.
48. *IHQ*, XX, p. 237, *IO*, IV, p. 100, Kalibhanā Plates of the sixth year of Mahābhavagupta I; *OHRJ*, XV, p. 115, Plates of Devānanda; *EI*, XIV, p. 324. Bangarh grant of Mahīpāla I.
49. *IHQ*, IX, p. 751. Baud grant of Kanakabhañja; *JBORS*, II, p. 45; *IO*. IV, p. 218, Mārañja-Murā grant of Mahāśivagupta I; *EI*, XXXVII, p. 247, Thana Plates of Nāgārjuna.
50. *IA*, XVI, p. 201, grant of Candella Dhaṅga; *Ibid*. XVII, p. 117, Kalas Budrukh Plates of Bhillamarāja III; *EI*, XXIX, p. 79. Santiragama grant of Daṇḍimahādevī; *Ibid*. XIX, p. 41, Antirigam grant of Jayabhañja; IHQ, X, p. 473, Baud grant of fifty-eighth year of Raṇabhanja; *EI*, III, p. 345, *IO*, IV, p. 133, Cuttack grant of Mahābhavagupta I.
51. *IHQ*, XXI, p. 213, Taltalai Plates of Dharmamahādevī; *JASB*, XVII, p. 245 Angul Plates of Dharmamahādevī; *JBORS*, II, p. 405, Dhenkanal grant of Jayastambha; *EI*, XXIII, p. 108, Gaonri Plates; *Ibid*, XXIX, p. 48, Bangaon Plates; *Ibid*, *XV*, p. 293. Amgachi grant.
52. Brough, J., *op. cit.*, p. 4.
53. Quoted by Brough, J., *op. cit.*, pp. 172-176.
54. Ghurye, G.S., *op. cit.*, p. 174.
55. Suggested by Dr. B.P. Mazumdar.
56. *IA*, XVI, p. 203, 11.9-10 (text).
57. *EI*, XXIX, p. 12, 1.41 (text).
58. *Ibid*, II, p. 309, 11.38-39 (text).
59. *JASB*, N.S.I, p. 18, 11.33-34 (text); p. 20, 1.37 (text)/*IO* IV, p. 192.11.33-34 (text), p. 198, 1.37 (text).

60. *Ibid*, p. 13, 1.11 (text); *Ibid*, p. 113, 1.11 (text).
61. *EI*, XVIII, p. 297, 1.18 (text).
62. *Ibid*., XXII, p. 156, 1.28 (text).
63. *Ibid*, XXXVII, p. 261, 1.21 (text); *OHRJ*, XI, p. 158, 1.22 (text).
64. *EI*, XIV, p. 327, 1.47 (text).
65. *Ibid*, VIII, p. 141, 11.15-16 (text); *IO*, IV, p. 120, 11.15-16 (text).
66. Quoted by Brough, J., *op. cit*., pp. 103-105, 109-110.
67. *Ibid*, pp. 105-110.
68. *EI*, XXVIII, p. 282, 11.16-17 (text).
69. *JBORS*, II, p. 174, 11.11-12 (text).
70. *OHRJ*, IV, p. 75, 11.16-17 (text).
71. *EI*, III, p. 348, 11.11-12 (text). *IO*, IV, p. 140, 11.11-12 (text).
72. *Ibid*., XI, p. 94, 11.11-12 (text); *IO*, IV, p. 96, 11.11-12 (text).
73. *Ibid*., IV, p. 258, 1.16 (text), *IO*, IV, p. 239, 1.16 (text).
74. *JBORS*, II, p. 411, 1.16 (text).
75. *EI*, XXXVIII, p. 131, 1.23 (text).
76. *Ibid*., XXXIV, p. 96, 1.25 (text).
77. *OHRJ*, XII, p. 7, 1.18 (text).
78. *JBORS*, II, p. 407, 1.15 (text).
79. *EI*, VI, p. 139, 11.32-33 (text).
80. *Ibid*., III, p. 342, 1.14 (text); *IO*, IV, p. 107, 1.14 (text).
81. *Ibid*., p. 342, 1.16 (text), *IO*, IV, p. 107, 1.16 (text).
82. *Ibid*., p. 342, 11.12-13 (text); *IO*, IV, p. 107, 11.12-13 (text).
83. Ghurye, G.S., *op. cit*., p. 195.
84. Brough, J., *op. cit*., pp. 161, 162, 167, 168.
85. *JASB*, XVII, p. 249, 11.22-23 (text).
86. *JBORS*, II, p. 54, 11.1-2 (text); *IO*, IV, p. 220, 1.26 (text).
87. *JBORS*, II, p. 415, 11.23-24 (text).
88. *EI*, III, p. 342, 11.12-13 (text); *IO*, IV, p. 107, 11.12-13 (text).
89. Quoted by Brough, J., *op. cit*., p. 108.
90. *EI*, XXXIV, p. 100, cf: fn. 2.
91. *JBORS*, VI, p. 271, 1.25 (text).

92. *EI*, III, p. 342, l.10 (text); *IO*, IV, p. 106 l.10 (text).
93. *JASB*, N.S. XXVII, p. 223, l.24 (text).
94. Quoted by Brough, J., *op. cit.*, pp. 112, 115, 119.
95. *Ibid.*, pp. 113, 117, 120.
96. *Ibid.*, p. 115.
97. *JBORS*, II, p. 400, Dhenkanal grant of Kulastambha; *OHRJ*, XIII, p. 1, Angul Plates of Śāntikara, *EI*, XXXVIII, p. 128, Talcher Plates of Vinītatuṅga II; *Ibid.*, p. 124, Khargaprasad Plates of Vinītatuṅga II; *Ibid.*, XXXIV, p. 100, Asiatic Society's Plates of Gayāḍaṭuṅga; *IHQ*, IX, p. 751, Baud grant of Kanakabhañja; *EI*, XXV, p. 147, Ādipur Plates of Narendrabhañja; *Ibid.*, XXIV, p. 15, Juraḍa grant of Neṭṭabhañja; *Ibid*, XXIX, p. 189; *OHRJ*, I, p. 208, Dasapalla grant of Śatrubhañja; *EI*, XI, p. 98, Sonpur Plates of Śatrubhañja; *JAHRS*, III, p. 30, Phulsara C.P. of Kīrttirāja; *OHRJ*, XV, p. 115, Plates of Devānanda.
98. *EI*, XXVII, p. 327, cf. fn. 5.
99. Quoted by Brough, J., *op. cit.*, pp. 149, 151, 156.
100. Brough, J., *op. cit.*, p. xvii.
101. Ghurye, G.S., *op. cit.*, p. 195.
102. *Ibid.*, p. 195.
103. *OHRJ*, XI, p. 195, ll.15-17 (text); *IO*, IV, p. 125, ll.15-17 (text).
104. *EI*, III, p. 342, ll.10-11 (text); *IO*, IV, p. 106, ll.10-11 (text).
105. *EI*, XII, pp. 323-324, ll.18-19 (text).
106. *Ibid.*, XVIII, p. 297, ll.18-19 (text).
Commenting on the expression "*Virvamitravat* (*Viśvāmitravat?*) in a Caulukya grant from Satara dated 617 A.D., Ghurye observed that it demonstrates almost conclusively that the use of 'pravaras' in the specification of an individual along with his 'gotra' was in the 7th century Maharashtra an entirely new phenomenon.... Otherwise the 'vat' suffixed name of the eponym is not explicable." (Ghurye, G.S., *op. cit.*, p. 166). The phenomenon, however is not peculiar to Maharashtra. It is seen in Orissa as well.

107. *EI*, III, p. 342, 1.14 (text); *IO*, IV, p. 107, 1.14 (text); *EI*, III, p. 342, 1.16 (text); *IO*, IV, p. 107, 1.16 (text).
108. *Ibid.*, p. 342, 11.12-13 (text), *IO*, IV, p. 107, 11.12-13 (text).
109. *EI*, VI, p. 139, 1.33 (text).
110. *Ibid.*, XXVIII, p. 282, 1.17 (text).
111. *JAHRS*, III, p. 40, 11.19-20 (text).
112. Ghurye, G.S., *op. cit.*, p. 156.
113. Quoted by Kane, *HDS*, II, p. 113.
114. *Ibid.*, p. 111.
115. Kane, *HDS*, II, p. 110.
116. Quoted by Kane, *HDS*, II, p. 113.
117. *IA*, XI, p. 305, Plates of Śīlāditya II (Śīlāditya III ?), *saṁvat* 352/c. 671-672 A.D.; *EI*, XXI, p. 208, Jesar Plates of Śīlāditya III, *GE*; 347/c. 666-667 A.D.; *Ibid*, XXV, p. 25, Ellora Plates of Dantidurga, *Śaka* 663/c. 741 A.D.
118. *Ibid.*, XXXIV, p. 116, 1.23 (text).
119. *Ibid.*, VII, p. 26.
120. *JASB*, XVII, p. 144, 11.36-37 (text).
121. *EI*, IV, p. 243.
122. Quoted by Kane, *HDS*, II, p. 132.
123. *EI*, III, p. 349, 1.41 (text); *IO*, IV, p. 142, 1.41 (text).
124. *Ibid.*, XXIX, p. 57, 1.50 (text).
125. Kane, P.V., in *HDS*, II, p. 123, quoting the views of Gautama, Baudhāyana and Manu.
126. *EI*, XXXVII, p. 82, 1.19 (text).
127. *Ibid.*, I.p. 179, 1.46 (text).
128. *IHQ*, XX, p. 247, 1.13 (text), *IO*, IV, p. 153, 1.13 (text); *EI*, XVIII, p. 299, 11.26-28 (text).
129. Mazumdar, B.P., *The Socio-Economic History of Northern India*, p. 94.
130. *EI*, VI, p. 139, 1.34 (text).
131. Ghurye, G.S., *op. cit.*, p. 1.
132. Williams, M., *A Sanskrit English Dictionary*, p. 1062.
133. Winternitz, M., *HIL*, Vol. I (translated by S. Ketkar), p. 53.
134. Williams, M., *op. cit.*, p. 1062.
135. *JBBRAS*, N.S. I, p. 69, Plates of Dhruvasena II; *Ibid.*, p.

50, Goras Plates of Dhruvasena II; *EI*, I, p. 85, grant of Dhruvasena III, *JBBRAS*, N.S. I, p. 71, Plates of Śīlāditya III; *Ibid*., p. 73, Plates of Śīlāditya III (both *GE* 346/c. 666 A.D.).

136. Weber, A., *History of Indian Literature*, pp. 104, 70 and 87.

137. Ghosh, B.K., in *V.A.* p. 227.

138. Apte, V.M., in *V.A.* p. 441.

139. Winternitz, M., *op. cit.*, p. 170.

140. *EI*, XXXV, p. 281, Amreli Museum Plates of Dhruvasena II; *Ibid*, I, p. 85, a grant of Dhruvasena III; *IA*, XV, p. 335, grant of Dharasena IV; *EI*, IV, p. 74, Lunsadi Plates of Śīlāditya II (Śīlāditya III?) *G.S.* 350/c. 669-670 A.D.; *JBBRAS*, N.S.I, p. 73, grant of Śīlāditya III; *EI*, XXII, p. 114, Jesar Plates of Śīlāditya III *Valabhī saṁvat* 357/c. 676-677 A.D.; *Ibid*., XXXVII, p. 37, Bhadresar Plates of Bhīmadeva I.

141. *EI*, VI, p. 133, grant of Daṇḍimahādevī; *Ibid*, XXXIV, p. 96, second set of Talcher Plates of Gayāḍatuṅga *Ibid*, XII, p. 325, Baud grant of twenty-sixth year of Raṇabhañja; *IHQ*, X, p. 473, Baud grant of fifty eighth year of Raṇabhañja; *EI*, XXIV, p.15, Juraḍa grant of Neṭṭabhañja; *Ibid*, III, p. 340, *IO*, IV, p. 105, Patna Plates of Mahābhavagupta I, sixth year; *JASB*, N.S. I, p. 5, *IO*, IV, p. 112, Patna Museum Plates of Mahābhavagupta I, sixth year; *JBORS*, II, p. 45, *IO*, IV, p. 218, Mārañja-Murā grant of Mahāśivagupta I; *EI*, IV, p. 254, *IO*, IV, p. 237, Kudopali grant of Mahābhavagupta II; *EI*, XXVI, p. 74, Baripada Museum Plates of Devānanda; *JAHRS*, III, p. 30, Phulsara C.P. of Kīrttirāja.

142. *EI*, VII, p. 26, Cambay Plates of Govinda IV; *IA*, XII, p. 247, Sāngli grant of Govinda IV; *EI*, V, p. 188, Deoli Plates of Kṛṣṇa III.

143. *EI*, XXIX, p. 79, Santiragama grant of Daṇḍimahādevī, *IHQ*, XXI, p. 213, Taltalai Plates of Dharmamahādevī, *JBORS*, II, p. 400, Dhenkanal grant of Kulastambha; *Ibid*, p. 167, Tasapaikera charter of Raṇabhañja; *EI*, XIX, p. 41, Antirigam grant of Yaśabhañja; *Ibid*., VIII, p.

138, *IO*, IV, p. 118, Nagpur Museum Plates of Mahābhavagupta I; *IHQ*, XX, p. 237, *IO*, IV, p. 100, Kalibhanā Plates of sixth year of Mahābhavagupta I; *JASB*, N.S. I, p. 14, *IO*, IV, p. 167, Patna Museum Plates of eighth year of Mahāśivagupta I.

144. Mahāvīracarita, *op. cit.*, I, p. 2, 1.6.
145. Williams, M., *op. cit.*, p. 444.
146. Weber, A., *op. cit.*, p. 63.
147. *IA*, I, p. 14, C.P. of Dharasena I; *JBBRAS*, N.S.1, p. 28, Plates of Śīlāditya I; *Ibid.*, p. 69, grant of Dhruvasena II; *Ibid*, p. 50, Goras C.P. of Dhruvasena II, *Ibid*, pp. 71 and 73, Plates of Śīlāditya III *G.S.* 346/c. 666 A.D.
148. *JBORS*, II, p. 405.
149. Williams, M., *op. cit.*, p. 369.
150. *IA*, VII, p. 70, grant of Dharasena II; *Ibid*, p. 73, grant of Dharasena IV; *Ibid.*, p. 76, grant of Kharagrāha II, *JBBRAS*, XI, p. 335, grant of Śīlāditya, *EI*, XXVII, p. 197, PWM Plates of Dadda III.
151. *OHRJ*, XIII, p. 1, Angul C.P. of Śāntikara; *EI*, XXV, p. 157, Ādipur Plates of Narendrabhañja; *IHQ*, XX, p. 245, *IO*, IV, p. 151, Kalibhanā Plates of thirty-fourth year of Mahābhavagupta I, *OHRJ*, XI, p. 192, IO, IV, p. 124, Gaintala Plates of Mahābhavagupta I.
152. Weber, A., *op. cit.*, pp. 52 and 55.
153. Ghosh, B.K., in *VA op. cit.*, p. 233.
154. *EI*, XXXIV, p. 116, 1.23 (text).
155. *JASB*, XVII, p. 144, 11.35-36 (text).
156. *IHQ*, XXI, p. 220, 1.35 (text).
157. *IA*, I, p. 16. It must be mentioned here, that the charter says nothing about the donees being brothers. However, the names of their fathers, their *gotras* and *śākhās*, their original homes and places of residence being the same, it may be assumed that they were brothers.
158. *Harşacarita, op. cit.*, II, p. 23, 1.24 (text).
159. *KS*, pp. 137-138, 11.44-45 (text).
160. *EI*, XIII, p. 291, 1.15 (text).
161. *Karpūramañjarī*, i, 77.
162. *EI*, IV, p. 80, 1.54 (text).

163. Kane, P.V., in *IHQ*, XIV, p. 242.
164. Quoted by Kane, in *HDS*, II, p. 241.
165. *JBBRAS*, N.S.I, p. 72, 1.49 (text) and also, p. 71.
166. Mazumdar, B.P., *op. cit*., p. 82.
167. Krishnamachariar, M., *op. cit*., p. 741.
168. *EI*, XI, p. 175, fn. 5.
169. Quoted by Kane, in *HDS*, II, pp. 250-251.
170. *OHRJ*, XIII, p. 1, Angul C.P. of Śāntikara; *EI*, XXXIV, p. 96, Talcher Plates of Gayāḍatuṅga, *Ibid*, XXV, p. 147, Ādipur Plates of Narendrabhañja, *Ibid*, XI, p. 95, *IQ*, IV, p. 184, Nibinnā grant of Mahāśivagupta I *Ibid*, XXIII, p. 73, Indian Museum Plates of Devendravarman III, *Gaṅga* 308/c. 804-806 A.D.
171. *EI*, XXXIII, p. 215, Mahudi Plates of *V.S.* 1074/c. 1017 A.D.
172. *JASB*, XVII, p. 137, Jājilpārā grant; *EI*, XIV, p. 324, Bangarh grant of Mahīpāla I, *Ibid*, XXII, p. 150, Irda Plates.
173. Williams, M., *op. cit*., p. 481.
174. Quoted by Kane, in *HDS*, II, p. 251.

## Chapter IV

# Economic Life and Status

It is easy to presume, that the impetus for the migration of the majority of Brāhmaṇas during the period under survey, c. 475-1030 A.D., came from their search for a more settled life with better economic prospects than what they had known in their ancestral homes. Subsequently after they had taken up residence in new areas, some of them became recipients of land-grants. As a result, sometimes plots of land, but mostly a village, or at times villages accompanied by various privileges, were made over to them.

**Economic Prospects of the Donated Lands**

In some cases, definitely cultivated plots of land were donated to the immigrant donees, as can be seen from the charters which mention wells, ponds and reservoirs as being included in the grants. Maitraka Dharasena I gave to two Brāhmaṇa brothers, two fields and a well. Likewise, the Brāhmaṇa Bhaṭṭi in *G.S.* 287/c. 608 A.D., received from Śīlāditya I, a plot of land and a well. By a charter of *G.S.* 346/c. 666 A.D., Śīlāditya III, made a donation of two fields and a well to three Brāhmaṇas. Another Brāhmaṇa by a separate grant issued in the same year by the same king, became the recipient of two fields, each with a well in its vicinity. The Lunsadi Plates of Śīlāditya II (Śīlāditya III ?) of the *Gupta* year 350/c. 669-670 A.D., record that two Brāhmaṇa brothers coming from Dvīpa or Diu, were given a pond and some pieces of land. The Brāhmaṇa Saggala, received a well called Dhoraka together with land in the village of Kukkapadra from Śīlāditya III, recorded in his Jesar Plates of *GS* 347/c. 666-667 A.D. Another set of the Jesar Plates issued by Śīlāditya III in the *Valabhī* year 357/c. 676-677 A.D., records the grant of some plots of land together with a reservoir, to an unnamed Brāhmaṇa. All these pieces of land which lay near wells, ponds and reservoirs, must have been cultivable. Otherwise, the inclusion in the grants, of these irrigation facilities, probably meant to help in agriculture, loses its purpose.

Mention may be made here of the Sankheda Plates of Gurjara Dadda II, issued in *K.S.* 392/c. 642 A.D. A *śibara* described by Mirashi, who edited the charter, as a farmhouse, was included in the field that was given to the Brāhmaṇa Sūrya. The presence of a farmhouse near the field may mean, that the land was either cultivable, or had already been brought under the plough.

To form an idea of the economic gains of the beneficiaries from the donated lands and villages, a study of those areas should be made. The Maitrakas generally endowed their donees with more fields and plots of lands rather than with whole villages. Mostly these lay in cultivable areas, as is proved by the fact, that almost in every case, the donated fields were adjacent to plots of land in the possession of other Brāhmaṇas and householders. Besides, as quite frequently, ponds, wells and rivers lay in the vicinity, it is likely that the donees could get irrigation facilities. In a copper plate grant of Dharasena I, the field that the brothers Ajuna and Mankasvāmin received, was surrounded on the south, west and north, by fields belonging to Vattu, Kuṭumbi Vinhala and the Brāhmaṇa Shashṭibhava. To the east of the field was a well whose owner was Vinhala. The Amreli Museum Plates of Dhruvasena II, dated in the year 323/c. 642-643 A.D., record the grant of a plot of land bounded on the east, west and north by *brahmadeya* fields. Dharasena IV granted to the Brāhmaṇa Aditiśarman, two fields lying in two villages. Near one of these was a *bhṛishṭī* or the raised ground near a tank. This implies that on the borders of the field, was a tank, near which was the field of the Brāhmaṇa Vairabhaṭa.

Unlike these plots of land which existed in sqarsely populated localities, there were others which lay at the junction of villages, and not far from the public thoroughfare. In the *Gupta* year 347/c. 666-667 A.D., Śīlāditya III by his Jesar Plates, donated to Saggala a well and a hundred *pādāvartas* of land, broken up into three pieces. The largest of these was bounded on the east and west by fields owned by an *upādhyāya* and one Bhāsikya. To the south, lay three royal wells and to the north was the river Vaṅśatikā. The same river formed the northern boundary of the second plot of land. The embankments of the two wells Śirādaṇḍaka on the south and Dhoraka on the west, made up the southern and western boundaries. Bordering on the east, was the village of Kaṇṇasomaka. There were three *brahmadeya* fields belonging to Taṭṭa and Caṭṭa on the east, south and west of the third plot, to the north of which ran a rivulet or sāriṇī. Ten years later, another set of Jesar Plates also issued by Śīlāditya III, in the *Valabhī* year 357/c. 676-677 A.D., records the donation of a hundred and four *pādāvartas* of land. These were broken up into five pieces, of which two had originally been in the possession of a family which, however, was no longer in existence, at the time when the grant was made. One of these two, was surrounded on the east and south by fields owned by the Brāhmaṇa Aṇahaka and by Chachcha and Māṭrila. A field known as Pattinapāṇaka-*durgakṣetra* lay to the north, while to the west was a field called Maḍhavānaka. In addition to the latter, on the west was a road leading towards a village named Koraṭapadraka. The second piece of land was hemmed in on all sides by fields. Two lying to the north and south belonged to the Brāhmaṇa Aṇahaka, while to the east was the *brahmadeya* field of Śaṅkara. A householder called Bhoṭuka had a field which lay towards the western boundary of the plot. The three other pieces which formed a part of the endowment, were at the time of the grant, under the cultivation of Kikkaka. The largest of these lay to the south-west of the village of Suptāvasadhī. Two fields called Pattiaṇaka and Māṭṛsthāna and another belonging to the Brāhmaṇa Saṅgaka, lay to the south and west of this plot of land. The fourth piece of land was near a public road which ran along that land's eastern boundary. To its south lay the *grāmaśikhara* or the mound, on which stood a village. A nobleman named Varuṇa had a well, whose embankment stood to the west, while in the north, was a field belonging to one Karkkaka. Close to the west of the smallest of the five pieces of gifted land, ran a public road. On the three other sides were *brahmadeya* fields. To the north lay the one belonging to Śaṅkara, to the east, the one owned by Chamasa, and to the south was the field known as Dāsānaka.

Like the Maitrakas, some of the Gurjaras, made grants in habitable areas. The field that Dadda II granted to the Brāhmaṇa Sūrya, by his Sankheda Plates of *K.S.* 392/c. 642 A.D., was well placed, standing at a junction of three villages. On the east was the boundary of the village of Kṣīrasara, on the north, that of Kukkuṭavallikā, and on the south the village of Āṭavīpāṭaka, with a road going to the village of Suvarṇārapalli. To the west lay a *brahmadeya* field and a tank. A later king of the same dynasty, Jayabhaṭa III, issued from Navasari, a set of plates in *K.S.* 456/c. 705-706 A.D. By this charter, Devasvāmin was given a field. The village of Golikā formed the eastern boundary of the field, while to the west was a road leading to the village Dhāhaddha. On the north and south, were fields belonging to Brāhmaṇas, and a couple of tanks.

The evidence of the above-mentioned records, points to one definite fact. Neither the Maitrakas nor the Gurjaras made grants of land in totally isolated or barren regions. The presence of cultivable fields of others in the vicinity of the donated plots, together with the existence of wells, rivers and tanks indicate that they must have been cultivable for at least some time in the year. It may also be suggested that there was in Gujarat at least in the time of the Maitrakas and Gurjaras, a considerable demand for landed property. Besides, when the plots of land stood close to villages and near public roads, they were more easily accessible.

The practice of granting cultivable lands in Gujarat continued in the later half of the eighth and early years of the ninth century. Candrāditya by his Hilol Plates of the year 470, gave two pieces of land surrounded by *brahmadeya* fields to Bhaṭṭa Mātragaṇa. Later Karkka Suvarṇavarṣa by his Baroda grant of *Śaka* 734/c. 812 A.D., made a grant of the village of

Vaḍapadraka. It was bounded on the east, west and north by the villages of Jambuvāvikā, Aṅkoṭṭaka and Vagghāchchha, and on the south by the tank called Mahāsenaka.

In later years, the granting of whole villages became the order of the day. The imperial Rāṣṭrakūṭas gave to their donees, villages with well defined boundaries in fairly populous areas. In *Śaka* 836/c. 914-915 A.D., the Brāhmaṇa Siddhapabhaṭṭa received from Indra III, the village of Kurundaka. It was surrounded on all sides by villages: Vāraḍapallikā to the east, Nāmbhītaṭaka to the south, Valīśa to the west and Vavviyaṇa to the north. Govinda IV in *Śaka* 855/c. 933 A.D. by his Sāngli grant gave to Keśava Dīkṣita, a village called Lohāgrāma, bounded on the east, south, west and north by the villages of Ghoḍegrāma, Vañjulī, Viñchavihavajha and Sonnahi respectively. Likewise, the village of Rikkaṭi donated by the Kolhapur Copper Plate of Akālavarṣa in the *Śaka* year 882/c. 960 A.D., had to its east Sirigrāma and Māligrāma, to the south Koḍovali and Ciñcavāṭa, to the west Yerurage and Coke, and to the north, Mundasage. It is rather difficult to assess to what extent the soil of the three donated villages mentioned above, was cultivable. However, the inclusion of *dhānya* and *hiraṇya* in the list of the rights transferred to the donees, presupposes the cultivation of some crops in those donated lands and the enjoyment of some kind of taxes levied in cash. Besides, as the villages stood in the midst of others, and were habitable, the Brāhmaṇa donees could look for other sources, to supplement their income from the land.

The nature of the endowment as recorded in the Deoli Plates of Kṛṣṇa III, is somewhat different. The village of Tālapuruṁṣaka, which formed the subject of the grant in *Śaka* 862/c. 940 A.D., had on one side the river Kanhanā which ran along its southern boundary. To the north lay Vadhīragrāma, and to the east and west, the villages of Mādaṭaḍhiṇḍhara and Mohama. The waters of the river might have helped to make Tālapuruṁṣaka agriculturally more fruitful. The existence of adjacent villages also indicates, that the gifted villages was not in a barren area.

A special mention should be made of the Cambay Plates of Govinda IV, issued in *Śaka* 852/c. 930 A.D. The village Kevañja that was donated to the Brāhmaṇa Nāgamārya, was surrounded on all sides by villages. To its south and west were Sāmagama and Sīhuka, while the village of Kāvikā formed its northern and eastern boundaries. As the grant was a token for the priestly fees for the performance of *śrādha* and sacrifices, like *rājasūya, vājapeya*, and *agniṣṭoma*, it is certain that Nāgamārya was a priest of the highest order. It is therefore likely that such a priest was given a village whose lands were cultivable. Further, as the donated village was in the vicinity of Kāvikā, which is described in the charter, as a holy place, it is not unreasonable to presume, that the donor saw also the prospect of supplementary income for the donee. He might have been occasionally commissioned to perform funeral ceremonies and sacrifices by other persons at Kāvikā particularly, or in the adjacent villages.

Like the Rāṣṭrakūṭas, the Caulukyas of Aṇhilvāḍa gave to their donees villages, surrounded by villages. In *V.S.* 1051/c. 994-995 A.D., Mūlarāja I granted to Dīrghācārya, the village of Varaṇaka. To its east was Dhanāra village, to the south Guṁdāuka, to the west Voḍha-*grāma* and to the north Metravāla. Another Brāhmaṇa Bhaṭṭāraka Ājapāla received from Bhīmadeva I, in *V.S.* 1086/c. 1030 A.D., the village of Mansūra in the Cutch region. Its eastern, southern, western and northern boundaries were formed by the villages of Ghaḍhadika, Aikayikā, Dharavadrikā and Prajhārikā respectively. That the villages themselves were populated, is proved by the fact, that the inhabitants of the villages were asked to pay the usual taxes to the donees. Besides, the levying of *bhāga, bhoga* and *hiraṇya* means that they were not totally devoid of crops and agricultural produce, although the soil of Cutch is not very fertile.

Two charters of the Śilāhāras of northern Konkan, however, present a different picture. Nāgārjuna of this family, issued in the *Śaka* year 961/c. 1039 A.D., the Thana Plates, recording the grant of the village of Muṁjavalī to one Mādhava Paṇḍita. In describing the property, a rather unusual term has been used—*pūrvva-prasiddhāya-bhaṭṭhaukāsādisahitaḥ* (text, lines 68-69). The words *bhaṭṭha* and *ukkāsa* have been explained by the editor M.G. Dikshit. According to him, *bhaṭṭha* means low-land in which inferior crops are grown and which is subjected to sea-waves in high tides. *Ukkāsa* refers to fallow, uncultivable land, barren on account of rocky soil. It is clear therefore, that the village lay near the sea, as a result of which the salty water destroyed the quality of the soil, making it unfit for cultivation. In another charter, that of Mummuṇirāja, of *Śaka* 971/c. 1049 A.D., the donated village Kichchita, was bounded on the east by the Śrī-Enara hills and the rivulets running from it, and on the south by the Sāmvīna river. To the north and west were the two villages Nīmvā and Mātara. So the village of Kichchita perhaps stood in a hilly terrain, and although not in totally desolate surroundings, might have been sparsely populated. Besides, as neither charter mentions the levying of any taxes connected with crops, they were agriculturally not very fruitful to the beneficiaries.

The charters of the Paramāras, however, make no mention at all about the boundaries of their donated lands. The Gaonri Plates of Vākpati II and the Banswara, Betma, Ujjain and Mahudi Plates of his nephew Bhojadeva, merely give the names of the transferred villages and the districts in which they lay. Absence of boundary marks pre-supposes that the donated lands were not in the midst of thickly populated areas, where land-owners must have been few. The greater specification of boundary marks shows that too many owners had holdings in a small well-settled area.

One exception among the Paramāra records, was the Depalpur grant of Bhoja, dated *V.S.* 1079/c. 1022 A.D. By this charter, he gave to the Brāhmaṇa Vacchala, thirty-four *aṁśas* of level land, measuring four ploughs. This particular method of assessing the size of the land, probably indicates, that the donated area though small in size, was cultivable.

The Pālas of Bengal and Bihar, unlike the Rāṣṭrakūṭas and Paramāras, hardly ever handed over a whole village to their donees during the period under review. By the Jājilpārā grant of Gopāla II, the two *pallis* of Kāṣṭhagṛha and Mahārāja in the village of Ānandapura were granted to Śrīdharaśarman who could also collect the *dvārikādāna* or toll levied at the gate. Vigrahapāla III in his eleventh regnal year, issued the Belwa Plates. By this charter, a plot of land in the recently cultivated village of Lovanikāma was bestowed on Jayānandadevaśarman. The Bangaon Plates issued in the seventeenth year of the same king records, that a Brāhmaṇa received a piece of land in Vasukāvartta village in the Tirhut division of modern Bihar. It yielded a revenue of about five hundred standard coins. Although the charters are silent about the surroundings in which these lands stood, some suggestions can be made about their location. As they were mostly parts of villages, they were not situated in isolated areas. The collection of toll at the gates of the village, also points to this. Besides, the villages lay in the fertile regions of North Bengal and North Bihar, which means that they were cultivable. Moreover the soil was conducive to the growth of *āmra* and *madhuka* trees. The donees could either sell the fruits or lease out the trees, both of which would add to their profits.

In Assam, as in Bengal, cultivable plots of land were given to Brāhmaṇa donees. Indrapāla by his Guakuci Plates, granted to the Brāhmaṇa Devadeva, some land with an output of rice. The pieces of land were surrounded on all sides by other cultivated fields.

Coming to Orissa, very rarely do the charters give any indication of either the location or the surroundings of the donated plots. In a record from Baud, Kanakabhañja made a donation of two *pāṭakas* of land called Jamarāpura and Sihipura, surrounded by Māharapuragrāma to the east, Kopāsimyāgrāma to the south-west and Tela-*nadī* to the north. The Brāhmaṇa Harivaṁśa who was the recipient could use the waters of the river both for irrigation, as well as to levy a tax on fish therein, as fishing rights were included among his privileges. Similarly, Śulki Jayastambha allowed these rights to the donees of two grants from Dhenkanal, indicating the existence of rivers near the donated villages, although no mention of the boundaries has been made.

It is possible that in Orissa, population was sparse and hence the number of land-owners was small. So relatively little information has been given about the boundaries of the donated lands. The Śulkis Bhauma-Karas, Bhañjas and Tuṅgas of Orissa, do not refer to *bhāga, bhoga, dhānya* or *hiraṇya*, which constituted the chief benefits from the soil. Sometimes, however, as in the case of the Bhauma-Karas, the income from weavers, milkmen and vintners accrued to the donees. This implies, that the lands which had been given to the donees, were situated in fairly well-settled areas. The Somavaṁśis alone permitted their beneficiaries not only to levy taxes like *bhāga, bhoga* and *hiraṇya*, but also in addition, the right to enjoy the income from trees like *āmra* and madhuka. Perhaps, the Raipur-Bilaspur-Sambalpur region over which they held sway, was comparatively more fertile and helpful for the growth of crops.

From a study of the above, a point that gradually emerges is, that throughout the period c. 475-1030 A.D., the rulers of the various dynasties generally adopted a policy to settle migrant Brāhmaṇas in habitable areas, where there was already an existing population. It is only very rarely, that we come across a village lying in hilly tracts or in an inaccessible area e.g. in the charters of the Śīlāhāras. The majority of the plates of the period under review, describe how fields surrounded by cultivated fields and villages bordered by settled villages were given in charity. Even in Orissa, where no mention is made of the boundaries, there is nothing to suggest total isolation or absolute lack of human habitation. Keeping this in mind, it is difficult to agree with some learned scholars, that lands were granted to Brāhmaṇas invariably with the sole purpose of extension of cultivation. This might have been true of the village of Kichchita (Thana Plates of Mummuṇirāja), where the Sāmvīna river ran along the southern boundary. But it is hard to apply the theory of extension of cultivation, even to Muṁjavatī of the Thana Plates of Nāgārjuna. Standing on the sea-shore and vulnerable to saline water, the inscription itself reveals, that the donated plot was unfit for cultivation. As for the innumerable other villages and lands that changed hands in the course of the six centuries under discussion, it would be going too far to suggest, that even as late as the eleventh century, they had been left empty and barren, and that the first time they were settled or brought under the plough, was when they were mentioned in the land-grant charters.

**Measurements**

The area of the donated plots are indicated usually by terms like *nivartana, pādāvarta, māla, droṇa* and *kulya* throughout the period. The Abhona Plates of Kalacuri Śaṁkaragaṇa of *K.S.* 347/c. 596-597 A.D., record the grant of a hundred *nivartanas* of land in Vallisikā village. D.C. Sircar correctly points out, that the term *nivartana* meaning an area of land, was not the same in different ages and localities.[1] So it is not possible to assess the exact measurement of the endowed land. A hundred and twenty *pādāvartas* of land in Kālāsamaka village went to Bhaṭṭi, the donee of a grant of Śīlāditya I of *G.S.* 287/c. 608 A.D. *Pāda* as a linear measure, is ordinarily equal to twelve *aṅgulas* or nine inches in length. But a *pādāvarta* must have been a bigger measure. Scholars have conjectured this measurement in terms of feet. Relying on the calculations of Fleet and D.C. Sircar, that a hundred *pādāvartas* was equal to a hundred feet each way, or ten thousand square feet,[2] Bhaṭṭi received from Śīlāditya I a fairly large plot of land measuring about fourteen thousand and four hundred square feet. Dhruvasena II by his charter of *G.S.* 312/c. 632 A.D., gave away to Mātrakāla, a field called Sārasakedāra in Hastikapallikāgrāma. The field has been described as *vrīhipiṭakacatuṣṭayavāpa*. As *piṭaka* is a measure of capacity,[3] the field could probably yield four *piṭakas* of paddy. The Amreli Museum Plates of the same ruler, issued in the year 323/c. 642-643 A.D., however, merely state, that a plot of land on the northern border of the village of Machchhoṭikā, was given to Somaśarman, with no details about its area. Likewise, Śīlāditya II (Śīlāditya III ?) in *saṁvat* 352/ c. 671-672 A.D., gave to Magopadatta, a field consisting of two plots of lands. In the *Kalacuri* year 456/c 705-706 A.D., Devasvāmin received from Gurjara Jayabhaṭa III, a field measuring sixty-four *nivartanas* in the Śamīpadraka village.

Two charters from Orissa, record grants, only plots of land in a village. An immigrant Brāhmaṇa Ṛṣivaka acquired by a

Dhenkanal grant of Śulki Jayastambha,[4] land in the village of Llolapura. Dharmamahādevī by her Angul Plates, granted land measuring *daśa-māla* or ten *mālas* in Deśaṇa-*grāma*, to Śrīdharabhaṭṭa. The editor of this charter P. Banerji thinks, that *māla* may denote the same measure as *mā*, which is a South Indian measure, about one-twentieth of a *veli*. According to K.C. Panigrahi, there is in Orissa, a land-measure called *māṇa*, which is the equivalent of about three-fifths of an acre.[5] If *māṇa* is the same as *māla*, then the land that Śrīdharabhaṭṭa received, may have been about six acres.

In the early years of the eleventh century, Devadeva, a Brāhmaṇa migrant to Assam, received from Indrapāla of Kāmarūpa, a plot or plots of land yielding two thousand *droṇas* of rice, as recorded in the Guakuci Plates. The term *droṇa* here, has been used in the sense of weight. There was no single and uniform standard weight covered by this term, throughout North India. A Gwalior Inscription mentions *droṇa* as a measure current in Gopagiri or Gwalior (*Gopagirīya-māpyena*).[6] Kauṭilya's *Arthaśāstra*, II. 19, refers to at least four types of *droṇa*, containing 162½, 175, 187½ and 200 *palas*. According to D.C. Sircar, a *droṇa* was often regarded as equal to four *āḍhakas*. Scholars of Bengal hold that it was a weight between a maund and fourteen seers to two maunds approximately.[7]

Two Paramāra charters also refer, not to villages, but to measures of land. By the Banswara grant of Bhoja of *V.S.* 1076/c. 1019 A.D., a hundred *nivartanas* of land were made over to the Brāhmaṇa Bhāila, in the Ghāghradora-*bhoga* of Sthālī-*maṇḍala* at Vaṭapadraka. Three years later, in *V.S.* 1079/c. 1022 A.D., Bhoja issued the Depalpur Plates whereby thirty-two *aṁśas* or portions of level land measuring about four ploughs, at Kirikaikā, in the western *pathaka* of Ujjain, were donated to Vacchala.

Caulukya Bhīmadeva I by his Muṁdaka grant, of *V.S.* 1086/c. 1030 A.D., gave to the Brāhmaṇa Vāsudeva, merely a *hala* of land in Muṁdaka-*grāma*. A *hala* meaning a plough measure, indicates an area which could be cultivated with one plough in a day. The larger the number of ploughs utilized, the greater would be the area cultivated. Of course, the capacity of the plough to cultivate, would depend on the quality of the soil. Like *nivartana, hala* too was not exactly the same in different ages and localities. D.C. Sircar gives two alternative equivalents of *hala* as being one-fourth of a *Sīrā* or half of a *kula*.[8]

By the Belwa grant of the Pāla king Vigrahapāla III the village Lovanikāma in Puṇḍravardhana-*bhukti*, was partitioned, and the Pāla king Vigrahapāla III, gave a cultivated plot of three *Kulyas* seven and a half *droṇas* and eleven *udamānas* to Jayānandadevaśarman. There is some controversy, regarding the interpretation of *kulya*. A *kulyavāpa* is usually taken to mean an area of land which could be sown with a *kulya* measure of seed, while a *droṇavāpa* according to various ancient lexicons, was equal to one-eighth of a *kulyavāpa* in area. Monier Williams explains the term *kulya* as a winnowing basket or a measure of eight *droṇas*, meaning thereby, that a *kulyavāpa* of land would be required to be sown by eight *droṇas* of seed. D.C. Sircar agrees with this, and describes a *kulya* as a measure of capacity, equal to eight *droṇas*.[9] R.C. Majumdar too, on the basis of the Paharpur Plates, which state, that four plots of land together measuring twelve *droṇavāpas*, corresponded to an area measuring one and a half *kulyavāpas*, points out, that one *kulyavāpa* was equal to eight *droṇavāpas* in an acre.[10] Pargiter, however, makes a *kulya* of land, a little more than an acre.[11] Maity disagrees with this view. He cites the Damodarpur Copper Plates which record, that one *kulyavāpa* of land was purchased on the north of Pañcakulyavāpaka, i.e. a village comprising five *kulyavāpas* of land. If one *kulya* is taken to be equal to one acre, the village would be approximately, little more than five acres in area. Maity therefore feels, that it is hardly likely that a village could be so small.[12] However, whatever a *kulyavāpa* may exactly have been, it is not possible to form any definite idea about the exact size of the land that Vigrahapāla III gave to the immigrant Brāhmaṇa, because the term *kulya* like *droṇa*, had no uniform standard.

It is obvious from the above discussion, that although the area of the donated lands has been mentioned in most of the charters that record grants of plots, different units of measurement have been used by the different ruling houses. This, together with the fact, that some of the terms do not have the same implication in all regions, and at all times, make it almost impossible to form a comparative estimate of the size of the holdings, or to assess their benefit to the donees.

**Characteristics of Donated Areas**

Unlike these charters which are silent as to whether the donated plots were granted in one piece, there are others dealing with grants of pieces of land scattered over varied distances. Dadda II by his two sets of Sankheda Plates issued in *K.S.* 392/c. 642 A.D., gave to the Brāhmaṇa Sūrya, two fields situated in two villages. One had to be sown with a *piṭaka* of paddy and lay on the eastern border of the village of Suvarṇārapalli. The other, which was on the south-eastern border of the village of Kṣīrasara, could be sown with ten *prasthas* of paddy. *Prastha* like *piṭaka* was a measure of capacity, sometimes regarded as one-sixteenth of a *droṇa*[13] Two fields, one in Kolamba in Kheṭaka, and the other in the village of Duhuduhu, belonging to Nāgarakapathaka, were donated to Aditiśarman by Dharasena IV. Buhler, who edited the plates, holds, that Nāgarakapathaka means the area immediately surrounding the town, i.e. Kheṭaka itself. Hence the two fields were perhaps not far from one another. Śīlāditya III in *G.S.* 346/c. 666 A.D., conferred on the Brāhmaṇa Yajñadatta, a field of a hundred *pādāvartas* and a well in Padmavaṭika-*grāma* in Kalākṣyeṭaka and another field of the same area, with a well in Hastavaprāhāra, all lying within Surāṣṭra.

In the next year, *G.S.* 347/c. 666-667 A.D., Śīlāditya III by his Jesar Plates, bestowed on Saggala, a hundred *pādāvartas* of land in the village of Kukkapadra. These hundred *pādāvartas* were broken up into three pieces, lying towards the western, the south-western and the eastern boundaries of the same village. Each of these was separated by fields belonging to other Brāhmaṇas, as well as by streams and rivers. Ten years later, a Brāhmaṇa who is merely referred to as a Dīkṣita, received one hundred and four *pādāvartas* of land, in the village of

Madasara, by another set of Jesar Plates of Śīlāditya III, of the *Valabhī* year 357/c. 676-677 A.D. This land was divided into five pieces, each of which like the plots given to Saggala, was surrounded by *brahmadeya* fields and by public roads. So in both these cases, the donated plots of land were not contiguous.

The practice of granting lands in different areas to the same donee, seems to have become less frequent in later years. A *viṣayapati* under Kakka II, by his Hilol Plates, gave to Bhaṭṭa Mātṛgaṇa, two pieces of land, one to the south of the village of Hilohila, and the other in Pādāṭaka-*grāma*. Kanakabhañja of Orissa, granted two *pāṭakas* Jamarāpura and Sihipura in Vābulāveṇḍaka to Harivaṁśa. A *pāṭaka* according to D.C. Sircar, could be a territorial division, or a portion of a field. It definitely was a part of a village, probably its outlying part.[14] According to the Gunaighar Copper Plate of c. 507-508 A.D., a *pāṭaka* appears to be a land measure equal to forty *droṇavāpas* in area. A village could have as many as four *pāṭakas*, as seen from a grant of Vijayacandra Gāhaḍavāla, dated c. 1161 A.D.[15] It is possible therefore, that the two *pāṭakas* given to Harivaṁśa, were situated in the same village. Gopāla II in his sixth regnal year, by his Jājilpārā grant, granted to Śrīdharaśarman, the two *pallis* of Kāṣṭhagṛha and Mahārāja, situated in the *agrahāra* of Ānandapura in Puṇḍravardhana-*bhukti*. According to P.N. Misra, the editor of the plates, the word *palhkā* or *palli* denotes both a village and a smaller section of it. As the two donated *pallikās* lay within an *agrahāra*, which itself usually indicates a village, they must have been parts of it.[16]

It is difficult to explain why lands broken up into small pieces or fields lying in different villages should have been granted to a donee. It may be, that such grants were made in populous areas where adjacent plots were already in the possession of others. However, whatever might have been the reasons the fact remains, that such grants were agriculturally not very remunerative. Scattered plots of lands, require separate boundaries and are expensive to cultivate. Fragmentation of lands granted to one donee would also mean, that the

Brāhmaṇa perhaps would not be able to look after all the plots of land himself, as in some cases, they were situated in different villages. As a result, he might have had to lease it to tenants, already living in the vicinity of the granted plots, who would cultivate the lands for him. He himself would share the income accruing therefrom, in the position of a landlord.

Apart from the grant of fields and plots of land, the charters also record grant of single villages to immigrant Brāhmaṇas. Bhūtakumāra, who received Loṇāpadraka-*grāma* from Śīlāditya III in *G.S.* 342/c. 661-662 A.D., and Bhaṭṭa Āchchaḍa of the Prince of Wales Museum Plates of Jayabhaṭa IV, issued in *K.S.* 486/c. 735-736 A.D., who was given the village of Mannātha were two such Brāhmaṇas. Likewise Siddhapabhaṭṭa in *Śaka* 836/c. 914-915 A.D., was endowed with the village of Tenna and Paṅḍita Delha received the village of Nalataḍāga in *V.S.* 1076/c. 1019 A.D., by the Betma grant of Paramāra Bhoja. Bhaṭṭa Śubhadāma, in the fifty-eighth year of Raṇabhañja and Govinda in the sixth year of Mahābhavagupta I became recipients of Turullā-*grāma* and Jambūgrāma respectively.

Besides these, sometimes, we come across a few Brāhmaṇas who were given more than one village as endowments. Brāhmaṇa Nārāyaṇamitra or Nārāyaṇa an emigrant from Ānandapura received from the Maitrakas, Dharasena IV and Kharagrāha II, the villages of Desurakṣitijja and Paṅgulapallikā.[17] Daṇḍimahādevī, the Bhauma-Kara queen in Orissa, by her Santiragama charter, gave to Bhaṭṭa Mākyadeva, Santīra-*grāma* and another locality called Komyosaṅga, which are unidentified, but which lay within Dakṣiṇa Tosala. Likewise, Neṭṭabhañja, issued a set of plates, referring to the grant of Rāigrāma and Seḍagrāma, both of which are yet unidentified, to the Brāhmaṇa Bhaṭṭa Dāuli. Mahābhavagupta I by his Cuttack Plates issued in his thirty-first regnal year, granted four villages, Raṇḍā Alāṇḍalā and Tūleṇḍā near Bolangir and Arkigrāma near Sambalpur to Mahattama Sādhāraṇa. His son Mahāśivagupta I, endowed Yaśakara with two villages Mārañja and Murā in the Kośala country, by his Mārañja-Murā grant issued in his third year. Later in his twenty-fourth and twenty-eighth years, Mahāśivagupta I, by two sets of

Patna Plates, benefited tha Brāhmaṇa Mohodadhi, bestowing on him the villages Ḍelā-ḍelī and Luttarumā on the banks of the river Ṭel in the Kośala country. In the absence of identification of most of these villages, it is difficult to assess how far spread out they were from one another. However, it is likely, that like the Brāhmaṇas who received scattered plots of lands, these recipients of two or more villages in Orissa too, had to depend on others for the supervision of at least parts of the lands donated to them.

Mention must be made here of the immigrant Brāhmaṇas, who had already emigrated from their ancestoral homes sometime before they received grants of land. They at times took up residence in the neighbourhood of the lands or villages, which they were to receive later, and sometimes, in places at some distance from them. One such Brāhmaṇa was Bhobika, who had left the Gauḍa country and was residing in the village of Charmmanihauha or Chamarwara, in the old Baroda state. Later on by the Prince of Wales Museum Plates of Govindarāja, dated *Śaka* 732/c. 810 A.D., he received the village of Usauṇaka two miles to the north-east of Chamarwara. Another Brāhmaṇa Vāsudeva and his son Rāmadeva, having emigrated from Śrāvasti, were living in the Yamagarta-*maṇḍala*. before Gayāḍatuṅga by his second set of Talcher Plates, donated to them, Vāmāitāllo-*grāma*, also in the Yamagarta-*maṇḍala*. Devaśarman who was to share the village with them, had originally lived in a village in North Bengal, and at the time of the grant, was a resident of Sāvira *bhaṭṭa-grāma* in Oḍra-*viṣaya*. It is possible, that these and other Brāhmaṇas like them, on receipt of the grant, did not think it necessary to migrate to the donated village. Instead they preferred to live where they had already settled down. For the supervision of the lands and villages that they had received, they might have let out the latter to tenant farmers who would look after them and cultivate them, while the donees could enjoy the income as landlords.

A peculiar feature to be noted is, that none of the immigrant donees of the Pālas and their feudatory officers, during the period under survey, with the exception of the temple and priests mentioned in the Khalimpur Plates, received whole villages from their patrons. Gopāla II, by his Jājilpārā grnat, donated to Śrīdharaśarman, two *pallis*, Kāṣṭhagṛha and Mahārāja, lying within the *agrahāra* of Ānandapura. The Bangarh grant of Mahīpāla I, records, that the village of Kuraṭapallikā, with the exception of Chūṭapallikā, with the low ground that belonged to the royal domain in the Gokalikā-*maṇḍala* of Puṇḍravardhana-*bhuktī* was given to Bhaṭṭaputra Kṛṣṇādityaśarman.

Two hypothetical reasons, may be suggested for the absence of grants of whole villages to Brāhmaṇa immigrants in Bengal. Perhaps, villages in North Bengal, were already populated by Brāhmaṇa families, which made it difficult to hand over entire villages to other Brāhmaṇas coming from outside. Alternately, the dearth of local Brāhmaṇas which is attested to by emigrations from Bengal, during the period of the decline and disintegration of the Pāla empire, might have had something to do with this. It may be, that the pālas eager to welcome new Brāhmaṇas to their kingdom, preferred to increase their number, by settling two or more Brāhmaṇa families in one village, rather than allotting one village to one family. However, whatever the reason might have been, the donees enjoyed a wide range of important tax privileges, which added to their income from their donated portions.

**Collective Landgrants**

Frequently plots of lands and villages were granted collectively to a group of Brāhmaṇas. In some cases, their numbers were three or four. The Nogawa Plates of Dhruvasena II of *GS* 320/c. 639-640 A.D., describe how a hundred *bhuktis* of land were granted to two Brāhmaṇas Agnisvāmin and Saṅgaravi. About a hundred years later in *Śaka* 663/c. 741 A.D., Rāṣṭhrakūṭa Dantidurga, donated a village to Māula, Ādityabhaṭṭa and Govisara. Vinītatuṅga II of Orissa by his Talcher Plates, granted Maddhamaṇḍa-*grāma* to be enjoyed as a *sahayoga* by two Brāhmaṇas, Naraka and Lakhādita. Mahābhavagupta I by the Patna Plates of his sixth year, granted the village of Vakaveḍḍā to Dāmaka, Vāsudeva,

Koṇḍadeva, and a fourth Brāhmaṇa whose name is not recorded. Ādityabhaṭṭa, Yajñubhaṭṭa and Khaṇḍidevabhaṭṭa, three Brāhmaṇa migrants from Bengal, were to share Sividi in Kandalivāda village, as known from the Cheedivalasa Plates of Eastern Gaṅga Devendravarman issued in the *Gaṅga* year 397/c. 893-894 A.D.

Sometime Brāhmaṇa co-donees far exceeded the number of those mentioned above. Śīlāditya I by his Navalakhi Plates of *G.S.* 286/c. 545-546 A.D. (?) (c. 605-606 A.D.), made a grant jointly to forty-four Brāhmaṇas. All of these had emigrated from Samgapurī.

Whereas all the donees of the charters discussed above, were immigrants, a number of land grants were made collectively to Brāhmaṇas both local and coming from elsewhere. One such instance is provided by the Nogawa Plates of Dhruvasena II of *saṁvat* 321/c. 640-641 A.D. One of the two donees of the charter had emigrated from Udumbaragahvara. The Bonda Plates of Mahāśiva Tīvara, give the names of twenty-five Brāhmaṇas, two of whom had come from Lāṭa and Avanti. By the Kaira Plates of Gurjara Dadda II, dated in the *Kalacuri* year 380/c. 629-630 A.D., forty Brāhmaṇas received the village of Śirīshapadraka. One among them had emigrated from Jambūsaras and another from Bhṛgukachchha. The others were resident Brāhmaṇas. Two other charters issued by Śīlāhāra Mummuṇirāja in *Śaka* 970/c. 1048-1049 A.D. and *Śaka* 971/c. 1049 A.D., record grants to Brāhmaṇas, some of whom were immigrants. The donees of the former, among whom one was from Madhyadeśa, were to share the revenues of some villages in the Bassein region of Maharashtra. A Brāhmaṇa from Lāṭa, one from Madhyadeśa and one from Gauḍa, figure among the donees of the latter, and were granted the village of Kichchita.

Most of the records on collective landgrants do not state the individual shares to be enjoyed by each donee. But sometimes immigrant Brāhmaṇas were singled out for greater attention. By his Cambay Plates of *Śaka* 852/c. 930 A.D., Govinda IV, bestowed six hundred *agrahāras* and three lacs of gold coins on a number of Brāhmaṇas. But only one of them

Nāgamārya, whose original home was at Kāvikā, but who at the time to the grant was living in Mānyakheṭa, was given a whole village, that of Kevañja. In the same way, Bhillamarāja III by his Kalas Budrukh Plates of *Śaka* 948/c. 1025 A.D., gave the village of Kalaśa to twenty-five Brāhmaṇas, the chief among whom was Maṅamvanāyaka from Takkārikā in Madhyadeśa.

Only one charter, the Gaonri Plates of Vākpati II of *V.S.* 1038/c. 981 A.D., specifies the shares of each Brāhmaṇa donee. Most of the twenty-six beneficiaries had left their homes in different places to come and settle in the Malwa region. It is remarkable that one of them, Sarvānanda, an emigrant from Koṇopā in Magadha, not only enjoyed the largest share, but was further granted the village of Kaḍahichchhaka, five years later, in *V.S.* 1043/c. 986 A.D. He was made the sole proprietor of this village. It seems therefore, that at times, preference was shown to immigrants over local Brāhmaṇas.

Collective landgrants by their very nature might indicate fragmentation of holdings. The size of the villages granted and the portion of each donee is very rarely known. Yet it is definite, that whenever plots of land in a village had to be divided among a number of Brāhmaṇas, each individual shere could not have been very large, specially where the donees numbered more than twenty, sometimes rising even to forty-four, as in the case of the Navalakhi Plates.

Sometimes migrant donees related to one another, were granted lands at the same time, by a single charter. This trend seems to have been a common factor throughout the period under discussion. Dharasena I donated two fields and a well to two brothers, Ajuna and Mankasvāmin. The Goras Copper Plate of Dhruvasena II of *GE* 313/c. 634 A.D., records a grant of two plots of land to Devakula and his cousin Bhāda. Three Brāhmaṇas shared two fields and a well, by a grant of Śilāditya III of *GS* 346/c. 666 A.D. One of them was Soma, the others being Piṭṭaleśvara and his son Nāga. The Lunsadi Plates of Śīlāditya II (Śīlāditya III ?) of *G.S.* 350/c. 669-670 A.D., give the names of two uterine brothers Īśvara and Bhaṭṭi who became co-beneficiaries of a pond and some pieces of land. Śryāśraya Śīlāditya by his Mudgapadra grant of *K.S.* 420/c.

668-669 A.D. bestowed a village on two cousins Revāditya and Varasyaka. Gayāḍatuṅga by his second set of Talcher Plates gave Vāmāitāllo-*grāma* to Devaśarman, Vāsudeva and his son Rāmadeva. The Patna Museum Plates of the sixth year of Mahābhavagupta I, benefited two brothers Keśava and Apya. Three brothers Duvanandī, Thiranandī and Bhaganandī from Bengal, migrated to the Kanara district, where Kulika Vīra Pracaṇḍadeva by his Hindol Plates, gave to them the village of Vaḍapāṭi.

But most remarkable is the case of the Asiatic Society's Plates of Gayāḍatuṅga. In it twenty-two Brāhmaṇas were jointly granted a village called Toro-*grāma*. According to D.C. Sircar the editor of the charter, all the twenty-two donees, probably belonged to the same family. They were divided into eleven groups, and each group was given a specific share. There were divisions within some of the groups, e.g. Rāmadeva and his five brothers together counted as one, enjoying one-eighteenth of the output of the village, and Śrīghoṣa and his three brothers could have one-twelfth.

The grant of lands and villages conjointly to members of one family implies, that Brāhmaṇas with a common origin and common affiliations could strengthen themselves financially, and in course of time could become a force to be reckoned with. It must be pointed out, however, that while the Maitrakas and Somavaṁśi Mahābhavagupta I were prepared to transfer lands together with accompanying tax privileges, either to Brāhmaṇa brothers or cousins, or even to two generations of one family, Śryāśraya Śīlāditya, Gayāḍatuṅga and Vīra Pracaṇḍadeva, were reluctant to do so, as their grants make no mention at all of the taxes that the donees could enjoy. Rather, in the case of Gayāḍatuṅga, they were required to pay a *tṛṇodaka* or a nominal tax to the king. So while some donors willingly encouraged property rights of specific immigrant families, others did not intend their donees to become financially independent of the control of their patrons.

**Extent of Grants, Revenues and other Privileges**

What gave the land grants any real meaning, was the transfer of the accompanying right to collect a varied number of taxes, which were levied on the land or the village.

Sometimes, however, this privilege was absent. Viceroys like Śrayāśraya Śīlāditya, and others e.g. Devānanda of the Nanda family, the Śulkis Jayastambha and Raṇastambha, the Bhañjas, Kanakabhañja, Neṭṭabhañja and Vidyādharabhañja, Vinītatuṅga II of the Tuṅga family, the Kulikas Vipracandra and Vīra Pracaṇḍadeva, Sinda Ādityavarman and Siṁharāja, and the Śīlāhāras Nāgārjuna and Mummuṇirāja, held back from all their migrant donees, the authority to levy taxes. Others like Caulukya Bhīmadeva I, Daṇḍimahādevī, Dharmamahādevī, Kulastambha, Gayāḍatuṅga, Raṇabhañja, Śatrubhañja and Narendrabhañja differentiated between one and another immigrant Brāhmaṇa donee in this matter. Caulukya Bhīmadeva I granted tax privileges to the donee of the charter of *V.S.* 1086/c. 1030 A.D. and the Bhadresar Plates of *V.S.* 1117/c. 1060 A.D. but not to the Brāhmaṇa of the Muṁdaka grant of *V.S.* 1086/c. 1030 A.D., whereby the Brāhmaṇa received only a *hala* of land. Dharmamahādevī denied tax rights to the donee of the Angul Plates, but allowed them to the Brāhmaṇa of the Taltalai charter. The donees of Raṇabhañja, with the exception of Śubhadāma of the Baud charter of his fifty-eighth year, were to enjoy tax privileges. It is difficult to understand why such distinctions should have been made. In the case of Bhīmadeva I, the donation of merely a *hala* of land, too small for any substantial taxes to be levied on it, may explain the exclusion of tax privileges from the Mumdaka grant, and their inclusion in his two other sets of plates, which record grants of whole villages. But as regards the others, no valid explanation is possible, except perhaps the whims and prejudices of the ruling class. Some scholars of course believe, that tax privileges were granted in every case, as the donation of a land or village always implied the accompaniment of these rights. They attribute the omission of their mention in some of the charters as carelessness on the part of the scribes and engravers. However, the fact,that it was the authority to levy taxes, that gave any grant its actual significance makes it difficult to accept the argument, that such an important feature should have been left out merely by mistake of the writer or engraver of the land grant charters. These, in ancient times, were regarded as valid, legal documents, clearly stating the rights and privileges of the beneficiaries.

**Revenues from Donated Areas**

The taxes that usually accrued to immigrant donees through land charters, were *bhāga, bhoga, uparikara, udraṅga, dhānya, hiraṇya, kara, bhūta-vāta-pratyāya, nidhi* and *upanidhi*. Scholars give various interpretations of these terms. Altekar's view that *bhāga* and *bhoga* were synonymous with *udraṅga* and *uparikara* respectively,[18] cannot be accepted. All the four terms occur together in many of the Maitraka records. The plates of Guhila Bhāvihita and those of the Paramāras Vākpati II and Bhoja, mention both *bhāga* and *bhoga* as well as *uparikara*. It seems therefore, that these terms had individual significance. *Bhāga* denoted the land revenue. Although inscriptions make no mention of its rate of assessment, some idea can be gathered from the literature of the period. Varying rates have been suggested by different scholars, for crops grown during different seasons. They are also based on the nature and fertility of the soil. However, the highest rate for *bhāga* seems to have been one-sixth and the lowest one-tenth.[19] *Bhoga* probably meant periodical supplies of fruits, firewood, flowers and the like, which the villagers furnished to the king.[20]

*Dhānya*, as gathered from the word itself, was probably a tax on paddy, collected from the people. *Hiraṇya* which occurs frequently in the records of the period, literally means gold. However, as U.N. Ghoshal points out,[21] it may have been a tax levied in cash upon certain special kinds of crops, as distinguished from the tax in kind, which was charged upon the ordinary crops. *Dhānya* and *hiraṇya*, have been translated by editors of land grants, as the state's share of grain and gold, possibly implying taxes on crops, realized both in kind and in cash.

*Udraṅga* and *uparikara* have been explained by U.N. Ghoshal, as taxes on permanent and temporary tenants.[22] D.C. Sircar explains *uparikara* as an additional tax, or tax paid by temporary tenants, and agrees with U.N. Ghoshal, that *udraṅga* was a tax on permanent tenants.[23] L. Gopal gives two synonyms for *udraṅga* and *uparikara*. According to him, they are identical with the expression of *Sakḷiptopakḷiptaḥ* dues on land, as these expressions do not appear anywhere together.[24] He cites the Hyderabad Plates of Pulakeśin II, where the expression *sakliptaḥ, soparikaraḥ* is used while enumerating the privileges. So L. Gopal concludes, that *sakliptaḥ* is the same as *sodraṅgaḥ*, while *sopakliptaḥ* and *soparikaraḥ* are identical with one another. As *klipta* occurs in the *Arthaśāstra*, in the sense of a fixed tax, he feels, that *upakliptaḥ* can be identified with *uparikara* which means the extra cess on cultivators over and above the fixed revenue of the state. S.K. Maity gives another interpretation for *udraṅga*. He argues, that as the *Rājataraṅgiṇī* of Kalhaṇa contains the word *draṅga* used in the sense of a watch-station, the word *udraṅga* probably meant a police tax levied on the district for the maintenance of the local police station.[25] It may, however, be pointed out, that Maity gives no explanation for the prefix *u* added to the word *draṅga*, which makes it difficult to agree with him. In the inscriptions of the Pālas, Paramāras, Somavaṁśis and Kalacuris, the term *kara* finds a place with other named and unnamed taxes, which could be collected by the donee, in forms like *sa-kara, samasta bhāga-bhoga kara, hiraṇya* etc. That *kara* did not mean a specific revenue income, is clear from the mention of other taxes ending with *kara*, e.g. *uparikara* and *bhāga-kara*. According to B.P. Mazumdar,[26] *soparikara* referred to in many inscriptions, e.g. the Betma grant of Bhoja dated in *V.S.* 1076/c. 1019 A.D. has never been regarded by any scholar as consisting of two taxes, *upari* and *kara*. He points out that in the Kudopali Plates of Mahābhavagupta II, the expression *sarvvo-parikara* is immediately followed by *karādānasahito* and concludes, that *uparikara* here clearly means one type of *kara* or tax. He further states, that as *bhāga* is essentially a land-revenue term and is mentioned in many Somavaṁśi charters, along with *kara*, it is certain, that *kara* in the period under review, cannot be the regular land revenue. When terms like *a-kiñcit-karagrāhya*, or *a-kiñcit-kara-pragrāhya*, were used, they meant, that the donee got the privilege of being free from all taxation. *Kara* in those cases, was no specific tax, but indicated all revenue income or taxes in general.

Coming to the term *bhūta-vāta-pratyāya*, this has been explained differently by scholars. Mirashi takes the expression to denote taxes on things manufactured or imported into the village. This belief is based on Altekar's view, that *bhūta* meant articles manufactured in the village itself, while *vāta* referred to those imported into the village, in short, the general excise and octroi duties collected at the village.[27] D.C. Sircar, however, disagrees. According to him, *bhūta-vāta-pratyāya* was the income that might arise out of changes in the natural or climatic conditions,[28] which implies, that it may have been a tax levied on agricultural products.

As for *nidhi* and *upanidhi*, which occur frequently in charters from Orissa, D.C. Sircar describes them as treasure hoard, or hidden treasures under the ground.[29]

It must, however, be pointed out, that all these taxes were not levied by all the ruling houses. In the earlier period, the Maitrakas seem to have exacted the largest number of taxes from their subjects. Consequently, when they granted a field or a village, they handed over all of these taxes, like *dhānya, hiraṇya, udraṅga, uparikara* and sometimes *bhāga, bhoga* and *bhūta-vāta-pratyāya* to their donees. As regards the early Gurjaras, it is remarkable, that additions were made to the list of taxes in successive generations. In the days of Daḍda II, *udraṅga* and *uparikara* were the two specifically mentioned taxes, as seen from his Kaira Plates of *K.S.* 380/c. 629-630 A.D. and the two sets of Sankheda Plates of *K.S.* 392/c. 642 A.D. Under Dadda III, *dhānya* and *hiraṇya* too came to be levied. The beneficiary of his Prince of Wales Museum Plates, dated *K.S.* 427/c. 676-677 A.D., was to enjoy these, together with *udraṅga* and *uparikara*. Later, Jayabhaṭa III and Jayabhaṭa IV added *bhūta-vāta-pratyāya* to the other four and allowed all these to their immigrant Brāhmaṇa donees. Guhila Bhāvihita by his charter issued in the *Harṣa* year 48, transferred to his donee, the right to collect only *bhāga, bhoga, uparikara* and *bhūta-vāta-pratyāya*. Avanijanāśraya Pulakeśirāja, like Dadda II, permitted the Brāhmaṇa Kāñcala to levy only *udraṅga* and *uparikara.*

In alter years, *haraṇya* seems to have been a common tax in the Rāṣṭrakūṭa, Pāla, Paramāra and Kalacuri kingdoms. The Rāṣṭrakūṭas sometimes levied it along with *uparikara*, *udraṅga* and *dhānya*, while the Pālas preferred *bhāga, bhoga* and *kara*. The Paramāras like the Pālas, apart from *hiraṇya*, allowed *bhāga*, and *bhoga* to their donees, adding to them *uparikara* as well. Karṇa Kalacuri, issued in the *Cedi* year 793/c. 1042 A.D., the Benares Plates, transferring to the beneficiary, rights to *bhāga, bhoga kara* and *hiraṇya*, and adding to them the right to mines. Bhīmadeva I by his grant of *V.S.* 1086/c. 1030 A.D., and by his Bhadresar Plates of *V.S.* 1117/c. 1060 A.D., gave away *bhāga, bhoga* and gold to his donees.

In Orissa, while the charters of the Bhauma-Karas mention only *uparikara*, those of the Tuṅgas and Bhañjas, lay stress on *nidhi* and *upanidhi* alone. Two exceptions, however, must be mentioned. Devadevadāma, the donee of the second set of Ādipur Plates of Narendrabhañja, was entitled to collect *uparikara*, instead of *nidhi* and *upanidhi*. Likewise Yaśabhañja by his Antirigam Plates, gave to his donee the right to levy *bhāga, bhoga* and *hiraṇya*, and not *nidhi* and *upanidhi*. The Somavaṁśi charters give the names of the largest number of taxes, *bhāga, bhoga, hiraṇya, uparikara*, *nidhi, upanidhi* and the general tax indicated by *kara*. The donees of the Cheedivalasa Plates of Eastern Gaṅga Devendravarman of the *Gaṅga* year 397/c. 893-894 A.D., were allowed *bhāga*, and *bhoga*.

From the discussion of the nature of these taxes described above, it appears, that *bhāga, dhānya* and *hiraṇya*, were the three items of taxation on crops, which could yield the major income. Where these were not transferred to immigrant Brāhmaṇas, they could avail themselves in some states, merely of *uparikara* or an extra cess, *bhoga* or supplies of fruits and flowers, *bhūta-vāta-pratyāya* or income from articles of trade, as well as that from treasure troves. Although the rate at which these taxes were levied in each kingdom, is not known, yet it would not be wrong to suggest that the donees of the period under survey, who were permitted to collect the first group of taxes, i.e. *bhāga, dhānya* and *hiraṇya* in the Maitraka, Gurjara, Guhila, Rāṣṭrakūṭa, Pāla, Paramāra, Caulukya, Somavaṁśi and Eastern Gaṅga kingdoms, perhaps could become financially more solvent, than their counterparts who were deprived of them.

It must, however, be kept in mind, that sometimes records do not mention all the taxes specifically. But they use expressions like *sarvvākara, sarvvādāna-saṁgrāhya, sarvvādāya-sametaḥ, karādāna sahitaḥ* and *ādibhiḥ*, to denote unnamed taxes in general, as can be seen from the records of the Rāṣṭrakūṭas, Kalacuris, Pālas, Paramāras and Somavaṁśis. It may mean that though only some taxes are mentioned as being handed over to the donees, others too may have been given as indicated by the use of the above mentioned terms.

Apart from these specifically mentioned tax privileges, Brāhmaṇa donees of the period were also entitled to levies on fruit bearing trees, pasture grounds, trees, animals and fish. Gopāla II, Mahīpāla I and Vigrahapāla III, allowed their donees to enjoy the yields of *āmra* and *madhuka* trees, and at the same time, handed over grazing grounds or *gocara* to them. The Paramāra charters make no mention of fruit trees specifically, but lay down that their donees were to receive pasture lands and trees along with the other privileges. Karṇa Kalacuri by his Benares Plates of *Cedi* 793/c. 1042 A.D., the Somavaṁśis, the Bhañjas Neṭṭabhañja and Kanakabhañja and Saurāditya from Bihar, by a grant of *V.S.* 1077/c. 1020 A.D., gave up their rights to fruit trees in favour of their immigrant donees. Likewise, Yaśabhañja by his Antirigram Plates, Kīrttirājadeva by his Phulsara Copper Plates, Śīlāhāra Nāgārjuna by the Thana Plates of *Śaka* 961/c. 1039 A.D., Caulukya Mūlarāja I by his Balera Plates of *V.S.* 1051/c. 994-995 A.D. and Bhīmadeva I by the Bhadresar Plates of *V.S.* 1117/c. 1060 A.D., all bestowed on their beneficiaries, the authority to enjoy the trees, grass and creepers lying within their donated shares. Among the Rāṣṭrakūṭas, Govinda IV by his Cambay Plates of *Śaka* 852/c. 930 A.D., transferred the right over fruit trees to his donees, while the village of Rikkaṭi was granted to the Brāhmaṇa Govindabhaṭṭa, along with rows of trees, by the Kolhapur Copper Plate of Akālavarṣadeva, dated *Śaka* 882/c. 960 A.D.

Charters from Orissa enumerate some other benefits which were not enjoyed by donees of the period in other regions. Fishery and hunting rights were allowed by Jayastambha and Kanakabhañja. Jayastambha also gave to the Brāhmaṇas, the privilege to collect tolls and ferry dues. Under the Bhauma-Karas, the income of weavers, *gokūṭa* or milkmen and *śauṇḍika* or vintners too, accrued to the migrant donees.

The system of collecting toll duties at gates, was prevalent in the Pāla kingdom as well. Gopāla II by his Jājilpārā grant, gave two plots of land in a village to an immigrant Brāhmaṇa, along with prospective *dvārikādāna*. According to P.N. Misra, the editor of the charter, the term means a tax or toll collected at the gates. Hence together with the revenue from the land and other taxes, Śrīdharaśarman could enjoy the income from toll duties as well.

Donation from markets has been mentioned in only two charters from Bengal. The Khalimpur Plates of Dharmapāla, where an endowment of four villages was made for the maintenance of a temple of the god Nunna-Nārāyaṇa, include the *haṭṭikā* or possibly small market attached to the villages, in the grant. Similarly, the donee of the Irda Plates of Nayapāla, enjoyed the right to markets. According to R.S. Sharma, the beneficiary of the Khalimpur Plates, would not allow as much a free hand to traders, with regard to the markets, as the state would do.[30] But this conclusion is not supported by facts. It is, however, possible that in both cases, merely the income from the markets was handed over to the donees.

The Thana Plates of Śīlāhāra Mummuṇirāja of *Śaka* 970/c. 1048-1049 A.D. record the grant of neither a village, nor a plot of land. The revenues of certain villages and fields, a house-tax and the produce of some fields, partly in food-grains and partly in the form of *drammas*, were assigned to the donees. The house-tax was levied at the rate of one *dramma* per house, and the plates state, that the *kumāragaḍyāṇas* derived from them, were pooled together and distributed among the donees. The term *kumāragaḍyāṇa* has not been explained by

Mirashi, the editor of the charter. D.C. Sircar,[31] describes *kumāragaḍyāṇaka* as a tax, probably of one *gaḍyāṇa* or gold coin, levied on the occasion of a prince's birth. It seems therefore, that in addition to the revenues of the villages, the Brāhmaṇa donees of the plates, were to enjoy a special tax which was received by the royal family on a particular occasion.

Some charters from Maharashtra contain the term *abhyantarasiddhi*. The donees of the Ellora Plates of Rāṣṭrakūṭa Dantidurga of *Śaka* 663/c. 741 A.D., a grant of Indra III dated in the *Śaka* year 836/c. 914-915 A.D., and another of Sinda Ādityavarman of *Śaka* 887/c. 965-966 A.D., all received this privilege. *Abhyantarasiddhi* has been explained by Bhandarkar, as the right of internal adjudication of a lawsuit, meaning that the donees were given the authority to settle internal disputes within their villages. Mirashi too describes the term *antaḥsiddhika* as the power of internal adjudication. However, as D.C. Sircar[32] points out, expressions like *tribhog-ābhyantarasiddhi* or *bāhy-ābhyantara-siddhi* render this doubtful. He explains, that *bāhya* may mean the income from the sale of things imported into a village or revenue from external sources collected mainly in cash, or taxes payable to the king. *Tribhog-ābhyantara* according to him, was the right to enjoy one-third of the revenue, the other two parts going in equal shares to gods and Brāhmaṇas. So he concludes that *abhyantarasiddhi*, means payment of revenue, or inland taxes to the village authorities, and not to the king. Hence when the right of *abhyantarasiddhi* was transferred to a donee, it implied, that henceforth, he was to enjoy some taxes which until then had been received by the village authorities.

Some other privileges were sometimes enjoyed by immigrant Brāhmaṇas. They were to receive the income arising from the fines imposed on persons committing one or many of the *daśāparādhas*. Maitraka, early Gurjara and Rāṣṭrakūṭa charters, included this right among the others handed over to Brāhmaṇa beneficiaries. Ghoshal's explanation that the term refers to the right of a donee to be exempted, at least in part, from the ordinary penalties for the commission of some traditional offences, has been refuted by L. Gopal.[33] He points out, that there is nothing in the records to show that the expression refers to an immunity to be enjoyed by the donee. The context in which it appears in the charters, shows that it was one among the sources of revenue, that the kings gave up in favour of their donees. As he puts it, if the term had signified an immunity, it would have been written as *adaśāparādhadaṇḍaḥ*. Hence the granting of *daśāparādha* meant that the donee could collect the fines arising therefrom.

Charters from Assam and Bengal mention the word *caurod-dharaṇa*. D.C. Sricar[34] says, that according to some scholars it indicated the right to punish thieves or impose fines on them. He himself explains it as the right to recover stolen property. So the rulers of Bengal and Assam in some cases, allowed their beneficiaries to levy fines on thieves or to seize stolen property.

At times donees were also given the right to subject the villagers to *viṣṭi* or forced labour. The term *sotpadyamānaviṣṭika* occurs in some of the Maitraka and Rāṣṭrakūṭa records. This implies, that the "right to get unpaid labour whenever that may be due from the tenants" (Sircar, D.C. *IEG* p. 406), was transferred to the donees.

It may be mentioned here, that there is some disagreement between scholars, as regards the position of the people who were liable to be forcibly employed by the donees. L. Gopal believes, that although they were not slaves, these people can be regarded as serfs, albeit in a restricted sense, if performance of service for others, is taken to be the essence of the status of serf. But D.C. Sircar does not agree. According to him, the Indian kings or landlords of the early period, demanded free labour from the subjects. The charters creating rent-free holdings state specifically, that the right to unpaid labour from the tenants was transferred to the donee who was himself exempted from all obstruction or troubles, including the supply of free labour to the kind. But the obligation was not of the feudal king, as nobody was tied to the soil. They were not compelled to serve the king or landlord, when they gave up the possession of the property. Hence their obligation and status were not the same as those of serfs.

Accompanying the privileges, were certain immunities, safeguarding the immigrant donees. The most important of these was the immunity from all taxes and imposts. Moreover the donated land or village was to be free from interference by royal officials, as well as the billeting of *cāṭas* and *bhaṭas*. Besides, as mentioned in the records, the donees were reassured with the undertaking, that their villages would be free from all oppressions.

All donated lands, however, were not rent-free. With regard to immigrant Brāhmaṇas, there are a few instances of *kara-śāsanas* available from Orissa. Migrant Brāhmaṇas receiving villages from the Śulkis, Tuṅgas, Bhañjas and Somavaṁśis, had sometimes to pay a sum of money, as a rent to the king, although the word *kara* is not always used. Instead one also comes across the term *tṛṇodaka* in this connection. *Tṛṇodaka*, literally meaning grass and water, implies that the rent paid, was equal to the value of grass and water. In other words, it was just a nominal rent to be paid by the Brāhmaṇa for the land that he enjoyed. In the Puri Plates of Kulastambha, the recipient of the village Paḍāra, had to give a fixed rent of ten *palas* of silver per annum. His Talcher Plates required, that although Singagrāma had been donated as a rent-free holding, the donee would have to pay annually, a nominal rent of the value of a *tṛṇodaka*, amounting to two *palas* of silver. The Juraḍa grant of Neṭṭabhañja provided that the royal tax for the donated village was assessed at four silver *palas*, and a further sum of four *palas* was due for the taxes called *khaṇḍapālamuṇḍamola*. According to D.C. Sircar,[37] *khaṇḍapāla* was probably a cess payable to the officer-in-charge of a *khaṇḍa* or sub-division of a district. The second set of Talcher Plates of Gayāḍatuṅga, fix the rent at four silver *palas* worth of *tṛṇodaka* to be collected from the donees while in his Asiatic Society's Plates, it was to be nine *palas* per annum. Mahābhavagupta I realized a *kara* of eight *palas* annually, from the four Brāhmaṇas who received Vakaveḍḍā village by a *kara-śāsana*. The same amount had to be paid by Keśava and Apya, the beneficiaries of his Patna Museum Plates of his sixth year. It is remarkable that the charters called *kara-śāsanas* often declared the grant to be rent-free. Anyway, the rent paid was nominal, and the donees in most cases, enjoyed other privileges.

Mention must be made here of the Phulsara Copper Plates of Eastern Gaṅga Kīrttirājadeva. It is clear from the plates, that the income from the donated villages, was twenty-four *rūpyākhas* or *ruākhas*, and also a *yuvarāja-chhāya*, which is interpreted by the editor S.N. Rajaguru, as a tax, of one and a half *rūpyas*. At the same time it is not possible to explain the figure twenty before *caturaviṁśa*, and whether it has been correctly read by the editor.

**Immigrants as Royal Officials**

Some Brāhmaṇas are known to have held administrative posts in the states to which they had migrated. The Kolagallu Inscription of Khoṭṭiga of *Śaka* 889/c. 967 A.D., mentions one Gadādhara from Bengal. He had the consecration of images and construction of wells, tanks and monasteries to his credit, and was probably in charge of the realm of Kārttikeya, which might have been a territorial unit granted to him. In the Bangaon Plates issued in the seventeenth year of Vigrahapāla III, the actual donor of the village, was a Brāhmaṇa named Ghaṇṭīśa, whose ancestors had emigrated from Kroḍāñca. He held the post of a *vidheya* and was making the grant out of his own lands. This means, that he was in possession of lands, which might have been granted either to him or to his ancestors probably by some Pāla ruler. Another migrant Brāhmaṇa, Mahattama Sādhāraṇa who received four villages by the Cuttack Plates of Mahābhavagupta I, served as his *mantrin*. Unlike these, there were others in humble service. An immigrant Brāhmaṇa Devu, has been described as a *kāladeśī*. He probably served as an astrologer, attached to the *sadākaṭaka* or permanent camp of Mahābhavagupta I. The king by the Kalibhanā Plates of his thirty-fourth year, gave to him Konnayillā-*grāma*. A Brahmaṇa qualified as a *pratihāra* or door-keeper, was the donee of a grant of Daṇḍimahādevī, and received a village from her.

It may be suggested that the Brāhmaṇas Gadādhara, Ghaṇṭīśa, and Mahattama Sādhāraṇa, who held administrative offices, and at the same time received lands from their patrons, must have been eminent persons. Besides, they were sufficiently wealthy and powerful, not only to undertake works of public utility from personal funds, as was the case with Gadādhara, but also to make grants of land from their personal property. It is to be noted, however, that none of the charters say anything, as to whether grants of land to such immigrant Brāhmaṇas in royal service, were made in lieu of salary.

Not all immigrant Brāhmaṇas, however, were endowed with lands and villages. Some inscriptions make mention of Brāhmaṇa writers and composers of charters and *praśastis*, who had emigrated from their ancestral homes. Among those were Iśāna, the composer of the Mahua Inscription of Vatsarāja, Vimalamati who had composed the Mandakila Tal Inscription of *V.S.* 1043/c. 986 A.D., and Bhaṭṭa Kakka, the writer of the Hansot Plates of Cāhamāna Bhartṛvaḍḍha II of *V.S.* 813/c. 756 A.D., who are not known to have received grants from their kings. Another Brāhmaṇa Sillaṇa who had emigrated from Oyarī-*grāma* in Madhyadeśa, to serve under Paramāra Vairisiṁha of Dhārā has been described as a *nāyaka*. He probably belonged to the military department, although nothing has been said, as to whether he was the recipient of any endowment. As a matter of fact, the records which mention these Brāhmaṇas, contain no hints whatsoever about their mode of payment, although it is probable, that they received their salary in cash.

The same can be said about the Brāhmaṇa poets and scholars like Bhāravi, Bhavabhūti, Rājaśekhara, and Lakṣmīdhara. They adorned the royal courts, and were undoubtedly favoured by their patrons, although the texts give no idea about their emoluments or salary.

**Concluding Remarks**

A study of the conditions governing the grants made to local Brāhmaṇas, can help to form a comparative idea, about the position of migrant Brāhmaṇas. In some cases, no distinctions were made between the local and immigrant Brāhmaṇas. Mahāśiva Tīvara by his Bonda Plates[38] and

Baloda Plates,[39] bestowed exactly the same privileges on his migrant and local donees respectively. Śryāśraya Śīlāditya allowed no tax privileges to either the resident or the migrant donees of his Navasari Plates of *K.S.* 421/c. 669-670 A.D., or his Mudgapadra grant of *K.S.* 420/c. 668-669 A.D.[40] Among the Rāṣṭrakūṭas, Indra III handed over similar rights of taxation to the resident and migrant dones of two grants of *Śaka* 836/c. 914-915 A.D.[41]. Coming to Orissa, both the local and immigrant donees were denied by Śulki Raṇastambha the privilege of collecting taxes.[42]

Unlike these donors who did not favour the resident Brāhmaṇas at the cost of the immigrants, or *vice-versa*, there were two ruling chiefs, who although granting lands to Brāhmaṇas coming from outside, refused to endow them with the privilege of levying various taxes. Whereas the immigrant donees of the Khargaprasad Plates and Talcher Plates of Vinītatuṅga II, were deprived of all taxes, the local Brāhmaṇa in a grant from Bonai, was to receive the *uparikara* arising from the village given to him.[43] Like Vinītatuṅga II, Neṭṭabhañja too permitted *bhoga* to be collected by a resident donee,[44] but denied it to the immigrant Brāhmaṇas of the Juraḍa grant and another charter.[45] A comparative study, therefore, reveals, that apart from the donees of Vinītatuṅga II and Neṭṭabhañja, the local and immigrant Brāhmaṇas, on the whole, received similar treatment and benefits from their patrons.

From the above discussion, certain trends, emerge, related to the economic position of the immigrant Brāhmaṇas. Certain features, e.g. granting of plots of lands as well as villages, and the system of donating lands collectively, both to members of the same family and to unrelated Brāhmaṇas, were common throughout the period c. 475-1030 A.D. But some changes too are visible. Whereas in the days of the Maitrakas and Gurjaras, usually widely spread out plots broken up into smaller separated pieces, were handed over to the same donee, by the same grant, this practice seems to have become less frequent in the time of the Rāṣṭrakūṭas. The grants of the Pālas, Paramāras and Somavaṁśis, resemble those of the Rāṣṭrakūṭas.

Besides, grants of whole villages were more common in later years, than in the earlier period. Coming to the tax privileges, while under the Maitrakas, *bhāga, bhoga, dhānya, hiraṇya, udraṅga* and *uparikara*, were all handed over to the donees of some of their charters, in none of the records of the other ruling houses, are all of them specifically mentioned as being granted to Brāhmaṇas. On the other hand, while the term *kara* came to be frequently used from the eighth century onwards, one hardly comes across the expression in the inscriptions of the Maitrakas, Gurjaras, Guhilas and Cālukyas. Moreover the system of exacting a nominal rent from some of the donees, seems to have been a later development.

As far as the financial position of the immigrant Brāhmaṇas is concerned, apart from those in royal service, who must have received something in the nature of a salary, many were benefited to a greater or lesser degree, on receipt of their land grants. It may be suggested, that those donees who received grants unaccompanied by tax privileges, were probably in the position of tenants of their donors. They would be responsible for ensuring the proper cultivation of the plots for their patrons. The revenues and taxes from those lands would go to add to the donor's private income, while the donees would be entitled to only the produce of the soil. In fact, the donors would still be the owners of the lands, and the donees would merely be in the position of non-paying permanent tenants, unlike the other immigrants who enjoying the tax privileges accompanying their grants, would become real owners of the lands that they received.

Among the latter, the owners of scattered plots of lands and those of two or more villages, might have appointed tenants or tenant-farmers, to look after parts of their grants. The same might have been the case with those who perhaps decided to live in the towns or villages, where they had first taken up residence, after emigrating from their ancestral homes, rather than migrating again to their donated villages. These two groups of people, as a result of their land grants could become landlords who were dependent on others for the cultivation and supervision of their fields and villages, but who enjoyed the income arising from them.

The richest of course, were the Brāhmaṇas who were endowed with more than one village, accompanied by important tax privileges. Nārāyaṇamitra of the Maitraka grants held two villages enjoying *bhāga, bhoga, dhānya, hiraṇya, udraṅga, uparikara* and *bhūta-vāta-pratyāya*. There were three donees of the Somavaṁśi charters, Mahattama Sādhāraṇa, Yaśakara and Mahodadhi, the first, the recipient of four villages, and the two others of two each. They were permitted to collect *bhāga, bhoga, uparikara, hiraṇya, nidhi* and *upanidhi*. These Brāhmaṇas deserve special mention.

It is difficult, however, to make any proper assessment of the relative financial position of immigrant Brāhmaṇa donees in the different kingdoms. The lack of any uniform standard unit of measurement of the area of the lands and villages granted, the dearth of information about the rates at which taxes were levied at different times, and the silence of some of the charters as regards the individual shares of the donees of the collective grants, all add to the problem. But on the whole, the immigrant Brāhmaṇas perhaps did not lose anything by seeking new horizons. While some of them entered into royal service, others were enabled to enjoy the produce of the soil as non-paying permanent tenants of their donors. Some became fairly wealthy proprietors of lands and villages, collecting taxes and income from them, and at times assuming the position of landlords.

## References

1. Sircar, D.C., *IEG*, p. 220.
2. *Ibid*, p. 225.
3. *Ibid*, p. 251.
4. *JBORS*, II, p. 409.
5. *JASB*, XVII, p. 250, cf. fn. 4.
6. *EI*, I, 154 ff.
7. Sircar D.C., *IEG*, p. 101.
8. *Ibid*, p. 125.
9. *Ibid*, p. 165.
10. Majumdar, R.C. (ed.), *HB*, I, pp. 652 and 665.

11. Pargiter, *IA*, 1910, p. 216.
12. Maity, S.K., *Economic Life In Northern India In The Gupta Period,* p. 53.
13. Sircar D.C., *IEG*, p. 257.
14. *Ibid*, p. 242.
15. *EI*, XXXV, p. 210, 11. 15-17 (text).
16. *JASB*, XVII, p. 139, fn. 5.
17. *IA*, VII, p. 73; *Ibid*, p. 76.
18. Altekar, A.S., *RAT*, p. 214.
19. Mazumdar, B.P., *Land Revenue in India*, pp. 22-23.
20. Ghoshal, U.N., *HRS*, p. 317.
21. *Ibid*, p. 75.
22. *Ibid*, p. 276.
23. Sircar, D.C,, *IEG*, p. 352; *Ibid*, p. 349.
24. Gopal, L., *JBBRAS*, XXXIII-XXXIV, pp. 168-169.
25. Maity, S.K. *op. cit*., p. 85.
26. Mazumdar, B.P., in *IHC* (1972), pp. 25-29.
27. *CII*, IV, p. 89; Altekar, A.S., *RAT*, p. 229.
28. *EI*, XXXIV, p. 171.
29. Sircar, D.C., *IEG*, p. 216.
30. Sharma, R.S., Indian Feudalism, p. 125.
31. Sircar, D.C., *IEG*, pp. 408, 432 and 435.
32. *Ibid*, pp. 3, 44 and 343.
33. Gopal, L., *op. cit*., pp. 169-170.
34. Sircar, D.C., *IEG*, p. 71.
35. Sircar, D.C., *JOIB*, XVI, 1966-1967, p. 169.
36. Sircar, D.C., *Ibid.*
37. Sircar, D.C., *JRAS*, 1952, p. 8.
38. *EI*, XXXIV, p. 111.
39. *Ibid*., VII, p. 102.
40. *Ibid*, XXXIV, p. 117 Mudgapadra grant, *CII*, IV, p. 123, Navasari Plates.
41. *EI*, IX, pp. 29 and 33.
42. *JBORS*, II, p. 396, *Ibid*, IV, p. 168.
43. *EI*, XXXVIII, pp. 124 and 128, Khargaprasad and Talcher Plates, *JBORS*, VI, p. 236, Bonai Plates.
44. *JBORS*, XVII, p. 104.
45. *EI*, XXIV, p. 15, Juraḍa grant, *Ibid*, XXVIII, p. 278.

# Conclusion

Movement of Brāhmaṇas from one part of India to another, seems to have been a common occurrence during the period c. 475-1030 A.D. Although less frequent in the days of the Maitrakas and Gurjaras, the number of migrations increased considerably in the years following c. 750 A.D. At the same time, it was generally after c. 750 A.D., that emigrations from places or localities like Varendrī, Śrāvasti, Ṭakāri, Kolāñca, Hastigrāma, Hastipada and Madhyadeśa began. Another noticeable fact as gleaned from epigraphs is, that although same Brāhmaṇas went to live under the Rāṣṭrakūṭas in Maharashtra, some under the Pālas in Bihar and Bengal, and some under the Paramāras in Madhya Pradesh, by far the largest number migrated to Orissa, where they settled down under the various ruling houses. But what is more peculiar is, that while Orissa attracted so many Brāhmaṇas from outside, none are heard of as having moved out of Orissa.

As regards the pattern of migration, while in the earlier days, movement was confined to short distances, e.g. within Gujarat itself, later Brāhmaṇas began to make longer journeys, in search of new homes. In the early centuries of the period under review, usually the tendency was to seek familiar surroundings. In most of the Maitraka charters, Brāhmaṇas emigrating from towns, moved to take up residence not in villages, but sometimes in the capital town of Valabhī and sometimes in other important cities like Kheṭaka or Kaira. Later the trend changed. Most of the immigrant Brāhmaṇas who settled in villages in Bengal, Bihar and Orissa, had originally lived in villages. Some, perhaps the more adventurous among the immigrants, sought a complete change of scene, leaving towns to settle in villages and *vice-versa*.

As for the reasons which forced Brāhmaṇas to migrate at all, the records to not furnish clear clues to help in the solution of the problem. Although the traditional theory is, that Brāhmaṇas were imported by Ādiśūra into Bengal, that legend has been proved to have no historical basis. However, the theory of invitation of Brāhmaṇas, from U.P. to come to Bengal, is unacceptable.

Although there is no mention of the causes of migration in the inscriptions, we may suggest, that to a certain extent, political factors may have been responsible for a number of migrations. In the years following the death of Devapāla in c. 850 A.D., the weakening of the Pāla empire, threatened time and time again by the ambitious designs of the Paramāras, the Kalacuris the Candellas, the Kambojas and the Somavaṁśis, led to a number of emigrations from Bengal. At the same time, the struggle over Kanauj, leading to hostilities between the Pālas, the Gurjara-Pratihāras and the Rāṣṭrakūṭas, set in motion further migrations within or from Northern India. Later, the invasions of Sultan Mahmūd also had the same result. Driven from their homes by these forces, and moving away from decadent localities, the prime factors behind most of these migrations were the basic desire for security and safety and the search for improved means of livelihood.

Seen from this aspect, the movements were justified. While some among the immigrants came to be employed as teachers, priests, military officials, ministers, writers and composers of inscriptions and sharters, most of them, sometimes individually, sometimes as a family, and sometimes as members of a large group of Brāhmaṇas, not related to one another, were endowed with lands and villages. The specific inclusion of wells, reservoirs and other irrigation facilities in grants of the early period, point to the fact, that the lands donated, were definitely cultivable. In later years too, mostly such villages must have been granted, which could be brought under the plough. Usually the transfer of lands was accompanied by the authority to collect taxes, which varied from kingdom to kingdom and period to period. Almost all the major ruling houses, like the Maitrakas, Gurjaras, Rāṣṭrakūṭas, Pālas,

Paramāras and Somavaṁśis, handed to their donees the right to levy various taxes from the soil, together with a number of other privileges. The minor rulers, however, e.g. the Bhauma-Karas and the Bhañjas, permitted merely extra taxes, i.e. those other than land-revenue and the control over treasure-troves to their beneficiaries. Sometimes the fields or two or three villages bestowed on the same donee, were widely spread out, and were not contiguous to one another. Brāhmaṇas who received lands like these, and those who having migrated earlier were already settled in a village, but were later given lands in another village, were perhaps unable to supervise the cultivation of donated lands. In the absence of identification of all villages and towns recorded in the charters, it is difficult to measure the distance between scattered plots of lands and villages, or between the places of residence of immigrant Brāhmaṇas and the villages donated to them. However, the possibility cannot be denied that such Brāhmaṇas may have had to appoint tenant farmers to cultivate at least parts of their gift lands. Consequently the donees themselves enjoyed the income and profits from the land, thereby assuming the position of landlords. It must, however, be mentioned, that there was no remarkable distinction between the local and immigrant Brāhmaṇas, the latter not gaining financially in comparison with their local counter-parts.

The immigrant Brāhmaṇas included within their ranks, men of various *gotras*. Gregarious by nature, sometimes members of the same *gotras*, with common Vedic affiliations, tended to live in the same place. For example, all migrant Brāhmaṇas coming from Hastigrāma, belonged to the Parāśara *gotra*, while those emigrating from Ṭakāri, Kolāñca and Muktāvathi, were members of the Bharadvāja, Śāṇḍilya and Kaśyapa *gotras* respectively. What led to the migration of men of these particular *gotras*, e.g. only the Bharadvājas from Ṭakāri, or only the Śāṇḍilyas from Kolāñca, is an enigma. As long as any evidence of the cause of their migration is not known, it will be improper to suggest any reason for their movement. Most of the Brāhmaṇas coming from centres in Madhyadeśa, ultimately settled in Orissa. While the majority were acquainted with at least one Vedic *śākhā*, quite a few among them were well versed in more than one *Veda*. It is remarkable, that all known Brāhmaṇa migrants from Ṭakāri of the Bharadvāja *gotra*, were students of the *Śukla Yajus*. As for the connection between *gotra* and *śākhā*, four of the five immigrant Gautamas, followed the Yajurvedic school, while all the Śārkarākṣis have been described as *Bahvṛchas*. The *Śukla* and *Kṛṣṇa* schools of the *Yajurveda* were the most popular. Subjects like logic, history and grammar were also studied. Some were qualified to be teachers, as can be seen from the epithets *upādhyāya* and *ācārya* added to their names. Others officiated as priests in temples and during religious and social functions. As regards their family life, this on the whole seems to have been characterized by bonds of affection, members of the same family living in close proximity with one another. Women, however, hardly find any mention in the charters dealing with immigrant Brāhmaṇas, and did not make a significant contribution to society as a whole.

As for the impact of the immigrant Brāhmaṇas, some positive contributions may be attributed to them. As they brought with them their ancient traditions, they helped to build up a society with uniform characteristics throughout Northern India. Some of them like Gadādhara of the Kolagallu Inscription and Prahāsa of the Silimpur Stone Inscription had to their credit erection of temples and charitable work. The more learned among them, encouraged the spread of education, while the immigrant poets, dramatists and grammarians, left behind them some immortal works. Other than these cultural contributions, as the Brāhmaṇas received lands and villages, they played an active part in the colonization and settlement of new areas in Gujarat, Orissa and Bengal. Their advent benefited them as well as their patrons. Some of them gradually developed into a fairly wealthy land-owning section, who, enjoying the privileges transferred to them by the ruling class came to constitute a loyal element in the population, ready to uphold and maintain the authority of the king.

# List of Inscriptions

1. Bonda Plates of Mahāśiva Tīvara, *EI*, XXXIV, p. 111.
2. Copper Plate of Maitraka Dharasena I, *IA*, I, p. 14.
3. Grant of Dharasena II, *saṁvat* 270/c. 589-590 A.D., *IA*, VII, p. 70.
4. Abhona Plates of Kalacuri Śaṁkaragaṇa, *K.S.* 347/c. 596-597 A.D., *CII*, IV, p. 38.
5. Navalakhi Plates of Śīlāditya I, *G.S.* 286/c. 545-546 A.D. (?) (605-606 A.D.), *EI*, XI, p. 174.
6. Grant of Śīlāditya I, *G.S.* 287/c. 608 A.D., *JBBRAS*, N.S.I, p. 28.
7. Kaira Plates of Gurjara Dadda II, *K.S.* 380/c. 629-630 A.D.,*CII*, IV, p. 57.
8. Lohaner Plates of Cāḷukya Pulakeśin II, *Śaka* 552/c. 630 A.D., *EI*, XXVII, p. 37.
9. Grant of Dhruvasena II Bālāditya, *G.S.* 312/c. 632 A.D., *JBBRAS*, N.S.I, p. 69.
10. Goras C.P. of Dhruvasena II, *GE.* 313/c. 634 A.D., *JBBRAS*, N.S.I., p. 50.
11. Nogawa Plates of Dhruvasena II, *G.S.* 320/c. 639-640 A.D., *EI*, VIII, p. 188.
12. Nogawa Plates of Dhruvasena II, *saṁvat* 321/c. 640-641 A.D., *EI*, VIII, p. 194.
13. Sankheda Plates of Dadda II, *K.S.* 392/c. 642 A.D., *CII*, IV, p. 75.
14. Sankheda Plates of Dadda II, *K.S.* 392/c. 642 A.D., *CII*, IV, p. 78.
15. Amreli Museum Plates of Dhruvasena II, *saṁvat* 323/c. 642-643 A.D.,*EI*, XXXV, p. 281.
16. Grant of Guhila Bhāvihita, *Harṣa* year 48, *EI*, XXXIV, p. 167.

17. Grant of Dharasena IV, *G.S.* 330/c. 649-650 A.D., *IA*, VII, p. 73.
18. Grant of Dharasena IV, *IA*, XV, p. 335.
19. Grant of Dhruvasena III, *saṁvat* 334/c. 653-654 A.D., *EI*, I, p. 85.
20. Grant of Kharagrāha II Dharmāditya, *G.S.*, 337/c. 656-657 A.D., *IA*, VII, p. 76.
21. Grant of Śīlāditya III, *G.S.* 342/c. 661-662 A.D., *IA* V, p. 212.
22. Grant of Śīlāditya III *Gupta saṁvat* 346/c. 666 A.D., *JBBRAS*, N.S.I., p. 71.
23. Grant of Śīlāditya III *Gupta saṁvat* 346/c. 666 A.D., *JBBRAS*, N.S.I., p. 73.
24. Jesar Plates of Śīlāditya III, *Gupta saṁvat* 347/c. 666-667 A.D., *EI*, XXI, p. 208.
25. Mudgapadra grant of Śryāśraya Śīlāditya, *K.S.* 420/c. 668-669 A.D., *EI*, XXXIV, p. 117.
26. Lunsadi Plates of Śīlāditya II, (Śīlāditya III ?) *G.S.* 350/c. 669-670 A.D., *EI*, IV, p. 74.
27. Grant of Śīlāditya II (Śīlāditya III ?): *saṁvat* 352/c. 671-672 A.D., *IA*, XI, p. 305.
28. Jesar Plates of Śīlāditya III, *Valabhī saṁvat* 357/c. 676-677 A.D. *EI*, XXII, p. 114.
29. Prince of Wales Museum Plates of Dadda III, *K.S.* 427/c. 676-677 A.D., *EI*, XXVII, p. 197.
30. Parlakimedi Plates of Eastern Gaṅga Anantavarman, *Gaṅga* 204/c. 700 A.D., *EI* XXVI, p. 65.
31. Navasari Plates of Jayabhaṭa III, *K.S.* 456/c. 705-706 A.D., *CII*, IV, p. 82.
32. Grant of Śīlāditya, *G.S.* 403/c. 722-723 A.D., *JBBRAS*, XI, p. 335.
33. Prince of Wales Museum Plates of Jayabhaṭa IV, *K.S.* 486/c. 735-736 A.D., *CII*, IV, p. 102.
34. Navasari Plates of Avanijanāśraya Pulakeśirāja, *K.S.* 490/c. 739-740 A.D., *CII*, IV, p. 137.
35. Ellora Plates of Rāṣṭrakūṭa Dantidurga, *Śaka* 663/c. 741 A.D., *EI*, XXV, p. 25.
36. Mahua Inscription of Vatsarāja, *EI*, XXXVII, p. 53.

37. Hansot Plates of Cāhamāna Bhartṝvaḍḍha II, *V.S.* 813/c. 756 A.D., *EI*, XII, p. 197.
38. Hilol Plates of the year 470, *EI*, XXXIV, p. 213.
39. Khalimpur Plates of Dharmapāla, thirty-second regnal year; *EI*, IV, p. 243.
40. Indian Museum Plates of Devendravarman III, *Gaṅga* 308/c. 804-806 A.D., *EI*, XXIII, p. 73.
41. Prince of Wales Museum Plates of Govindarāja *Śaka* 732/c. 810 A.D., *EI*, XXVI, p. 248.
42. Baroda grant of Karkka Suvarṇavarṣa, *Śaka* 734/c. 812 A.D., *IA*, XII, p. 156; *JASB*, N.S. VIII, p. 292.
43. Baripada Museum Plates of Devānandadeva, *EI*, XXVI, p. 74.
44. Jurerpur Plates of Devānandadeva, end of 9th century A.D., *EI*, XXVII, p. 325.
45. Grant of Devānandadeva, *OHRJ*, XV, p. 115.
46. Cheedivalasa Plates of Eastern Gaṅga Devendravarman, *Gaṅga* 397/c. 893-894 A.D., *JAHRS*, II, p. 146.
47. Phulsara Plates of Kīrttirājadeva, *JAHRS*, III, p. 30.
48. Dhenkanal grant of Śulki Jayastambha, *JASB*, N.S. XXVII, p. 322.
49. Dhenkanal grant of Jayastambha, *JBORS*, II, p. 405.
50. Dhenkanal grant of Jayastambha, *JBORS*, II, p. 409.
51. Dhenkanal grant of Jayastambha, *JBORS*, II, p. 412.
52. Dhenkanal grant of Kulastambha, *JBORS*, II, p. 400.
53. Talcher Plates of Kulastambha, *EI*, XII, p. 156.
54. Puri Plates of Kulastambha, *EI*, XXIX, p. 164.
55. Grant of Raṇastambha, *JBORS*, IV, p. 168.
56. Jambgaon grant of Indra III, *Śaka* 836/c. 914-915 A.D., *EI*, IX, p. 24.
57. Chinchani grant of Indra III, *Śaka* 848/c. 926-927 A.D., *EI*, XXXII, p. 45.
58. Cambay Plates of Govinda IV, *Śaka* 852/c. 930 A.D., *EI*, VII, p. 26.
59. Sāngli grant of Govinda IV, *Śaka* 855/c. 933 A.D., *IA*, XII, p. 247.
60. Deoli Plates of Kṛṣṇa III, *Śaka* 862/c. 940 A.D., *EI*, V, p. 188.

61. Jājilpārā grant of Gopāla II, sixth regnal year, *JASB*, XVII, p. 137.
62. Siyadoni Inscription of Devapāla, *EI*, I, p. 172.
63. Kolhapur C.P. of Akālavarṣadeva, *Śaka* 882/c. 960 A.D., *JBBRAS*, N.S. X, p. 21.
64. Grant of Sindạ Ādityavarman, *Śaka* 887/c. 965-966 A.D., *EI*, XXV, p. 164.
65. Kolagallu Inscription of Khoṭṭiga, *Śaka* 889/c. 967 A.D., *EI*, XXI, p. 260.
66. Dharmapuri grant of Paramāra Vākpati II, *V.S.* 1031/c. 974 A.D., *IA*, VI, p. 51.
67. Gaonri Plates of Vākpati II, *V.S.* 1038/c. 981 A.D.., *EI*, XXIII, p. 108.
68. Gaonri Plates of Vākpati II, *V.S.* 1043/c. 986 A.D., *EI*, XXIII, p. 111.
69. Mandakila Tal Inscription, *V.S.* 1043/c. 986 A.D., *EI*, XXXIV, p. 77.
70. Balera Plates of Caulukya Mūlarāja I, *V.S.* 1051/c. 994-995 A.D., *EI*, X, p. 76.
71. Jodhpur grant of Siṁharāja, *V.S.* 1054/c. 997 A.D., *EI* XXXVI, p. 45.
72. Bangarh grant of Mahīpāla I, ninth regnal year, *EI*, XIV, p. 324.
73. Grant of Candella Dhaṅgadeva *V.S.* 1055/c. 998 A.D., *IA*, XVI, p. 201.
74. Irda Plates of Nayapāla, *EI*, XXII, p. 150.
75. Santiragama grant of Daṇḍimahādevī, *EI*, XXIX, p. 79.
76. Grant of Daṇḍimahādevī, *EI*, VI, p. 133.
77. Grant of Vakulamahādevī, *EI*, XXXVI, p. 307.
78. Taltalai Plates of Dharmamahādevī, *IHQ*, XXI, p. 213.
79. Angul Copper Plates of Dharmamahādevī.
80. Angul C.P. of Śāntikara, *OHRJ*, XIII, p. 2.
81. Vakratentalī charter of Mahābhavagupta I, third regnal year, *EI*, XI, p. 93; *IO*, IV, p. 95.
82. Kalibhanā Plates of Mahābhavagupta I, sixth regnal year, *IHQ*, XX, p. 237; *IO*, IV, p. 100.
83. Patna Museum Plates of Mahābhavagupta I, sixth regnal year, *JASB*, N.S.I., p. 12; *IO*, IV, p. 112.

84. Patna Plates of Mahābhavagupta I, sixth year, *EI*, III, p. 340; *IO*, IV, p. 105.
85. Nagpur Museum Plates of Mahābhavagupta I, eighth year, *EI*, VIII, p. 138; *IO* IV, p. 118.
86. Gaintala Plates of Mahābhavagupta I, eleventh year, *OHRJ*, XI, p. 192; *IO* IV, p. 124.
87. Mahākosala Historical Society's Plates of Mahābhavagupta I, eleventh year *EI*, XXII, p. 135; *IO* IV, p. 212.
88. Cuttack Plates of Mahābhavagupta I, thirty-first year, *EI*, III, p. 345; *IO* IV, p. 138.
89. Kalibhanā Plates of Mahābhavagupta I, thirty-fourth year, *IHQ*, XX, p. 245; *IO* IV, p. 151.
90. Mārañja-Murā grant of Mahāśivagupta I, third regnal year, *JBORS*, II, p. 45; *IO* IV, p. 218.
91. Orissa State Museum Plates of Mahāśivagupta I, fourth year, *EI*, XXXVIII, p. 186; *IO* IV, p. 159.
92. Patna Museum Plates of Mahāśivagupta I, eighth year, *JASB*, N.S. I., p. 14; *IO* IV, p. 167.
93. Cuttack Plates of Mahāśivagupta I, ninth year *EI*, III, p. 351; *IO* IV, p. 177.
94. Nibinnā grant of Mahāśivagupta I, fifteenth year, *EI*, XI, p. 95; *IO* IV, p. 184.
95. Patna Plates of Mahāśivagupta I, twenty-fourth year, *JASB*, N.S.I., p. 16; *IO* IV, p. 190.
96. Patna Plates of Mahāśivagupta I, twenty-eighth year, *JASB*, N.S.I., p. 19; *IO* IV, p. 196.
97. Talcher Plates of Vinītatuṅga II, *EI*, XXXVIII, p. 128.
98. Khargaprasad Plates of Vinītatuṅga II, *EI*, XXXVIII, p. 122.
99. Asiatic Society's Plates of Gayāḍatuṅga, *EI*, XXXIV, p. 100.
100. Talcher Plates of Gayāḍatuṅga, *EI*, XXXIV, p. 96.
101. Talcher Plates of Gayāḍatuṅga, *EI*, XXXIV, p. 93.
102. Keśari Plates of Śatrubhañja, *EI*, XXV, p. 161.
103. Dasapalla grant of Śatrubhañja, *EI*, XXIX, p. 189; *OHRJ*, I, p. 208.
104. Sonpur Plates of Śatrubhañja, *EI*, XI, p. 98.
105. Ganjam grant of Śatrubhañja, *OHRJ*, IV, p. 67.

106. Baud grant of Kanakabhañja, *IHQ*, IX, p. 751.
107. Ādipur Plates of Narendrabhañja, *EI*, XXV, p. 147.
108. Ādipur Plates of Narendrabhañja, *EI*, XXV, p. 157.
109. Antirigam Plates of Jayabhañja, *EI*, XIX, p. 41.
110. Ganjam grant of Vidyādharabhañja, *EI*, XVIII, p. 296.
111. Antirigam Plates of Yaśabhañja, *EI*, XVIII, p. 298.
112. Juraḍa grant of Neṭṭabhañja, *EI*, XXIV, p. 15.
113. Russellkonda Plates of Neṭṭabhañja, *EI*, XXVIII, p. 258.
114. Grant of Neṭṭabhañja, *EI*, XXVIII, p. 278.
115. Singharā Plates of Raṇabhañja, *JBORS*, VI, p. 481.
116. Udated Baud grant of Raṇabhañja, *JBORS*, XX, p. 147.
117. Tasapaikera charter of Raṇabhañja, thirteenth year, *JBORS*, II, p. 167.
118. Dasapalla grant of Raṇabhañja, twenty-fourth year, *JBORS*, VI, p. 266.
119. Grant of Raṇabhañja, twenty-sixth year, *EI*, XII, p. 325.
120. Aidā Plates of Raṇabhañja, fiftieth year, *EI*, XXXVII, p. 257; *OHRJ*, XI, p. 155.
121. Baud grant of Raṇabhañja, fifty fourth year, *EI*, XII, p. 322.
122. Baud grant of Raṇabhañja, fifty-eighth year, *IHQ*, X, p. 473.
123. Cuttack Plates of Mahābhavagupta II, third regnal year, *EI*, III, p. 355; *IO* IV, p. 205.
124. Kudopali grant of Mahābhavagupta II, thirteenth year, *EI*, IV, p. 254; *IO* IV, p 237.
125. C.P. of Kramāditya, *V.S.* 1081/c. 1024-1025 A.D., *JBRS*, LI, p. 55.
126. Mahudi Plates of Paramāra Bhoja, *V.S.*, 1074/c. 1017 A.D., *EI*, XXXIII, p. 215.
127. Banswara grant of Bhoja, *V.S.* 1076/c. 1019 A.D., *IA*, XLI, p. 201.
128. Betma grant of Bhoja, *V.S.* 1076/c. 1019 A.D., *EI*, XVIII, p. 320.
129. Grant of Saurāditya, *V.S.*, 1077/c. 1020 A.D., *EI*, XXXV, p. 130.
130. Ujjain grant of Bhoja, *V.S.*, 1078/c. 1021 A.D., *IA*, VI, p. 53.

131. Depalpur grant of Bhoja, *V.S.* 1079/c. 1022 A.D., *IHQ*, VIII, p. 305.
132. Kalas Budrukh Plates of Bhillamarāja III, *Śaka* 948/c. 1025 A.D., *IA*, XVII, p. 117.
133. Muṁdaka grant of Caulukya Bhīmadeva I, *V.S.*, 1086/c. 1030 A.D., *EI*, XXXVII, p. 35.
134. Grant of Bhīmadeva I, *V.S.* 1086/c. 1030 A.D., *IA*, VI, p. 193.
135. Grant of Kulika Vipracandra, *EI*, XXXVIII, p. 63.
136. Hindol Plates of Vīra Pracaṇḍadeva, *OHRJ*, XII, p. 4.
137. Guakuci Plates of Indrapāla, *KS*, p. 137.
138. Bhadresar Plates of Bhīmadeva I, *V.S.* 1117/c. 1060 A.D., *EI*, XXXVII, p. 37.
139. Yādava charter from Devalili, *EI*, XXXVII, p. 74.
140. Silimpur Stone Inscription, *EI*, XIII, p. 283.
141. Thana Plates of Śīlāhāra Nāgārjuna, *Śaka* 961/c. 1039 A.D., *EI*, XXXVII, p. 247.
142. Benares Plates of Kalacuri Karṇa, *Cedi* 793/c. 1042 A.D., *CII*, IV, p. 241 f.
143. Thana Plates of Mummuṇirāja, *Śaka* 970/c. 1048-1049 A.D., *EI*, XXXVIII, p. 145.
144. Thana Plates of Mummuṇirāja, *Śaka* 971/c. 1049 A.D., *EI*, XXV, p. 53.
145. Belwa Plates of Vigrahapāla III, eleventh regnal year, *EI*, XXIX, p. 9.
146. Amgachi grant of Vigrahapāla III, twelfth year, *EI*, XV, p. 293.
147. Bangaon Plates of the time of Vigrahapāla III, seventeenth year, *EI*, XXIX, p. 48.

## Select Bibliography

Agrawal, V.S.—*Harṣacarita EK Sānskritika Adhyayana*, Patna 1964. Alberuni: *India*, translated and edited by E.C. Sachau, Volumes I and II (T.O.S.), London 1910.

Altekar, A.S.—*The Rāṣṭrakūṭas And Their Times*, Poona 1934.

Baṇabhaṭṭa:—*HARṢACARITA*, translated and edited by P.V. Kane, Delhi 1965.

__________. *KĀDAMBARĪ*, translated by M.R. Kale, Bombay 1924.

Bandyopadhyay, R.D.—*Vāṅglār Itihāsa*, Volume I, Nababharat Publications, Calcutta 1971.

Bhavabhūti—*MAHĀVĪRACARITA*, translated and edited by Todar Mall, London 1928.

__________—MĀLATĪ-MĀDHAVA, translated and edited by M.R. Telang and W.S. Paniskar, Bombay 1905.

Brough, J.—*The Early Brāhmaṇical System of Gotra and Pravara*, Cambridge 1953.

Chanda, R.—*Gauḍa-rāja-mālā*, 2nd edition, Calcutta 1978.

Chandra, S.—*Dependence and Disillusionment*, Delhi 1975.

Childe, G.V.—*What Happened in History*, Middlesex 1972.

Daṇḍin—*DAŚAKUMĀRACARITA*, translated and edited by M.R. Kale, Delhi 1966.

Dasgupta, K.K. (ed.)—:*The Topographical List of the Bṛhat-saṁhitā*, translated by J.F. Fleet, Calcutta 1973.

Dasgupta, S.N. and De S.K.—*History of Sanskrit Literature*, Classical Period, Volume I, Calcutta 1947.

Dey, N.—*Geographical-Dictionary of Ancient and Mediaeval India*, London 1927.

Ghoshal, U.N.—*Contributions to the History of the Hindu Revenue System*, Calcutta 1972.

Ghurye, G.S.—*Two Brāhmaṇical Institutions: Gotra and Caraṇa*, Bombay 1972.

Kalhaṇa—*RĀJATARANGIṆĪ*, translated and edited by M.A. Stein, Motilal Banarsidass, Delhi 1961.

Kane, P.V.—*History of Dharmaśāstras*, Volume II, Poona 1941.

Krishnamachariar, M.—*History of Classical Sanskrit Literature*, Madras 1937.

Maity, S.K.—*Economic Life in Northern India in the Gupta Period*, c. A.D. 300-550, Delhi 1970.

Majumdar, R.C.—*History of Ancient Bengal*, Calcutta 1971.

Majumdar, R.C. (ed.)—*History of Bengal*, Volume I, Patna 1971 (Reprint).

Majumdar R.C. and Pusalker, A.D. (ed.)—*The Vedic Age*, Bombay 1951.

__________ *The Classical Age*, Bombay 1970.

__________ *The Age of Imperial* Kanauj, Bombay 1955.

__________ *The Struggle for Empire*, Bombay 1957.

Mazumdar, B.P.—*Socio-Economic History of Northern India*, c. 1030-1094 A.D., Calcutta 1960.

Mirashi, V.V.—*Bhavabhūti*, Delhi 1974.

Misra, Y.—*The Hindu Sahis of Afghanistan and the Punjab*, Patna 1972.

Niyogi, P.—*Brahmanic Settlements in Different Sub-divisions of Ancient Bengal*, Calcutta 1967.

Rājaśekhara—*KARPŪRAMANJARĪ*, edited by Sten Konow and translated by C.R. Lanman (H.O.S.), Delhi 1963.

Ray, H.C.—*Dynastic History of Northern India*, Volumes I and II, Delhi 1973.

Roux, G.—*Ancient Iraq*, Paperback edition, 1966.

Sankalia, H.D.—*Studies in the Historical and Cultural Geography and Ethnography of Gujarat*, Poona, 1949.

Sharma, B.N.—*Social and Cultural History of Northern India*, Delhi 1972.

Sharma, D.—*Early Chauhan Dynasties*, Delhi 1975.

Sharma, R.S.—*Indian Feudalism*, Calcutta 1965, 1980.

Sharma, R.S. (ed.)—*Land Revenue in India*, Delhi 1971.

Sircar, D.C.—*Indian Epigraphical Glossary*, Delhi 1966.

__________ *Studies in the Geography of Ancient and Mediaeval India*, Delhi 1971.

__________ *Studies in the Society and Administration of Ancient and Mediaeval India*, Calcutta 1967.

__________ *Select Inscriptions Vol. II,* Delhi 1983

Somadeva—*KATHĀSARITASĀGARA*, translated and edited by Penzer (ten volumes), Delhi 1968.

Tripathi, R.S.—*History of Kanauj*, Delhi 1964.

Weber, A.—*History of Indian Literature*, London 1914.

Winternitz, M.—*History of Indian Literature*, Volume I, translated by S. Ketkar, Calcutta 1927.

**Inscriptions**

Mirashi, V.V.—*Corpus Inscriptionum Indicarum*, Volumes III and IV, Ootacamund 1955.

Majumdar, N.G.—*Inscriptions of Bengal*, Volume III, Rajshahi, 1929.

Rajguru, S.N.—*Inscriptions of Orissa*, Volume IV, Bhubaneshwar, 1966.

Bhattacharya, P.N.—*Kāmārūpa-Śāsanāvatī,* Rangpur, B.S. 1338.

Sircar, D.C.—*Select Inscriptions*, Volume I, Calcutta 1942.
Relevant volumes of Epigraphia Indica

**Journals, Encyclopaedia, Dictionary**

Indian Antiquary, Bombay.

*Indian Culture*, Calcutta.

*Indian Historical Quarterly*, Calcutta.

*Journal of the Asiatic Society of Bengal*

*Journal of the Asiatic Society*, Calcutta.

*Journal of the Andhra Historical Research Society*, Rajahmundry.

*Journal of the Bombay Branch of the Royal Asiatic Society*, Bombay.

*Journal of the Bihar Research Society*, Patna.

*Journal of the Bihar and Orissa Research Society*, Patna.

*Journal of the Oriental Institute of Baroda*, Baroda.

*Orissa Historical Research Journal*, Bhubaneshwar.

*Bhārat Koṣa*, Volume I. Vangiya Sahitya Parisat, Calcutta 1964.

*Encyclopaedia Britannica*, Volume XV, London, 1955.

*Encyclopaedia of the Social Sciences*, Volumes VII-VIII & IX-X. New York, 1951.

Williams, M.—*A Sanskrit English Dictionary*, Oxford 1899.

# Abbreviations for Index

a.m. —auspicious month
a.o. —auspicious occasion
B. —Brāhmaṇa other than donee
bk. —book
Bl. —Black
Br. —groups of Brāhmaṇas
c. —coin
car. —caraṇa
co. —country
com. —composer
comp. —complex
d. —donee
dn. —division
dt. —district
ep. —epithet
F. —character in Fable
f. —field
fn. —footnote
f. of go. —family of gotras
f.r. —funeral rites
g. —god
ga. —gaṇa
gd. —goddess
go. —gotra
gr. —group
gr. of go. —group of gotras
h. —hills
l. —language
l.g. —law-giver
m. —measure
m.l. —measure of land
m. of B. —mother of Brāhmaṇa
m. of d. —mother of donee
mo. —monastery
mod. —modern
M.M. —character in *Mālati-Mādhava*
mt. —mountain
o. —officer
p. —pravara
pr. —priest
R. —character in *Rāmāyaṇa*
r. —river
rg. —region
s. —sacrifice
sa —śākhā
sc. —school
sec. —section
st. —state
std. —students
sub. dn. —sub-division
t. —tax
ti. —tithi
tk. —tank
tl. —title
t.u. —territorial unit
u.l. —unit of land
u.m. —unit of measurement
v. —village
W. —White
w. —well
wr. —writer
wt. —weight

# Index